Glossary of Women's Studies

Glossary of Women's Studies

Dr. Eswari M

Dr. Anji A

Dr. M H Hullur

KALPAZ

ISBN: 978-93-5324-617-4

First Published, 2021

Published by

Kalpaz Publications
C-30, Satyawati Nagar,
Delhi – 110052
Ph.: 011-47034999, 9811692060
www.kalpazpublications.com
E-mail: kalpaz@hotmail.com

Printed at: Gyan Press, Delhi.

List of Glossary

A

1. AA-HA! Accelerated Action for the Health of Adolescents:
2. Abled/enabled person
3. Ableism
4. Ableist Language
5. Abstinence
6. Access and control over resources
7. Access
8. Accession
9. Activist (for justice)
10. Adolescence
11. Adolescent Health in All Policies (AHAP)
12. Adoption
13. Advocacy
14. Affirmative action
15. Affirmative consent
16. Ageism
17. Agency
18. Agender
19. AIDs
20. Ally/Allyship/Accomplice
21. Ally
22. Allyship
23. Anarcha-feminism
24. Androcentric
25. Androcentrism
26. Androcracy
27. Androgynous mind
28. Androgyny
29. Antifeminism
30. Anti-oppression
31. Aromantic
32. Asex
33. Asexual
34. Asexuality
35. Assigned female at birth (AFAB)
36. Assigned male at birth (AMAB)
37. Atheism Plus
38. Autonomy in Decision-making
39. Autonomy

B

40. Bamboo Ceiling
41. Bechdel Test
42. Beijing Conference
43. Beijing Declaration and Platform for Action
44. Benevolent Sexism
45. Biantagonism
46. Bias
47. Binary Thinking
48. Binary
49. Biological Determinism
50. Biological Sex
51. Biphobia
52. Birth control
53. Bisexual
54. Bisexuality
55. Black Feminism
56. Bloomerism
57. Bodily Autonomy
58. Body Positivity

59. Boy
60. Brass Ceiling
61. Broflake
62. Bropriation
63. Bropropriating
64. Butlerian

C

65. Canon/Canonisation
66. Capabilities Approach
67. Capitalism
68. Carceral Feminism
69. Care (Informal)
70. Care Economy
71. Care Work
72. Career Woman
73. Casual sex
74. CEDAW (The Convention on the Elimination of All Forms of Discrimination against Women)
75. Celibacy
76. Chicana Feminism (a.k.a. Xicanism)
77. Christian Egalitarianism
78. Cinderella Complex
79. Circular and Linear Thinking
80. Circular Thinking
81. Cisgender
82. Cissexism
83. Citizen and Citizenship
84. Civil Society
85. Class
86. Classism
87. Coalitions, Alliances, and Networks
88. Commission on the Status of Women (CSW)
89. Commodity Feminism
90. Commons
91. Community Managing Role
92. Community Organising
93. Community Politics Role
94. Complementarianism
95. Compulsory Heterosexuality
96. Condom
97. Conscientisation
98. Consciousness Raising
99. Constituency Building
100. Consumerism
101. Contraceptive
102. Control
103. Convention
104. Counter Narrative vs. Master Narrative
105. Creep(er)
106. Crimes of Honour
107. Critical Consciousness
108. Critical mass
109. Cross-dressing
110. Cult of True Womanhood
111. Cultural Appropriation
112. Cultural Capital
113. Cultural Critic
114. Cultural Hegemony
115. Culture
116. Customary Law

D

117. Date rape
118. De Facto Discrimination
119. De Jure Discrimination
120. Decent Work
121. Decision-making and Participation
122. Declaration on the Elimination of Violence against Women
123. Deconstruction
124. Democracy
125. Derailing
126. Deregulation
127. Development
128. Dichotomy
129. Difference Feminism

130. Differences in legal status and entitlements
131. Differential Access to and Control Over Resources
132. Disability
133. Disabled
134. Disadvantaged groups
135. Disaggregated Data (Sex)
136. Discrimination (Direct and Indirect)
137. Discrimination (Gender Discrimination)
138. Discrimination (Gender)
139. Discrimination (Systemic)
140. Discrimination against Girls and Women
141. Displaced Women
142. Diversity
143. Division for the Advancement of Women (DAW)
144. Domestic responsibilities
145. Domestic violence
146. Domestic Work
147. Domestic Worker
148. Domesticity
149. Double Burden
150. Double Consciousness
151. Double Day
152. Double Standard
153. Dowry deaths
154. Dowry
155. Dworkinian
156. Dworkinite

E

157. Ecofeminism
158. Economic Autonomy
159. Economic Democracy
160. Educational attainment
161. Emergency contraception
162. Emosogynist
163. Empowerment Feminism
164. Empowerment of Women and Girls
165. Empowerment
166. Engendered Citizenship
167. Epistemic Advantage
168. Epistemology
169. Equal Pay
170. Equal Representation of Women and Men (in UN system)
171. Equal Rights Amendment (ERA)
172. Equality of opportunity
173. Equality of Outcome
174. Equality vs. Equity
175. Equality
176. Equity (and Sustainable Development)
177. Equity Feminism (Conservative Feminism)
178. Equity
179. Essentialism
180. Ethnicity
181. Eve teasing
182. Exoticisation
183. Extractive Industries

F

184. Family planning
185. Family
186. Fatphobia
187. Fat-shaming
188. Female - to - Male (FTM)
189. Female
190. Female Gaze
191. Female Genital Mutilation (FGM)
192. Female Infanticide
193. Female vs. Woman
194. Female-headed household
195. Femicide
196. Feminazi
197. Feminine Ecriture (écriture féminine)
198. Feminine Mystique

199. Feminine
200. Femininity
201. Feminisation of Migration
202. Feminisation of Poverty
203. Feminism
204. Feminist
205. Feminist Advocacy
206. Feminist Epistemology
207. Feminist Leadership
208. Feminist Movement-Building
209. Feminist Movements
210. Feminist Popular Education
211. Feminist scholarship
212. Feminist Theory
213. Feminist Transgression
214. Feminisation of migration
215. Feminine Labour
216. Feminisation
217. First Wave Feminism
218. Fluid
219. Foresister
220. Fourth-Wave Feminism
221. Free Trade
222. Free-Market or Market Economies
223. Friedanian
224. FTM
225. Fundamentalisms

G

226. Gas Lighting
227. Gay
228. Gender - Nonconformity
229. Gender (Expression) vs. Sex
230. Gender (or Sexual) Division of Labour
231. Gender
232. Gender Accommodating
233. Gender Action Plan (GAP)
234. Gender Advisor
235. Gender analysis
236. Gender Analysis
237. Gender Analytical Information
238. Gender and Development (GAD)
239. Gender Apartheid
240. Gender as Cultural Construction
241. Gender Audit
242. Gender Awareness
243. Gender Aware-Policies can be Sub divided into two Policy Types
244. Gender Balance
245. Gender bias
246. Gender Binary
247. Gender Blindness
248. Gender budgeting
249. Gender Characteristics
250. Gender Conformity
251. Gender-Critical
252. Gender Discrimination
253. Gender Disparities
254. Gender Diversity
255. Gender Division of Labour
256. Gender Effect
257. Gender Empowerment Measure (GEM)
258. Gender Equality (Equality between women and men)
259. Gender Equality as a Development Objective
260. Gender Equality
261. Gender Equity
262. Gender Essentialism
263. Gender Expression/Gender Image
264. Gender Expression
265. Gender Fluid
266. Gender Fluidity
267. Gender Focal Point
268. Gender Gap
269. Gender Identity
270. Gender in Development (Condition and Position)
271. Gender in Development (GID)
272. Gender Indicators

273. Gender Inequality Index (GII)
274. Gender Issues
275. Gender Lens
276. Gender Mainstreaming / Integrating
277. Gender Mainstreaming
278. Gender Needs/ Interests (Practical and Strategic)
279. Gender Needs
280. Gender-Neutral Language
281. Gender Neutral
282. Gender Neutrality
283. Gender Norms
284. Gender Parity
285. Gender Parity Index (GPI)
286. Gender Pay Gap
287. Gender Performativity
288. Gender Perspective
289. Gender Planning
290. Gender Policies
291. Gender Presentation
292. Gender Queer
293. Gender Relations (Transforming)
294. Gender Relations and Gender Identity (Changes)
295. Gender Relations
296. Gender Role Stereotyping
297. Gender Role
298. Gender Roles and Responsibilities
299. Gender Sensitivity and Gender Awareness
300. Gender Sensitivity
301. Gender Sensitisation
302. Gender Socialisation
303. Gender Stereotypes
304. Gender Stratification
305. Gender Studies
306. Gender Training
307. Gender Violence
308. Gender, Institutions, and Development Data Base (GID-DB)
309. Gender
310. Gender-Based Constraints
311. Gender-Based Violence
312. Gender-Based Violence in Emergencies (GBVE)
313. Gender-Biased Sex Selection
314. Gender-Blind Policies
315. Gender-Blind
316. Gender-Blindness
317. Gender-differentiated impact
318. Gender-disaggregated data
319. Gender-dominated occupations
320. Gender-neutral Programming and Policies
321. Gender-responsive Programming and Policies
322. Gender-neutral Pronouns
323. Gender-Neutral, Gender-Sensitive, and Gender Transformative
324. Gender-nonconformity
325. Gender queer / Gender non-conforming / Gender non-binary
326. Gender queer/Genderfuck
327. Gender queer/Genderfuck
328. Gender-Redistributive Policies
329. Gender-related Development Index (GDI)
330. Gender-Responsive Budgeting (GRB)
331. Gender-Sensitive Budgets
332. Gender-Sensitive Programming and Policies
333. Gender-Sensitivity
334. Gender-Socialisation
335. Gender-Specific Torture and Ill-Treatment
336. Gender-Transformative Programming and Policies
337. Geographic Location
338. Gilmanian
339. Girl
340. Glass Ceiling

341. Glass Escalator
342. Global Care Chains
343. Global Gender Gap Index
344. Globalisation
345. Governance
346. Guerrilla Girls
347. Gynocriticism

H

348. Hegemonic Masculinity
349. Hegemony
350. Herstory
351. Heteronormative
352. Heteronormativity
353. Heteropatriarchy
354. Heterosexism/Heterosexual Privilege
355. Heterosexism
356. Heterosexual
357. Heterosexuality (Compulsory)
358. Hidden Sexuality Curriculum (Hidden Heterogender Curriculum)
359. Hierarchical
360. Hierarchy
361. HIV
362. Homonormativity
363. Homophobia
364. Homosexual
365. Homosociality
366. Honour Killings
367. Hooksian
368. Hostile Sexism
369. Household maintenance
370. Housewife
371. Human Papilloma Virus (HPV)
372. Human Rights with a Gender Perspective
373. Human Rights
374. Human Rights-Based Approach (HRBA)
375. Human Security
376. Human smuggling
377. Hyper masculinity

I

378. Identity Politics
379. Identity vs. Subjectivity
380. Ideology
381. Impairment
382. In the closet
383. Incest
384. Indigenous Feminism
385. Individualist Feminism
386. Inequalities in economic participation and opportunities
387. Inequalities in political power and representation
388. Informal Economy
389. Informal Labour
390. Inheritance
391. Institutional Power
392. Institutional Racism
393. Institutionalised Oppression
394. Institutionalised Sexism
395. Intention/Intentionality
396. Inter-Agency Network on Women and Gender Equality (IANWGE)
397. Intermediate Barriers/Causes
398. Internalised Misogyny
399. Internalised Oppression
400. Internalised Racism
401. Internalised Sexism
402. International Conference on Population and Development (ICPD)
403. International Day of the Girl Child
404. International Financial Institutions (IFIs)
405. Interpersonal Racism
406. Intersectional Analysis
407. Intersectional Feminism
408. Intersectionality
409. Intersex

410. Invisibility of Feminine Labour
411. Invisible minority

K

412. Kyriarchy

L

413. Labour force
414. Lactivism
415. Lambda
416. Lateral Violence
417. Latinx(s)
418. Lesbian Feminism
419. LGBTQ
420. LGBTQ+
421. Liberal Feminism
422. Libfem
423. Lipstick Feminism
424. Livelihood
425. Logocentrism

M

426. Mainstream Feminism
427. Mainstreaming
428. Mako Mori Test
429. Male as Norm
430. Male Chauvinism
431. Male Gaze
432. Male Privilege
433. Male supremacy
434. Male-Dominated Society
435. Malestream
436. Male-to-Female (MTF)
437. Malnutrition
438. Man
439. Mansplain (verb) Mansplainy (adjective)
440. Mansplaining
441. Manspreading
442. Manterrupting
443. Marginalisation
444. Marginalise
445. Marginalised Group
446. Marginalised
447. Market
448. Marxist Feminism
449. Masculinity
450. Matriarchy
451. Matrilineal / Matrilocal
452. Matrix of Domination
453. Measures
454. Men who have sex with men (MSM)
455. Men's Rights Activists (MRAs)
456. Menopause
457. Men's Rights Movement
458. Menstrual Hygiene Management (MHM)
459. Menstruation
460. Mentalism/Sanism
461. Metanarrative / Master Narrative
462. Method
463. Methodology
464. Microaggression
465. Millennium Development Goals (MDGs)
466. Misandry
467. Misogynoir
468. Misogyny
469. Missing women
470. Mobilise
471. Monogamy
472. Monosexism
473. Movement
474. Movement-Building
475. MTF: Male-to-Female
476. Multiple Discrimination

N

477. Naturalisation
478. Nature/Culture
479. Neo-liberalism
480. Neurodiversity

481. NGO Non-Governmental Organisation
482. NGO-isation
483. Nice Guy (TM)
484. Nineteenth Amendment
485. No Means No
486. Non-Binary
487. Non-Op
488. Non-Productive Activities
489. Not All Men

O

490. Objectification
491. Occupational Segregation
492. On T
493. Oppression
494. Other
495. Othering
496. Out or Out of the closet
497. Outreach (for organising)

P

498. Paglian
499. Pansexual
500. Paradigm
501. Parity in Education
502. Participant Observer
503. Participation
504. Participatory Action Research (PAR)
505. Participatory Development
506. Participatory Poverty Assessments (PPA)
507. Participatory Rural Appraisal (PRA)
508. Pass
509. Passing
510. Patriarchal Resistance
511. Patriarchy/Patriarchal
512. Patriarchy
513. Patrilineal/Patrilocal
514. Pay equity
515. Penis Envy
516. Performative
517. Performativity
518. Petro-sexual politics
519. Phallocentric
520. Phallocentrism
521. Phallogocentrism
522. Physical autonomy
523. Physical violence
524. Pink-collar worker
525. Planned parenthood
526. Political
527. Politics of Location
528. Politics
529. Polyamory
530. Polyandry
531. Polygamy
532. Positive parenting
533. Post feminism
534. Post-2015 Development Agenda
535. Postcolonialism
536. Postmodern feminism
537. Post–modernism
538. Post-Op
539. Power
540. Power with
541. Power within
542. Practical Gender Needs (PGN)
543. Practical Gender Needs and Strategic
544. Practical Needs
545. Prejudice
546. Pre-natal sex selection
547. Pre-Op
548. Present
549. Private and public spheres
550. Privatisation
551. Privilege
552. Problematise
553. Pro-choice
554. Production
555. Productive Roles

556. Productive Work
557. Profeminism
558. Program
559. Project
560. Prostitute
561. Prostitution
562. Protofeminism
563. Psychoanalysis
564. Public/Private Spheres
565. Purity Culture
566. Purple Washing

Q

567. Qualitative Methods
568. Quantitative Methods
569. Queer
570. Quotas

R

571. Race
572. Racialisation
573. Racism
574. Radfem
575. Radical Feminism
576. Rape (Date)
577. Rape (Marital)
578. Rape Culture
579. Rape schedule
580. Rape
581. Repression
582. Reproductive age
583. Reproductive health
584. Reproductive Justice
585. Reproductive Labour
586. Reproductive Rights and Sexual and Reproductive Health
587. Reproductive Rights
588. Reproductive Roles
589. Reproductive Tax
590. Reproductive Work
591. Resistance
592. Resonance
593. Resources
594. Respectability Politician
595. Respectability Politics
596. Richian
597. Rights (Sexual)
598. Rights
599. Role conflict
600. Rosie the Riveter

S

601. Safe motherhood
602. Safe sex
603. Safe Space (for Feminist Organising)
604. Sati or suttee
605. Second Shift
606. Second Wave Feminism
607. Security
608. Self-Identify
609. Self-Reliance
610. Separatist Feminism
611. Sex and Gender
612. Sex Identity
613. Sex Positive
614. Sex Role Stereotype
615. Sex Roles
616. Sex Strike
617. Sex Typing
618. Sex vs. Gender
619. Sex Worker-Exclusionary Radical Feminism
620. Sex
621. Sex-Disaggregated Data
622. Sexism in Medicine
623. Sexism
624. Sex-Positivity
625. Sex-Reassignment Surgery (SRS)
626. Sex-Shaming (f.k.a. "slut-shaming")
627. Sexual and domestic violence
628. Sexual and Reproductive Health and Rights (SRHR):

629. Sexual Assault
630. Sexual Consent
631. Sexual Division of Labour
632. Sexual Exploitation
633. Sexual Harassment / Gender Harassment
634. Sexual Health
635. Sexual Identity
636. Sexual minority
637. Sexual Objectification
638. Sexual Orientation
639. Sexual Reassignment Surgery (Sexual/Gender Confirmation Surgery)
640. Sexual Rights
641. Sexual Violence
642. Sexuality
643. Sexually transmitted infections (STIs)
644. Shakespeare's Sister
645. Showalterian
646. Single men
647. Single parent
648. Sisterhood
649. Situated Knowledge
650. Slut-Shaming
651. Slut Walk
652. Social Capital
653. Social Construction
654. Social Constructionism
655. Social exclusion
656. Social Justice
657. Social privilege
658. Social protection
659. Social Transformation
660. Socialist Feminism
661. Socialisation
662. Socialised
663. Socio-Economic Status
664. Socio-Economic Violence
665. Solidarity Economy
666. Son Preference
667. Special
668. Stand-alone Gender Programming and Policies
669. Standpoint theory
670. State
671. Stereotypes
672. Stereotyping
673. Strategic Gender Interests
674. Strategic Gender Needs
675. Strategic Needs
676. Straw Feminism
677. Straw Feminist
678. Strong Objectivity
679. Structural adjustment programmes (SAPs)
680. Structural Barriers/Causes
681. Structural Discrimination
682. Structural Gender Inequality
683. Structural Racism
684. Subject/Object
685. Subjectification
686. Substantive Equality
687. Suffrage
688. Supportive Policies (at the UN)
689. Sustainable Development
690. SWERF
691. Systems of oppression

T

692. Temporary Special Measures
693. TERF
694. The CEDAW Convention
695. The First Wave of Feminism
696. The Second Wave of Feminism
697. The Gaze
698. The Man (or, the boys' club)
699. The Personal Is Political
700. The Separate Spheres
701. The Third Wave of Feminism
702. Title IX

703. Tokenism
704. Tone-Policing
705. Top freedom
706. Total fertility rate (TFR)
707. Toxic Masculinity
708. Traditions
709. Trafficking in Persons
710. Trans Activism
711. Trans Female/Woman
712. Trans Feminine
713. Trans Inclusivity
714. Trans Man
715. Trans Masculine
716. Trans Woman
717. Trans/Transgender
718. Trans-Exclusionary Radical Feminism
719. Transfeminism
720. Transformational Leadership
721. Transformatory Potential
722. Transgender Person
723. Transgender
724. Transgenderist
725. Transition
726. Transmisogyny
727. Transnational Feminism
728. Transphobia
729. Transsexual
730. Transvestite
731. Transsexuality
732. Transvestite/Cross Dresser
733. Triangle
734. Trigger Warnings
735. Trigger
736. Triple Oppression
737. Triple Role/ Multiple Burden
738. Two-Spirit

U

739. UN System-wide Action Plan (UN SWAP)
740. UN Women
741. Universal Declaration of Human Rights
742. Unpaid Care Work
743. Unpaid Labour
744. Unprotected sex
745. Unsafe abortions
746. Unsafe sex
747. Unwanted sex

V

748. Verbal Violence
749. Victim Blaming
750. Violence (Domestic)
751. Violence against Women (VAW)

W

752. Wage Gap
753. Waves of Feminism
754. Welfare
755. Wellbeing
756. Whimpster
757. White Feminism
758. White Privilege
759. Whiteness
760. Whitesplaining
761. White-Supremacist, Capitalist Patriarchy
762. WID: Women in Development (WID)
763. Wikigender
764. Wittigian
765. Woke Misogynist
766. Wollstonecraftian
767. Woman
768. Womanism
769. Women of Colour Feminism
770. Women of Colour
771. Women's Economic Empowerment
772. Women's Human Rights
773. Women's Political Participation

774. Women's Studies
775. Women's Studies
776. Women-Only Space
777. Women's Suffrage
778. Womon Womyn
779. Womyn
780. Womyn-born Womyn
781. Womyn's Land
782. World Economic Forum's (WEF)

Y

783. Yes means yes

Glossary of Women's Studies

AA-HA!(Accelerated Action for the Health of Adolescents): A global partnership, led by WHO and of which UNICEF is a partner, that offers guidance in the country context on adolescent health and development and puts a spotlight on adolescent health in regional and global health agendas.

Abled/Enabled Person: Someone not disabled by society.

Ableism: A pervasive system of discrimination and exclusion that oppresses people who have mental, emotional, and physical disabilities. Deeply rooted beliefs about health, productivity, beauty, and the value of human life combine to create an environment that is often hostile to those whose physical, emotional, cognitive, or sensory abilities fall outside the scope of what is currently defined as socially acceptable. Also, see *disability*. (Rauscher and McClintock, 1997)

Ableist Language: Words whose literal or historical definition derives from a disability and have been used to marginalize others, and press disabled people.

Abstinence: Avoidance of sexual relations of any kind. For some, it may mean the decision to avoid only penetrative sex; for others, it may mean only engaging in 'outer course'. Reasons for abstinence could include contraception and prevention of pregnancy, disease, as well as religious belief.

Access and Control Over Resources: This concept has three parts: resources, access, and control. The first, resources, refers to means and goods, including economic (household income) or productive means (land, equipment, tools, work, credit); political means (capability for leadership, information and organisation); and time. Access and control have slightly different meanings. Access refers to the ability to use and benefit from specific resources (material, financial, human, social, political, etc.) whereas control over resources also entails being able to make decisions over the use of that resource. For example, women's control over land means that they can access land (use it), own land (can be the legal title-holders), and make decisions about whether to sell or rent the land. Access and control over resources is a key element of women's empowerment, and by extension, the achievement of gender equality.

Access: It is the means or rights to obtain services, products, or commodities. The Women's Equality and Empowerment Framework identifies "access" as one of the five levels of equality that are important in the process of women's development. Gender gaps in access to resources and services are one type of obstacle to women's development. Women's achievement of equality of access to resources and services is seen as an objective for women's equality; by the same token, women's mobilisation to achieve equality of access is an element of the process of empowerment.

Accession: The act whereby a state becomes a party to a treaty already negotiated and signed by other states. It has the same legal force as ratification. Accession usually occurs after the treaty has entered into force.

Activist (for justice): Someone who cares deeply about injustice, inequality, and/or the wellbeing of others and the planet, and who takes or organises political action with others and is driven by a belief in an alternative, and the hope and conviction that a better world is possible.

Adolescence: The second decade of life, from the ages of 10- 19. Young adolescence is the age of 10-14 and late adolescence age of 15-19. This period between childhood and adulthood is a pivotal opportunity to consolidate any loss/gain made in early childhood. All too often adolescents - especially girls - are endangered by violence, limited by a lack of quality education, and unable to access critical health services. UNICEF focuses on helping adolescents navigate risks and vulnerabilities and take advantage of opportunities.

Adolescent Health in All Policies (AHAP): An approach to public policies across sectors that systematically takes into account the implications of decisions for adolescent health, avoids harmful effects, and seeks synergies – to improve adolescent health and health equity. This is a strategy that facilitates the formulation of adolescent responsive public policies in all sectors, and not just within the health sector.

Adoption: Approval of the final text of a convention by the committee which wrote it. It is then open for signatures, ratification, or accession.

Advocacy: An organised, concerted effort by people and organisations to effect change in both the formal political and policy arena as well as social attitudes. There are many understandings, definitions, strategies, and applications for advocacy, including public interest advocacy, policy advocacy, social justice advocacy, citizen-centered and participatory advocacy.

Affirmative Action: A plan or programme designed to combat the effects of discrimination against an identified group based on sex, race, age, religion or ethnicity that has been disadvantaged in hiring, promotion, the award of contracts or access to employment opportunities. It can include systems of preferences designed to give additional considerations to individuals who are from groups that have suffered discrimination. The term 'positive action' or 'affirmative action' is preferable to 'revenge on discrimination'. (See also disadvantaged groups; discrimination; gender parity.).

Affirmative Consent: Affirmative consent (enthusiastic yes) is when both parties agree to sexual conduct, either through clear, verbal communication or nonverbal cues or gestures. It involves communication and the active participation of people involved. This is the approach endorsed by colleges and universities in the U.S., who describe consent as an "affirmative, unambiguous, and conscious decision by each participant to engage in mutually agreed-upon sexual activity." According to Yoon-Hendricks, a staff writer for Sex, Etc., "Instead of saying 'no means no, 'yes means yes' looks at sex as a positive thing." Ongoing consent is sought at all levels of sexual intimacy regardless of the parties' relationship, prior sexual history, or current activity ("Grinding on the dance floor is not consent for further sexual activity," a university policy reads). By definition, affirmative consent cannot be given if a person is intoxicated, unconscious or asleep.

Ageism: Prejudice against a person or people, because of her age; any idea, attitude, action or mental or institutional structure that subordinates or discriminates against a group or person because of age. Building multi-generational movements that build on the knowledge and experience of people of all ages is a major challenge for feminists. Young women's voices go unheard, while older feminists sometimes feel that their hard-won knowledge is dismissed by the younger generation is no longer relevant. Feminists point out that consumer capitalism influences perceptions of women and age, subverting traditional customs and values that honour older women while reinforcing negative stereotypes of older women, all in the service of creating a fear of aging that sells skin cream and other products. (Facio, 2011)

Agency: The capacity to take action or to wield power. Conventional social change efforts often involve top-down, expert-, and/or externally-driven approaches that treat primary beneficiaries as targets, rather than agents, of change. In contrast, movement-building and other empowerment approach is explicitly seeking to engage and support primary beneficiaries in defining and driving the change that they wish to see.

Agender: A term that describes people who lack a gender, or are without gender (genderless, gender- neutral, non-binary).

AIDS: Acquired Immune Deficiency Syndrome or the late stage of the chronic disease caused by the infection with Human Immuno Deficiency Virus (HIV), in which the immune system is weakened and unable to fight opportunistic infections. For many years, the term 'HIV/AIDS' was used freely in media reports to refer to the global epidemic. But increasingly, the accepted – and more accurate – terminology and usage have been to separate HIV and AIDS ('HIV and AIDS' instead of 'HIV/AIDS') because they are not the same, and because they are lumping them together tends to confuse the statistics for both as well. The 2007 terminology summary by the Joint United Nations Programme on HIV/AIDS (UNAIDS) encourages writers to "use HIV unless specifically referring to AIDS", for instance as in "HIV testing", and "children orphaned by AIDS". HIV epidemic and AIDS epidemic are acceptable.

Ally/Allyship/Accomplice: Allies are people who want to end oppression for marginalised individuals/groups but are not themselves part of the group. Allyship is not a self-proclaimed identity or performance, it is a lifelong process; it is bestowed, not proclaimed. This group prefers the term "accomplice" to ally because accomplices are not supporters, but are engaged in the fight, i.e. fighting *with* rather than fighting *for*.

Ally: A person who bridges communities through listening, trusting, and accountability to combat oppression and advance social justice and equity.

Allyship: An allyship may exist between those who are underprivileged and those who acknowledge their privilege (identity privileged). Identity privileged allies also challenge those who attempt to sub/consciously maintain the status quo.

Anarcha-Feminism: Feminism melded with anarchism, seeing the way to gender equality in the dismantling of hierarchical structures in society. Also called anarcho-feminism, and/or sexual identity or gender identity.

Androcentric: Dominated by or emphasising masculine interests or a masculine point of view.

Androcentrism: The centering and normalisation of men and men's perspectives, to the exclusion of women and non-binary people or A characteristic of sexism (that presents the male as the prototype or model for humanity and the masculine perspective as the default human point of view or as objective reality. In this form of sexism, men's lives and the masculine are privileged and taken as the embodiment of all human experience throughout history, whereas women's lives and the feminine are understood as "other." discourse A basic definition is the language of a given field or area of study, for example, medical discourse or legal discourse. Michel Foucault, a French philosopher concerned with the origins and dissemination of "knowledge," developed the idea that knowledge is produced, i.e., that what we know about and see in the world is not simply the "natural order" of things, but is shaped by the dynamics of power and dominant ideologies that are at play in any given society. Feminists such as Chris Wheedon and Judith Butler have built upon this theory to describe how knowledge, for example regarding "women's work" or women's roles in history, is not value-neutral but instead is the product and reflection of dominant attitudes and beliefs about race, class, gender, ethnicity, etc. While "conventional" knowledge is produced in the service of male-dominated societies, feminist activists can and do produce knowledge, for example, through lived experience, that is more conscious of power imbalances in society, and in doing so, alter discourse in favour of women's equality.

Androcracy: Government in which the rulers are men.

Androgynous Mind: Virginia Woolf introduced this term in A Room of One's Own (1929) to indicate the creative mentality that partakes of both masculine (andro) and feminine (gyno) qualities. Heilbrun and Bazin see it as a balancing of "the evanescent masculine and the eternal feminine" as typical of the enlightened state, yet Showalter and others have seen it as a "sexist myth in disguise," reifying binary stereotypes.

Androgyny: A term that combines the Greek words for man and woman is a state of ambiguous gender in which identifying sexual characteristics are uncertain or mixed. It differs from hermaphroditism, or intersexuality, a condition in which dual sexual characteristics are unambiguously present. To say that someone is androgynous is to say that he or she combines stereotypically male and female attributes.

Antifeminism: Antifeminism (also spelt anti-feminism) in opposition to some or all forms of feminism. Antifeminists in the late 19th century and early 20th century resisted women's suffrage, while antifeminists in the late 20th century in the United States opposed the Equal Rights

Amendment. Others, particularly in the 21st century, see antifeminism as a response to an ideology rooted in hostility towards men.

Anti-Oppression: An attempt to recognise and mitigate societal oppression to advance the equity.

Aromantic: A person who does not experience romantic attraction.

Asex: Having no obvious sex or sex organs. Asexual can also refer to a person who does not experience sexual attraction.

Asexual: A term a sexuality that is used to describe a person who does not experience sexual attraction. Note: be careful not to conflate sexual attraction with romantic attraction when thinking about asexuality; a person who identifies as asexual might have any number of romantic relationships, just relationships absent of sexual intimacy.

Asexuality: The lack of sexual attraction to anyone, or low or absent interest in sexual activity.

Assigned Female at Birth (AFAB): People who are declared to be female at birth based on how their genitals appear, and who are generally raised in a female gender role.

Assigned Male at Birth (AMAB): People who are declared to be male at birth based on how their genitals appear, and who are generally raised in a male gender role.

Atheism Plus: A social movement encouraging progressive atheists to embrace feminism and other social justice issues.

Autonomy in Decision-Making: Women's participation in all branches of government, signing of CEDAW optional protocol, positioning of various national machineries for the advancement of women.

Autonomy: The concept of autonomy refers to people's capacity to make free and informed decisions about their lives, enabling them to be and act following their aspirations and desires, given a historical context that makes those possible. Women's autonomy is often conceptualised as having three dimensions.

Bamboo Ceiling: The glass ceiling concept is applied specifically to the Asian or Asian-American people, particularly women.

Bechdel Test: An imprecise gauge of the presence of women in media, based on the proportion of works that feature two named women who converse about something other than a man. The term named after Alison Bechdel.

Beijing Conference: The United Nations Fourth World Conference on Women was held in the Chinese capital in 1995. It produced a declaration of the international community's commitment to the advancement of women and a platform of action that set out measures for action by 2000. The conference provided a clear commitment that the protection and promotion of the rights of women and girl children are a key part of universal human rights. The three previous world conferences were held in Mexico City in 1975, Copenhagen in 1980, and Nairobi in 1985. In many ways, the results of the Beijing conference furthered the progress made at the 1994 International Conference on Population and Development (ICPD) in Cairo, Egypt, where the advancement and empowerment of women and women's rights to control their fertility had already been negotiated. (See also **International Conference on Population and Development**.).

Beijing Declaration and Platform for Action: The Beijing Declaration and Platform for Action was adopted by the Fourth World Conference on Women: Action for Equality, Development, and Peace, Beijing, 15 September 1995. The document was agreed upon by world governments at the Conference and is a comprehensive outline of strategic steps to be taken to concretise and enhance the goals of CEDAW (See **CEDAW**). Although it is not, of its nature, a legally binding document, consisting of policy commitments rather than legal obligations, it is, nonetheless, a significant statement of principle, and has great symbolic value.

Benevolent Sexism: A subjectively positive orientation of protection, idealisation, and affection directed toward women that, like hostile sexism, serves to justify women's subordinate status to men (or) Less obvious. Kind of seems like a compliment, even though it's rooted in men's feelings of superiority. It's when men say women are worthy of their protection (off the sinking boat first) or that they're more nurturing than men (therefore should raise children). It's restrictive.

Biantagonism: Hatred or dislike of bisexual folk.

Bias: Inclination or attitude toward or against something, someone, or a particular group of persons; prejudice. (See also **discrimination; gender bias**.).

Binary Thinking: Black and white thinking, the inability to see "gray areas" or the middle between two opposing categories.

Binary: In the humanities and social sciences, a binary refers to a stable classification with two distinct and opposing parts. For example, some individuals view females and males as binary.

Biological Determinism: The idea that our genial makeup influences our personalities, and thus our personality can be connected to biological differences, and our interests are determined by these factors. People use this idea to create and reinforce gender stereotypes. For example, biologically, a woman can bear a child; she is the gentle, kind, main caretaker.

Biological Sex: The state of being male, female, intersex, or other as defined by physical markers such as sex organs, hormones, gametes, and chromosomes (or) refers to physiological and anatomical female or male characteristics with which a person is born. (Goodman and Schapiro, 1997)

Biphobia: Hatred/dislike of bisexual folk/bisexuals or aversion toward bisexuality and bisexual people as a social group/as individuals.

Birth Control: All methods of preventing birth, including abstinence and abortion. Birth control was initially used synonymously with family planning. (See also **Family Planning**.).

Bisexual: A person for whom their sexual attraction is more or less equally directed to a person of either sex.

Bisexuality: An identity for which sex and gender are not a boundary to attraction.

Black Feminism: Black feminism holds that the experience of black women gives rise to a particular understanding of their position concerning sexism, class oppression, and racism. The experience of being a black woman, it maintains, cannot be grasped in terms of being black or of being a woman, but must be elucidated via intersectionality, a term coined by legal scholar Kimberlé Crenshaw in 1989. Crenshaw argued that each concept—being black, being female—should be considered independently while understanding that intersecting identities compound upon and reinforce one another.

Black Feminism: Feminism focused on the representation of black women.

Bloomerism: An early form of feminism, named for American 19th-century women's rights activist Amelia Bloomer (1818-1894).

Bodily Autonomy: The principle of having control over one's own body. Relevant to discussions on reproductive justice.

Body Positivity: The advocacy of loving one's own body exactly as the way it is determined.

Boy: Boy is a young male human, usually a child or adolescent. When he becomes an adult, he is described as a man. The most apparent difference between a typical boy and a typical girl is the genitalia. However, some intersex children with ambiguous genitals, and genetically female transgender children, may also be classified or self-identify as a boy. The term boy is primarily used to indicate biological sex distinctions, cultural gender role distinctions or both. The term can be joined with a variety of other words to form these gender-related labels as compound words.

Brass Ceiling: The glass ceiling concept as applied to women in law and military professions.

Broflake: A derogatory term for a (usually white, heterosexual and conservative) man who is easily offended by advocacy for marginalised demographics.

Bropriation: (Of a man) the stealing of a woman's idea to present as one's own without giving due credit.

Bropropriating: Stealing an idea from a woman and putting it into the world as your own.

Butlerian: A term named after American feminist and gender theorist Judith Butler (b. 1956).

Canon/Canonisation: In the context of religion, granting Sainthood to the dead person of Roman Catholic Church. In feminist terms, as long as learning disciplines were controlled exclusively by white males, very few women or ethnically diverse authors were included in this list.

Capabilities Approach: Developed by economist and development expert Amartya Sen, the capabilities approach views the end goal of development as the expansion of the freedom of people to choose the kind of life they wish to live. Capabilities are "substantive human freedoms" – rather than focusing on income and wealth, they ask what choices people have, and what individuals are actually able to do and be. According to the United Nations Development Programme (UNDP), which has outlined the approach in its Human Development Reports (see HDR 2000), there are three essential capabilities: for people to lead long and healthy lives, to be knowledgeable, and to have a decent standard of living. Martha Nussbaum has written about the relevancy of the capabilities approach to women, contending that "women's issues have been at the heart of the approach from the start, both because of their urgency and because of the dire situation of women around the world helps us to see more clearly the inadequacy of various other approaches to development." Naila Kabeer has also recently examined the approach of gender mainstreaming in poverty eradication and the Millennium Development Goals. Although Kabeer believes that improvements can be made, she notes that the approach in many respects has been more successful in revealing the gender dimensions of poverty than other commonly used approaches.

Capitalism: An economic system in which products are produced and distributed for profit is benefitting privately owned capital goods and wages. Many feminists assert that a critique of capitalism is essential for understanding the dynamics of inequality, as universal economic restructuring based on capitalism reflects a particular ideology that celebrates individual wealth and accumulation at the lowest cost to the investor, with little regard for the societal costs and exploitation.

Carceral Feminism: An approach that sees increased policing, prosecution, and imprisonment as the primary solution to violence against women; adherents to this approach would likely reject the descriptor.

Care (Informal): Unpaid care for dependent children, the elderly, ill or disabled persons carried out by family members or others. The responsibility of informal care work is taken up by women with a major impact on their health and well- being. Informal care is largely invisible and the economic and social contributions of women carers are unacknowledged. Over 75% of informal carers worldwide are women.

Care Economy: An unpaid economy sometimes called the "domestic" or "reproductive" sector or "social reproduction" in which women do most of the work of maintaining the labour force and keeping the social framework in good order – both vital services for government and the commercial economy. The care economy produces and reproduces families and provides community-oriented goods and services such as healthcare, childcare, education, and the like as a part of the process of caring for people and often outside the money economy. The care economy overwhelmingly depends on women's labour. The value of the care economy is usually excluded from official economic statistics, making it hard to assess the gender impact of budget and policy decisions that touch on this sector. Work in the care economy is often not paid, though it may be supported by payments from the government. Conversely, government cutbacks on social programs or funding inadequacies in the provision of basic social services and essential utilities in infrastructure and other areas of basic needs can add substantially to women's burden of unpaid work in the care economy. (Also see **Domestic Work**)

Care Work: Care work encompasses care provided to dependent children, the elderly, the sick, and the disabled in care institutions or in the home of the person requiring care. Care policies and the provision of care services are intrinsically related to the achievement of equality between women and men. The lack of affordable, accessible, and high- quality care services, and the fact that care work is not equally shared between women and men have a direct negative impact on women's ability to participate in all aspects of social, economic, cultural, and political life.

Career Woman: A woman who considers her job, and success in her work, to be important in her life. This phrase is somewhat outdated and can carry sexist and derogatory connotations.

Casual Sex: Sexual encounters between people who barely know each other and where pleasure is generated by excitement and novelty, or between people who have sexual encounters but have no intention to develop the relationship into a long-term commitment. This is also referred to sometimes as recreational sex.

CEDAW (The Convention on the Elimination of All Forms of Discrimination against Women): An international convention adopted in 1979 by the UN General Assembly, is often described as an international bill of rights for women. Consisting of a preamble and 30 articles, it defines what constitutes discrimination against women and sets up an agenda for national action to end such discrimination. By accepting the Convention, States commit themselves to undertake a series of measures to end discrimination against women in all forms: • to incorporate the principle of equality of men and women in their legal system, abolish all discriminatory laws and adopt appropriate ones prohibiting discrimination against women; • to establish tribunals and other public institutions to ensure the effective protection of women against discrimination; and • to ensure elimination of all acts of discrimination against women by persons, organisations or enterprises. Countries that have ratified or acceded to the convention are legally bound to put its provisions into practice. They are also committed to submit national reports, at least every four years, on measures they have taken to comply with their treaty obligations. Optional Protocol to CEDAW 4 was adopted in 1999 by the General Assembly. States which ratify the Optional Protocol recognize the competence of the Committee on the Elimination of Discrimination against Women to consider petitions from individual women or groups of women who have exhausted all national remedies. The Optional Protocol also entitles the Committee to conduct inquiries into the grave or systematic violations of the Convention. CEDAW articulates the nature and meaning of sex-based discrimination and gender equality and lays out State obligations to eliminate discrimination and achieve substantiate equality. The convention covers not only discriminatory laws, but also practices and customs, and it applies not only to State action but also to the State responsibility to address discrimination against women by private actors. The convention covers both civil and political rights (rights to vote, to participate in public life, to acquire, change or retain their nationality, equality before the law and freedom of movement), and economic, social, and cultural rights (rights to education, work, health and financial credit). CEDAW also pays specific attention to particular phenomena such as trafficking, certain groups of women, such as rural women, and specific areas where there are special risks to women's full enjoyment of their human rights, such as matters related to marriage and the family. CEDAW also specifies the different ways in which States Parties are to eliminate discrimination, including through appropriate legislation prohibiting discrimination, or positive action to improve the status of women.

Celibacy: Abstinence from all sexual activities and sexual relations, especially for religious reasons.

Chicana Feminism (a.k.a. Xicanism): A movement for and by Chicanas and Latinas who work for gender equity through the arts and action.

Chicana Feminism: Chicana feminism, also called Xicanisma, is a socio-political movement in the United States that analyzes the historical, cultural, spiritual, educational, and economic intersections of Mexican-American women that identify as Chicana. Chicana feminism challenges the stereotypes that Chicanas face across lines of gender, ethnicity, race, class, and sexuality. Most importantly, Chicana feminism serves as a movement, theory, and praxis that help women reclaim their existence between and among the Chicano Movement and American feminist movements.

Christian Egalitarianism: All people are equal before God and in Christ; have equal responsibility to use their gifts and obey their calling to the glory of God; and are called to roles and ministries without regard to class, gender, or race.

Christian Feminism: Christian feminism is a school of Christian theology that seeks to advance and understand the equality of men and women morally, socially, spiritually, and in leadership from a Christian perspective. Christian feminists argue that contributions by women, and an acknowledgment of women's value, are necessary for a complete understanding of Christianity. Christian feminists believe that God does not discriminate on the basis of biologically determined characteristics such as sex and race, but created all humans to exist in harmony and equality, regardless of race or gender. Christian feminists generally advocate for anti-essentialism as a part of their belief system, acknowledging that gender identities do not mandate a certain set of personality traits. Their major issues include the ordination of women, biblical equality in marriage, recognition of equal spiritual and moral abilities, reproductive rights, integration of gender neutral pronouns within readings of the Bible, and the search for a feminine or gender-transcendent divine. Christian- feminists often draw on the teachings of other religions and ideologies in addition to biblical evidence, and other Christian- based texts throughout history that advocate for women's rights.

Cinderella Complex: A phrase coined by feminist author Collette Dowling to describe women who have an unconscious fear of independence and desire to be taken care of.

Circular and Linear Thinking: Linear thinking tends to be a goal-driven, solely pursuing the lines dictated by logic and evidence in pursuit of its goals or conclusions; circular thinking explores "around" a subject, often pausing for multiple viewpoints, networking in ways that may not seem to bear directly on the problem at hand, and as a result this type of thinking tends to develop ideas within a larger context, thus locating multiple perspectives in its conclusions.

Circular Thinking: This is not to be confused with circular reasoning, a fallacy that embeds the conclusion as part of the argument, "begging the question."

Cisgender: The term for a person whose biological sex "matches" the gender that society associates with that sex (i.e. being biologically female and also identifying as a woman, as opposed to being born biologically female and identifying as a male).

Cissexism: Transphobia as normalised by social systems (or) assumptions or erasure of Trans folk.

Citizen and Citizenship: A citizen is most commonly understood as an inhabitant of a specific country who owes allegiance to its government and is entitled to the protection and rights it provides. From this legal definition, 'citizenship' is viewed as the exercise of rights and responsibilities. Even as governments exert legal control on who is and isn't a citizen, definitions of citizenship vary with different understandings of democracy and the role of the state. The prevalent narrow view is that a government decides who legitimately belongs (excluding immigrants); citizens' rights are limited to voting and using public services and infrastructure. Alternatively, a social justice notion of citizenship and being a citizen is dynamic – makers and shapers – as opposed to the above "users and choosers" definition (Gaventa, 1997). From a feminist point of view, citizenship involves claiming voice and accountability in all areas of life – public, private, and intimate – to challenge power hierarchies and exercise rights. (VeneKlasen and Miller, 2002)

Civil Society: The space for voluntary collective action around shared goals and interests, outside both the market and the state but interacting with them. "It is often described as the space between the citizen and the state, where the will of citizens is manifested and mobilised outside of official (i.e., state) auspices," says the United Nations Development Programme (UNDP). Civil society organisations include nongovernmental organisations, trade unions, grassroots organisations, women's groups, academic, and research institutions, faith-based groups, cooperatives, local community groups, professional associations, youth organizations, and cultural groups. Government agencies, political representatives, political parties and for-profit businesses are not part of civil society. Repressive states control social relationships and organisations and often break down the values that enable people to work together.

Class: Definitions may vary; a working definition is that class is "a relative social ranking based on income, wealth, family lineage, education, status and/or power. (Yeskel and Leondar-Wright, 1997).

Classism: Oppression of poor people and the institutional, cultural, and individual set of practices and beliefs that assign differential value to people according to their socio-economic class; and an economic system that creates excessive inequality and causes basic human needs to go unmet. (Yeskel and Leondar-Wright, 1997).

Coalitions, Alliances, and Networks: While these terms are used differently in different contexts, they are often used interchangeably. Some distinctions are helpful in order to envision and tailor relationships to best suit their purpose and the needs of diverse members. Coalitions generally have a more formalised structure, for example employing staff or having standing committees, and usually, involve long-term relationships among the members. Alliances generally involve shorter-term relationships that come together around specific objectives and/ or at distinct moments. Networks tend to be loose, flexible associations of people and groups brought together by a common concern or interest to share information and ideas. (VeneKlasen and Miller, 2002)

Commission on the Status of Women (CSW): The Commission on the Status of Women (CSW) is a functional commission of the United Nations Economic and Social Council (ECOSOC). Established in 1946, the CSW is dedicated exclusively to gender equality and the advancement of the status of women. It is the principal global policy-making body, meeting annually to evaluate progress on gender equality, identify challenges, set standards and formulate concrete policies to promote gender equality and the advancement of women worldwide. CSW prepares recommendations and reports to ECOSOC on the promotion of women's rights in all fields: political, economic, civil, social and educational. CSW also prepares recommendations to ECOSOC on problems relating to women's rights that require immediate attention.

Commodity Feminism: A variety of feminism that co-opts the movement's ideals for profit. Ivanka Trump has been accused of peddling this brand of feminism, using her #WomenWhoWork campaign to sell her eponymous lifestyle brand.

Commons: Concept from the 18th century pre-capitalism period referring to resources that the public shares. Commons include tangible and intangible resources like parks, air and space, clean water, traditional knowledge, biodiversity, and the Internet—areas of common interest and necessity to which all members of a society have or should have access. Commons embody the efforts of multiple individuals and inputs; i.e. no single individual or entity can claim private ownership of common resources (e.g., government- funded scientific research, intellectual property). The current stage of capitalism includes a major offensive against the public commons, through privatisation of land, and resources as seen in the expansion of extractive industries like mining, oil and timber production onto public and indigenous lands, for example. Today, activists are "reinventing" and "reclaiming" the commons to democratise access to these vital resources and ensure that we protect them for current and future generations. But most of all what they are doing is defending the few spaces of commons left from encroachment.

Community Managing Role: This is one of "women's triple roles" which refer to the reproductive, productive, and community managing roles.

Community managing role activities are undertaken primarily by women, as an extension of their reproductive role, to ensure the provision and maintenance of scarce resources of collective consumption such as water, healthcare and education. This is voluntary unpaid work undertaken in 'free' time (OR) Activities undertaken primarily by women at the community level, as an extension of their reproductive role, to ensure the provision, and maintenance of scarce resources of collective consumption such as water, healthcare, and education. This is voluntary unpaid work undertaken in 'free' time.

Community Organising: Community organising is a process by which a group of people come together around a shared concern or problem and work together to find a solution that includes taking measures to influence the policies or culture surrounding them. Community organising often starts by addressing a concrete, unmet practical need and evolves to address the structural causes of the problem, thereby transforming power. A critical element of organising is the development of community leaders, using the organising process to better understand political dynamics change, and organising. (VeneKlasen and Miller, 2002)

Community Politics Role: Activities are undertaken primarily by men at the community level, organising at the formal political level, often within the framework of national politics. This work is usually undertaken by men and may be paid directly or result in increased power and status.

Complementarianism: A theological view that men and women have different but complementary roles and responsibilities in marriage, family life, religious leadership, and elsewhere; these separate roles preclude women from specific functions of ministry within the Church.

Compulsory Heterosexuality: It is the idea that heterosexuality is assumed and enforced by a patriarchal society. This refers to the idea that heterosexuality can be adopted by people regardless of their personal sexual preferences. Heterosexuality is viewed as the natural inclination or obligation by both sexes. Consequently, anyone who differs from the normalcy of heterosexuality is deemed deviant or abhorrent. Adrienne Rich popularised the term *compulsory heterosexuality* in her 1980 essay titled "Compulsory Heterosexuality and Lesbian Existence". Rich's first concept of compulsory heterosexuality only included women, however, later revisions of the idea have included how compulsory heterosexuality affects men. Common examples include the assumption that children will grow up to marry a person of the opposite sex, children must steer away from having friends of the opposite sex, and sexual education books that exclusively discuss heterosexuality, the concept of "coming out", religious and secular organisations that assume all members are heterosexual and believing that if one can pretend to be heterosexual that is better than being non- heterosexual. Compulsory heterosexuality is seen as ignorant, a contributor to homophobia by marginalising non-heterosexuals, treating heterosexuality as the superior default, and decreasing awareness of the large number of people within the population who are not heterosexual.

Condom: A flexible sheath (usually made of thin latex or polyurethane) designed to cover the penis (male condom) or vulva (female condom) during sexual intercourse for contraceptive purposes or as a means of preventing sexually transmitted infections (STIs). Both the male and female condoms, if used consistently, prevent the spread of STIs including HIV, an issue that adds to the controversy around condom use among conservative groups.

Conflict Theories: Conflict theories are perspectives in sociology and social psychology that emphasize a materialist interpretation of history, dialectical method of analysis, a critical stance toward existing social arrangements, and political programme of revolution or, at least, reform. Conflict theories draw attention to power differentials, such as class conflict, and generally contrast historically dominant ideologies. It is therefore a macro-level analysis of society.

Conscientisation: This means the process of becoming aware of the extent to which problems arise not so much from an individual's inadequacies, but rather from the systematic discrimination against a social group that puts all members of the system as a whole at a disadvantage. In women's development, conscientisation, therefore, involves the process by which women collectively analyse and understand the gender discrimination which they are up against. This is the basis for action to overcome and dismantle the obstacles which have been holding them back. In the Women's Equality & Empowerment Framework, women's and men's conscientisation is seen as the crucial step in the process of empowerment. It is crucial to the process of development in general. Through conscientisation, both men and women come to understand the nature of the obstacles they face, and the need therefore to mobilise for collective action. The process of discussion and understanding of common problems is a critical phase, for it enables and motivates men and women to move from being mere beneficiaries to being actors and active participants in their development. Conscientisation involves the identification of disparities and the analysis of their underlying causes.

Consciousness Raising: Consciousness-raising (also called awareness raising) is a form of activism, popularised by United States feminists in the late 1960s. It often takes the form of a group of people attempting to focus the attention of a wider group of people on some cause or condition. Common issues include diseases (e.g. breast cancer, AIDS), conflicts (e.g. the Darfur genocide, global warming), movements (e.g. Greenpeace, PETA, Earth Hour), and political parties or politicians. Since informing the populace of public concern is often regarded as the first step to changing how the institutions handle it, raising awareness is often the first activity in which any advocacy group engages. However, in practice, raising awareness is often combined with other activities, such as fundraising, membership drives, or advocacy, to harness and/or sustain the motivation of new supporters, which may be at its highest just after they have learned and digested the new information. The term *awareness- raising* is used in the Yogyakarta Principles against discriminatory attitudes and LGBT stereotypes, as well as the Convention on the Rights of Persons with Disabilities to combat stereotypes, prejudices, and harmful practices toward people with disabilities.

Constituency Building: Activities aimed at strengthening the involvement of those most affected by an issue in the design and leadership of advocacy. Effective constituency building enhances the organisation and political voice of people and lends legitimacy and leverage to change efforts. However, by focusing on constituencies solely to legitimize and bolster policy claims without concern for the longer- term questions of power and citizenship, some of these efforts have been criticized as "instrumentalist," and worse, have alienated communities otherwise interested in supporting change. (VeneKlasen and Miller, 2002).

Consumerism: The practice of purchasing the goods and services one needs or perceives as needed to sustain life and wellbeing (as opposed to building or creating things yourself or sharing them cooperatively within a community, for example). Consumerism represents a way of life, a way of projecting a social identity based on the things you buy. The neo-liberal free- market economy relies on consumerism to drive economic growth. Public and economic policies promote consumption, for example, by making it cheap to borrow money or by allowing employers to eliminate expensive labour standards, thereby making their products cheaper for the consumer while media is used to induce new needs and desires.

Contraceptive: A chemical agent and/or physical device for the prevention of fertility. Contraceptives prevent sexual intercourse from resulting in conception. A woman's right to control her fertility through any means she chooses is a tenet of the women's reproductive health rights agenda. In many societies, gender roles dictate that women are responsible for contraceptive use. In others, gender roles also make women responsible for contraceptive use, but gender relations dictate that they cannot use contraceptives without their partners' permission. Many contraceptives used by women (e.g., oral contraceptives, intrauterine devices, and implants) have undesirable side effects. A key goal in improving the quality of reproductive health services is to make contraceptives safe for women and to broaden responsibility for their use to men, in part by broadening the choice of contraceptives for both men and women. (See also **Family Planning; Reproductive Health; Reproductive Rights**.).

Control: It means the ability to direct, or influence events so that one's interests are protected. The Women's Equality & Empowerment Framework recognises women's equality of control with men as the most important or "highest" aspect of women's development - where women ensure that resources and benefits are distributed so that both women and men get equal shares. Whereas conscientisation and participation are essential to the process of women's empowerment, it is only gender equality in control which provides the outcome.

Convention: An international agreement among nations. Such agreements may have different names: treaty, covenant, convention, or pact.

Counter Narrative vs. Master Narrative: Counter- narratives challenge or question the master narratives upheld by those who have power. Master narratives support the values and beliefs of a dominant group.

Creep(er): A strange person who you strongly dislike; an unpleasant or obnoxious person; someone who causes you to feel nervous and afraid.

Crimes of Honour: (See Honour Killing).

Critical Consciousness: An ever-evolving questioning awareness about the world and how power operates. A strategy and objective of feminist movement building, consciousness-raising includes developing an understanding of how personal experiences are linked to and influenced by political and economic systems; history and awareness of current events; and the dynamics of power. It engages an understanding of self, including the simultaneity of privileges and oppressions (e.g., race, class, gender). For women, developing a critical understanding of our situation helps us to overcome self-doubt fostered by subordination and sexism enabling us to recognize and tap into our power and link with others to address common issues. (Vene Klasen, 2006).

Critical Mass: The minimum number of a non-majority group necessary before change can occur in an institution or structure affecting the status of that group. It is also the level at which change can be self-sustaining. According to the United Nations, the critical mass threshold is estimated to be 30 to 35 percent participation by a non-majority group. Reaching the numerical goal of 30 percent participation does not automatically lead to desired change, as it is also dependent upon the quality of the participation, the decision-making authority of those participants and the environment still dictated by the majority group. Still, achieving critical mass in organisations is considered by many experts to be a necessary and priority goal in attaining gender equality. (See also **Tokenism**.).

Cross-Dressing: Act of dressing as the Opposite gender as against of one's birth sex.

Cult of True Womanhood: An ideology of the upper and middle classes during the nineteenth century which perpetuated the domestic sphere of women and determined their place as the homemaker. It has deep roots in Christian ideology and the affirmation of Christian ideals. There are four cardinal virtues equated to The Cult of True Womenhood: 1. Piety: perpetuating religious standards; women are understood to be more religious than men. 2. Purity: virginal; pure in all aspects of life. 3. Submission: A woman is to comply with her husband's rules and desires; to obey the male of the house. 4. Domesticity: women's domain is in the home, outside of the public sphere. The women were responsible for making the home a "haven" as well as having responsibility for raising the children. The Cult of True Womanhood is also related to the "Angel of the Home" in regards to its religious overtones and motifs.

Cultural Appropriation: Taking intellectual property, traditional knowledge, cultural expressions, or artifacts from someone else's culture without permission. This can include unauthorised use of another culture's dance, dress, music, language, folklore, cuisine, traditional medicine, religious symbols, etc.

Cultural Capital: A type of noneconomic currency that may facilitate an individual's social mobility. According to the French philosopher, Pierre Bourdieu (1986), cultural capital can be embodied (e.g., mastering a craft); objectified (e.g., collecting visual art); and institutionalised (e.g., publishing scholarship).

Cultural Critic: A feminist critic who critiques the social practices of the status quo that reinforce marginalisation.

Cultural Feminism: Cultural feminism is the notion that there is a "female nature" or "female essence" or related attempts to revalidate attributes ascribed to femaleness. It is also used to describe theories that commend innate differences between women and men.

Cultural Hegemony: A term used by Antonio Gramsci, depicts the Marxist philosophy of cultural domination of ruling society to the working class. Here, it is use of ordinary practices and shared values as a means by which one group can dominate a diverse culture.

Culture: Refers to aspects of a social environment that are used to communicate values such as language, dress, food, traditions, and rituals. In political terms, culture can be a binding quality that strengthens the solidarity of communities, for example, by reclaiming traditional cultures, resisting dominant cultures, and building "cultures of resistance." At the same time, "respect for culture" is an oft-used argument to resist social changes toward equality and justice. Culture is ever-changing, influenced by dominant economic, political and social dynamics, and varies from one context to another, for example, standards of beauty or notions of what constitutes a family. It is not a single body of beliefs immune to external influences or changes over time.

Customary Law: In many countries, a system of civil law runs parallel to indigenous and religious systems of customary law. Customary law often applies in matters concerned with family law, and thus has a great deal of impact on women's everyday lives, as it deals with issues such as marriage, divorce, inheritance, and child custody. The duality of legal systems in some countries, where both civil and customary law exist side by side, hinders the implementation of international human rights instruments like CEDAW. This is because these instruments are civil law instruments, which cannot be codified into customary law. Furthermore, where customary law is practiced in a way that marginalises or discriminates against women as equal citizens, it is highly unlikely that human rights principles such as the right to equality and the provisions of other international instruments will be considered.

Date Rape: A form of unwanted sexual vaginal, anal, or oral intercourse or any other sexual contact involving the use of force, or threat of force or deception perpetrated by an acquaintance of the rape survivor. It is also called acquaintance rape. Unsuccessful attempts are also included within the term 'rape'. Groups within a society, where, fewer opportunities to have access to resources such as education, health, credit, and power. Some examples of disadvantaged groups are ethnic groups, older adults, children, and disabled persons. Women and girls in these groups tend to have even fewer opportunities than their male counterparts; in other words, they are doubly disadvantaged/doubly marginalised. They are very often invisible in media reports that make these groups seem homogenous, especially when details about them – such as the sex and age of persons within them – are not disaggregated. (See also **Discrimination; Gender-Disaggregated Data)**

De Facto Discrimination: The practice of many immigration officials in various countries is to find a woman traveling alone with her minor children "suspicious" while men traveling with their children are seldom questioned.

De Jure Discrimination: In some countries, the law states that women (citizens) who marry foreign men lose their citizenship and/or property rights. On the other hand, men (citizens) married to foreigners do not lose their citizenship and/or property rights.

Decent Work: Decent work is the availability of employment in conditions of freedom, equity, human security, and dignity. According to the International Labour Organisation (ILO), decent work involves opportunities for work that is productive and delivers a fair income, security in the workplace and social protection for families, better prospects for personal development and social integration, freedom for people to express their concerns, organise and participate in the decisions that affect their lives and equality of opportunity and treatment for all women and men. United Nations Economic and Social Council have also given a General Comment that defines decent work and requires satisfaction of Article 6 of the International Covenant on Economic, Social and Cultural Rights.

Decision-Making and Participation: Women's participation in public life, specifically in the realm of public decision-making, is a key measure of the empowerment of women and a strategy for bringing about gender equality. The Beijing Platform for Action has two related strategic objectives: Take measures to ensure women's equal access to and full participation in power structures and decision-making (G.1) and Increase women's capacity to participate in decision-making and leadership (G.2). Women's equal participation in decision-making is not only a demand for simple justice or democracy but can also be seen as a necessary condition for women's interests to be taken into account. Without the active participation of women and the incorporation of women's perspective at all levels of decision-making, the goals of equality, development, and peace cannot be achieved. It is important to recognize that decision-making refers to many different areas of public life, including but unlimited decision-making positions in Governments, legislative bodies, and political parties.It is also necessary to seek the equal representation of women and men in decision-making positions in the areas of art, culture, sports, the media, education, religion, and the law, as well as employer organisations and trade unions, transnational and national corporations, banks, academic and scientific institutions, and regional and international organisations, including those in the United Nations system.

Declaration on the Elimination of Violence Against Women: In 1993, the General Assembly adopted the Declaration on the Elimination of Violence against Women, which serves as a complement to CEDAW in efforts to eliminate violence against women. The Declaration defines "violence against women" as any act of gender-based violence that results in, or is likely to result in, physical, sexual or psychological harm or suffering to women, including threats of such acts, coercion or arbitrary deprivation of liberty, whether occurring in public or in private life. It establishes that violence against women shall be understood to encompass, but not be limited to physical, sexual, and psychological violence occurring in the family, within the general community and perpetrated or condoned by the state. Finally, it argues that states should condemn violence against women and should not invoke any custom, tradition, or religious consideration to avoid their obligations concerning its elimination.

Deconstruction: "Strategy of critical analysis...directed towards exposing unquestioned metaphysical assumptions and internal contradictions in philosophical and literary language" (OED). Deconstructive analysis shows the text's failure to fulfill its "project" by exposing overly simplistic binary assumptions, gaps (aporia) in the message and by showing the absence of those obscure present.

Democracy: System of decision- making in which power is exercised by the people. Democracy depends not only on the structures that allow decision-making by the people but also on whether those people are free, informed, and safe to have input into and control over decisions that impact their lives. For feminists, questions of democratic participation in the household, sexual realm, media, knowledge creation, and the economic sphere are as important as the quality of participation in the public arena.

Derailing: Posting a comment on a thread that is off-topic from the original post.

Deregulation: The removal or watering-down of government rules and regulations, including consumer, labour and environmental protections, that constrain or increase the cost of the operation of corporations and other economic actors, often to protect the public good. Also see **neo-liberalism.**

Development: It is here used to mean both the improved material well-being (welfare) of people and the process by which this improved well-being is achieved. The concept of development also includes an element of equality - that material benefits from the development process should be fairly distributed, especially to benefit those most in need - the disadvantaged and the most vulnerable. Therefore, the special interest in women's development arises because women are a majority amongst the most disadvantaged. According to the United Nations Development Programme (UNDP), development is about "expanding the choices people have to lead lives that they value… it is about much more than economic growth..." In the United Nations system, the concept of human development is utilised. It is measured by the human development index (HDI) along with other indicators, such as the Gender-Related Development Index (GDI). The HDI includes three basic components: longevity, knowledge and standard of living. Longevity is measured by life expectancy, knowledge, is measured by a combination of adult literacy and average years of 5 schoolings, and standard of living is measured by purchasing power, based on real GDP per capita adjusted for the local cost of living (known as **'Purchasing Power Parity'**).

Dichotomy: It means "two divided parts." It refers to a division of unity or system into two mutually exclusive, opposing categories. The dichotomy is a way of thinking that sees everything in purely "either/or" terms, for example, male/female, good/back, obscuring complexity in analyses of difference. Feminists speak of sexual dichotomy, meaning the division of humanity into two sexes, the female and the male, which are defined by exclusion and that requires that every human being belongs to one or the other sex. Sexual dichotomy is a manifestation of sexism in that it denies the possibility that biological females can have masculine characteristics and biological males, feminine characteristics.

Difference Feminism: The term was developed by Carol Gilligan, a theory that posits fundamental biological, psychological, and spiritual differences between men and women. The concept has many variations, including reverse gender polarity (the view that women are superior to men), and notions of gender complementarily. Difference feminism holds that there are differences between men and women but that no value judgment can be placed upon them and both genders have equal moral status as persons.

Differences in Legal Status and Entitlements: There are many instances in which equal rights to personal status, security, land, inheritance, and employment opportunities are denied to women by law or practice.

Differential Access to and Control Over Resources: Productive, reproductive and community roles require the use of resources. In general, women and men have different levels of both: access to the resources needed for their work, and control over those resources. Access: the opportunity to make use of something. Control: the ability to define its use and impose that definition on others. Economic/Political/Social/Time/Resources: Resources can be economic: such as land or equipment; political: such as representation, leadership and legal structures; social: such as childcare, family planning, education; and also time — a critical but often scarce resource.

Disability: Disability is defined within specific contexts and depends on historical and cultural issues. A person with a disability is defined as someone who experiences a physical or mental condition that limits the ability to perform a major life activity such as walking, breathing, seeing, hearing, thinking or working. Major types of disabilities include: perceptual, illness-related, physical, developmental, mental/emotional, chronic/acute, and environmental. (Rauscher and McClintock, 1997)

Disabled: The way that having a disability affects some people with impairments – they are disabled by society. Also, an identity and cultural term that address the person with disabilities.

Disadvantaged Groups: Groups within a society that have fewer opportunities to have access to resources such as education, health, credit, and power. Some examples of disadvantaged groups are ethnic groups, older adults, children, and disabled persons. Women and girls in these groups tend to have even fewer opportunities than their male counterparts; in other words, they are doubly disadvantaged/doubly marginalised. They are very often invisible in media reports that make these groups seem homogenous, especially when details about them – such as the sex and age of persons within them – are not disaggregated. (See also **Discrimination; Gender-Disaggregated Data**.).

Disaggregated Data (Sex): For a gender analysis, all data should be separated by gender to allow differential impacts on men and women to be measured. Sex disaggregated data is quantitative statistical information on differences and inequalities between women and men. Sex disaggregated data might reveal, for example, quantitative differences between women and men in morbidity and mortality; differences between girls and boys in school attendance, retention, and achievement; differences between men and women in access to and repayment of credit; or differences between men and women in voter registration, participation in elections and election to office.

Discrimination (Direct and Indirect): Discrimination occurs in various forms in everyday life. As defined by the ILO (2003a). Any distinction, exclusion, or preference made based on race, colour, sex, religion, political opinion, national extraction, or social origin which has the effect of nullifying or impairing equality of opportunity and treatment in employment or occupation is discriminatory. Alongside racial discrimination, gender discrimination can be seen as one major form of discrimination. Discrimination can be distinguished into two forms: direct and indirect. The first form arises if, without being less qualified, certain groups of society are explicitly excluded or disadvantaged by the legal framework due to characteristics such as gender. Indirect discrimination occurs if intrinsically neutral rules or laws negatively affect certain groups, e.g. female workers. Discrimination of part-time workers against full- time employees is still present in nearly every country. As a major proportion of part-time workers are female, this disadvantages women as well.

Discrimination (Gender Discrimination): "Any distinction, exclusion or restriction made based on sex which has the effect or purpose of impairing or nullifying the recognition, enjoyment or exercise by women, irrespective of their marital status, based on equality of men and women, of human rights and fundamental freedoms in the political, economic, social, cultural, civil or any other field" [United Nations, 1979. 'Convention on the Elimination of all forms of Discrimination against Women,' Article 1]. Discrimination can stem from both law (de jure) or practice (de facto). The CEDAW Convention recognizes and addresses both forms of discrimination, whether contained in laws, policies, procedures, or practice. • de jure discrimination e.g., in some countries, a woman is not allowed to leave the country or hold a job without the consent of her husband. • de facto discrimination e.g., a man and woman may hold the same job position and perform the same duties, but their benefits may differ.

Discrimination (Gender): The Convention on the Elimination of all Forms of Discrimination against Women (CEDAW), approved by the United Nations in 1979, states that "Discrimination against women shall mean distinction, exclusion, or restriction made based on the sex which has the purpose of impairing or nullifying the recognition, enjoyment, or exercise by women, irrespective of their marital status, based on equality of men and women, of human rights and fundamental freedoms in the political, economic, social, cultural, civil or any other field". It refers to any distinction, exclusion, or restriction made on the basis of socially constructed gender roles and norms, which prevents a person from enjoying full human rights.

Discrimination (Systemic): Systemic discrimination is caused by policies and practices that are built into the ways that institutions operate, and that have the effect of excluding women and minorities. For example, in societies where the belief is strong that whatever happens within the household is the concern of household members only, the police force and judiciary, organisations within the institution of the state are likely routinely to avoid addressing questions of domestic violence, leading to systemic discrimination against all the women who experience violence within the home.

Discrimination against Girls and Women: Discrimination against girls and women means directly or indirectly treating girls and women differently from boys and men in a way that prevents them from enjoying their rights. Discrimination can be direct or indirect. Direct discrimination against girls and women is generally easier to recognize as the discrimination is quite obvious. For example, in some countries, women cannot legally own property; they are forbidden by law to take certain jobs; or the customs of a community may not permit girls to go for higher education. Indirect discrimination against girls and women can be difficult to recognize. It refers to situations that may appear to be unbiased but result in unequal treatment of girls and women. For example, a job for a police officer may have minimum height and weight criteria which women may find difficult to fulfill. As a result, women may be unable to become police officers.

Displaced Women: Displaced persons are those who have fled or been driven from their communities to other localities within their country of nationality. According to the UNHCR, more than 75% of displaced persons are women and their children, they are subjected to physical and sexual violence as much during their flight as when they arrive in the country of asylum, be it from members of the armed forces, immigration agents, bandits, pirates, local populations, individuals belonging to rival ethnic groups or other refugees.

Diversity: The key physical and social differences among people as shaped by class, gender, ethnicity, sexuality, etc. Diversity as a political principle for feminist organising is about the inclusion of different types of people in a group, an organisation or an agenda. It refers to the complex, enriching, and natural and socially defined variations among women and within an individual woman and group of women understood within the context of the shared experience of all women living in a world defined by patriarchy. While diversity is an important aspiration of many feminist movements, it is also a source of conflict due to variations of power and privilege.

Division for the Advancement of Women (DAW): International Research and Training Institute for the Advancement of Women (INSTRAW) Office of the Special Adviser on Gender Issues and Advancement of Women (OSAGI) United Nations Development Fund for Women (UNIFEM): The main roles of UN Women are: To support governmental entity, such as, the Commission on the Status of Women in their formulation of policies, global standards and norms. Also to help the Member States to implement the standards; standing ready to provide suitable technical and financial support to those countries that request it, and to forge effective partnerships with civil society. To hold the UN system accountable for its commitments on gender equality, including regular monitoring of system-wide progress.

Domestic Responsibilities: Tasks performed inside a household to ensure that the basic needs of its members are met, such as cooking, cleaning, and taking care of children or older adults. Traditionally, a person is not paid for performing these tasks, and power or status is not necessarily accorded because of these responsibilities. In many societies, the person responsible for the household is in a subordinate position within it and most often, women and girls are responsible for all household tasks, even if they work outside the home. It is this traditional, the gender-based division of household responsibilities that can limit girls' access to education when they are kept out of school or leave early to assume domestic responsibilities. But at the same time, the sharing of household responsibilities is much more common these days in many societies. Domestic responsibilities are not the sole obligation of female members in a household. (See also **Gender-Based Division of Labour; Household Maintenance; Reproductive Labour**.).

Domestic Violence: Pattern of coercive behaviour, whether physical, psychological, or sexual, against any member of a family or household, including by an intimate partner. Domestic violence against women and girls ranges from humiliation and economic coercion to physical assault, usually at the hands of intimate partners, husbands, brothers, uncles, or males within or associated within the household. Same-sex domestic violence occurs, though much less frequently than violence by males against females.

Domestic Work: Domestic work covers work in the home (one's own or another's), including many different activities, situations, and relationships and specific tasks such as cleaning, laundry and ironing; shopping, cooking and fetching water; caring for the sick, elderly, and children; looking after pets; sweeping and garden-tidying. Domestic work fundamentally involves power relationships and is usually undervalued, unpaid, largely invisible, and seen almost exclusively as "women's work" as a result of the sexual division of labour. In all societies, domestic work is assigned to women based on gender criteria; while men may occasionally share in these tasks, nowhere do men do equal work in the home. When women work outside the home in the labour market, other women (or children) are brought in to do domestic work, when finances permit, or women work double workdays, rather than men of the household doing more of the caring work.

Domestic Worker: Domestic workers perform a range of tasks (see above) for and in other peoples' households. They may cook, clean, and wash the laundry, and look after children, the elderly, or persons with disabilities. They may work as gardeners, guardians or family chauffeurs. Most of them are women. They are often excluded, de jure or de facto, from labour laws and social protection. (ILO). Domestic workers are involved in many types of employment relationships that almost always involve elements of race, ethnicity, age, poverty, and class: most domestic workers are and obliged by economic need to leave their own homes to work in those of usually wealthier people. The vast majority of domestic work is done through private arrangements between individuals, someone hired in, or a family member, sometimes with a written contract but usually with none. This makes domestic work a frequently unregulated and unsupervised sector, where women domestic workers face discrimination, labour law violations, and sexual harassment and abuse with little legal or social recourse. In some countries, domestic workers have organised in innovative and influential organisations to collectively transform this situation. (IDWN-International Domestic Workers Network).

Domesticity: About being devoted to one's home life. If one is domestic, he or she might refer to themselves as the caregiver, stay-at-home-dad/mom, homemaker, devoted wife/husband, mother/father, etc.

Much of the time spent would be doing household tasks and chores. Some of these might include cooking, cleaning, caring for the children, managing family's appointments, laundry, grocery shopping, etc. Domesticity may take up as much time as a "full-time" job, if not more. This term is often associated with a woman's role in the family.

Double Burden: A term used to describe the workload of people who work to earn money, but who are also responsible for significant amounts of unpaid domestic labour. This phenomenon is also known as *The Second Shift* as in Arlie Hochs' child's book of the same name. In couples where both partners have paid jobs, women often spend significantly more time than men on household chores and caring work, such as childrearing or caring for sick family members. This outcome is determined in large part by traditional gender roles that have been accepted by society over time. Labor market constraints also play a role in determining who does the bulk of unpaid work. Efforts have been made to document the effects of this double burden on couples placed in such situations. Many studies have traced the effects of the gendered division of labour, and in most cases, there was a notable difference between the time men and women contribute to unpaid labour.

Double Consciousness: A term describing the internal conflict experienced by subordinated groups in an oppressive society. It was coined by W. E. B. Du Bois about African American "double consciousness," including his own, and published in the autoethnographic work, *The Souls of Black Folk*. The term originally referred to the psychological challenge of "always looking at one's self through the eyes" of a racist white society, and "measuring oneself by the means of a nation that looked back in contempt". The term also referred to Du Bois' experiences of reconciling his African heritage with an upbringing in a European-dominated society. The term has since been applied to numerous situations of social inequality, notably women living in patriarchal societies.

Double Day: It means the extended working day that indicates a double burden.

Double Standard: A set of principles that applies differently and usually more rigorously to one group of people or circumstances than to another; especially a code of morals that applies more severe standards of sexual behaviour to women than to men.

Dowry Deaths: It means to be deaths of married women who are murdered or driven to suicide by continuous harassment and torture by their husbands and in-laws over a dispute about their dowry, making women's homes the most dangerous place for them to be. Dowry deaths are found predominantly in India, Pakistan, Bangladesh, and Iran. India reports the highest total number of dowry deaths with 8,391 such deaths reported in 2010, meaning there are 1.4 deaths per 100,000 women. Female dowry deaths account for 40 to 50 percent of all female homicides recorded annually in India, representing a stable trend over the period 1999 to 2016. Adjusted for population, Pakistan, with 2,000 reported such deaths per year, has the highest rate of dowry death at 2.45 per 100,000 women.

Dowry: Money or goods that a woman brings as a gift to her husband upon marriage. Originally a wedding gift of money, jewelry, clothing, or household items made to a daughter from her family, dowry was seen as a type of insurance in case of mistreatment by the bride's new family or a failed marriage. After being around for centuries, the use of dowry has fallen by the wayside and has been outlawed in many countries, largely because of the abuse of women it has led to in many cases. Where it continues in some cultures, it has become common for the groom and his family to demand a dowry of considerable amounts of money or goods (e.g., car, refrigerator, home electronics) at the time of marriage. The most extreme form of dowry-related abuse occurs when women are burnt to death (bride burning) by their husbands or in-laws, often because of disappointment with the woman's dowry. In other cultures, it is the groom's family that pays the dowry to the bride's family, usually with livestock or equivalent goods.

Dworkinian: Relating to American radical feminist Andrea Dworkin (1946-2005). The term means a supporter of Andrea Dworkin and her philosophy.

Ecofeminism: A joining of feminism with ecological concerns based on a perceived connection between the causes of the subjugation of women and the environment.

Economic Autonomy: Right to work and earn one's income, distribution of paid and unpaid work between women and men.

Economic Democracy: A vision in which access to and control over the world's resources – material, financial, human, and natural – are shaped by democratic, transparent, and accountable systems and institutions. Governments, international financial institutions, civil society actors, private companies, and others are all influential in determining whose economic and social interests are advanced and how, yet they lack effective mechanisms for democratic participation. Most people don't know how to engage with these entities or hold them accountable for economic injustices, and the entities block efforts to do so. Policies are based on economic theories and beliefs such as free-market economies and consumer-driven capitalism, rather than resulting from an open debate on serving the public good. In the absence of economic democracy, these policies enable the consolidation of wealth and further marginalise and exploit women, serving as the basis for shredding social safety nets, human rights, and environmental protections.

Educational Attainment: In most countries, women have a lower literacy rate, lower level of enrolment in primary, secondary and tertiary education.

Emergency Contraception: A contraceptive method used after unprotected intercourse is also known as the morning-after pill. The emergency contraception pill (ECP) should be used as soon as possible after unprotected sexual intercourse, health experts say. It prevents ovulation, fertilisation, and/or implantation of the egg. However, once the process of implantation has begun, the ECP will not cause an abortion. (See also **Contraceptive**.).

Emosogynist: Zach Braff in *Garden State*, according to Jezebel. He's emotional, full of angst, and seems like a feminist, but what he wants is a real-life manic pixie dream girl to manipulate and eventually discard after he finds himself.

Empowerment Feminism: Beyoncé's Formation comes on at the club, and you and your friends hit the dance floor hard. Empowerment feminism emphasizes "feeling," though some feminists would argue feeling amazing is not a great gauge of how society is supporting your self-expression and flourishing. Sheryl Sandberg's perpetually controversial Lean In, which focuses on how women can make changes to achieve greater success in the workplace, is another example of empowerment feminism.

Empowerment of Women and Girls: The empowerment of women and girls concerns their gaining power and control over their own lives. It involves awareness-raising, building self-confidence, expansion of choices, increased access to and control over resources and actions to transform the structures and institutions which reinforce and perpetuate gender discrimination and inequality. This implies that to be empowered they must not only have equal capabilities (such as education and health) and equal access to resources, and opportunities (such as land and employment), but they must also have the agency to use these rights, capabilities, resources, and opportunities to make strategic choices and decisions (such as is provided through leadership opportunities and participation in political institutions). In addition, UNESCO explains, "No one can empower another: only the individual can empower herself or himself to make choices or to speak out. However, institutions including international cooperation agencies can support processes that can nurture self-empowerment of individuals or groups". Inputs to promote the empowerment of women should facilitate women's articulation of their needs and priorities and a more active role in promoting these interests and needs. Empowerment of women cannot be achieved in a vacuum; men must be brought along in the process of change. Empowerment should not be seen as a zero-sum game where gains for women automatically imply losses for men. Increasing women's power in empowerment strategies does not refer to power over, or controlling forms of power, but rather to alternative forms of power: the power to; power with and power from within which focus on utilising individual and collective strengths to work towards common goals without coercion or domination.

Empowerment: A process involving a range of activities from individual self-assertion to collective mobilisation and resistance aimed at upending systemic forces and power dynamics that work to marginalise women and other disadvantaged groups. Empowerment begins when individuals recognize the systemic forces of inequality that influence their lives and consciously act with others to change existing power relationships. (Batliwala, 1994) (Or) The goal of empowerment is to address and eliminate discrimination by providing "marginalised groups with methods to obtain full privilege within society. Individually, empowerment implies self-confidence in one's skills and a sense of belonging necessary to succeed in achieving one's goals" (Grand Rapids Community College, 2012, para. 10). A criticism of empowerment is the perpetuation of inequity when one group has power over another to grant access to privilege.

Engendered Citizenship: Concept in which rights and responsibilities of individuals in the formal political arena are applied across all social relationships and institutions, specifically, the family which is conventionally understood as the "private" sphere and therefore not subject to the formal laws and policies of the public sphere. (Molyneaux, 1997)

Epistemic Advantage: This is a term used within feminist theory when attempting to acquire knowledge from the individual lives and experiences of different women. The term is used to describe how women and other minority groups, can have a much clearer understanding of how the power structure works within a given society because they are not members of the dominant group. Uma Narayan, a leading feminist theorist writes about epistemic advantage in her essay entitled, "The Project of Feminist Epistemology: Perspectives from a Nonwestern Feminist". Narayan defines epistemic advantage as "(the oppressed) knowing of the practices of both their contexts and those of their oppressors," (*Feminist Theory Reader*, p. 315). As the feminist movement has moved into the 3rd wave, women's 'intersecting identities' have become increasingly important. There has been an acknowledgment that women of different social locations (concerning race, class, nationality, sexuality, etc.) will have different experiences. Thus, these varying perspectives provide different women with 'advantages' in understanding their specific social locations within a given society's hierarchal power structure. Uma Narayan points out that while it is in the interest of various subordinate groups to know the dominant group, the dominant group does not have the same need. Women of colour often have a clearer understanding of how not only the gender hierarchy plays out in their daily lives, but the racial and class hierarchies as well. African-American feminist movements and Mexican-American feminist movements are only a few of the many marginalised groups that have made efforts in discussing their own 'epistemic advantage' within American society. The Combahee River Collective wrote in "A Black Feminist Statement" about the particular struggles of African-American women. They write: "We have spent a great deal of energy delving into the cultural and experiential nature of our oppression out of necessity because none of these matters have ever been looked at before. No one has ever mentioned the multilayered text of black women's lives," (*Feminist Theory Reader*, p. 167). Thus, it is African-American women's experiences from their specific social location that allows them their epistemic advantage. Although oppressed groups can have an advantage concerning knowledge of the power hierarchy we must remain sensitive to, and aware of, the effects of oppression among various groups and/or individuals. Karen J. Warren points this out in her book *Ecological Feminism* in which she explains that we "must avoid the potential glorification of oppression that may accompany the positing of 'epistemic advantage' to marginalised groups," (p. 131). One of the primary tenets of feminist thought is to focus on the lived experience of women without creating or maintaining any form of hierarchy within various epistemologies and that all women's experience is of value and importance.

Epistemology: An epistemology is a theory of knowledge. Feminists and gender researchers have argued that traditional epistemologies exclude the possibility that women can be "knowers" or agents of knowledge; they claim that the voice of science is a masculine one and that history is written exclusively from the point of view of men (of the dominant class and race). They have proposed alternative epistemologies that legitimate women's knowledge.

Equal Pay: Equal remuneration for men and women workers for work of equal value.

Equal Representation of Women and Men (in UN system): The goal of gender balance/equal representation of women and men applies throughout the United Nations system, and in every department, office, or regional commission, overall and at each level. It applies not only to posts subject to geographical distribution but to all categories of posts, without regard to the type or duration of the appointment, or the series of Staff Rules under which the appointment is made, or the source of funding. Equal representation of women and men in the United Nations system is a longstanding mandate. Articles 8 and 10 of the UN Charter, for example, stipulate that there shall be no restrictions on the eligibility of men and women to participate under conditions of equality in its principal and subsidiary organs. The Universal Declaration of Human Rights also states that there can be no distinction or discrimination based on gender. Acting on these principles, the General Assembly has repeatedly called for gender balance. Most recently, on 4 February 2009, the General Assembly asked the Secretary-General to "review and redouble his efforts to make progress towards achieving the goal of 50/50 gender balance at all levels in the Secretariat and throughout the United Nations system".

Equal Rights Amendment (ERA): American suffragists designed the ERA in the 1920s as a way to guarantee equal rights for women under the United States Constitution. In 1972, after nearly 50 years of political strife, the ERA passed both houses of Congress; however, the states were unable to ratify the proposed amendment. To this day, 11 states have adopted constitutions or amendments, reminiscent of the ERA, to grant equal rights regardless of sex. These states include Alaska, California, Colorado, Connecticut, Illinois, Iowa, Maryland, Montana, Oregon, Utah, and Wyoming.

Equality Feminism: Equality feminism is a subset of the overall feminism movement that focuses on the basic similarities between men and women, and whose ultimate goal is the equality of the sexes in all domains. This includes economic and political equality, equal access within the workplace, freedom from oppressive gender stereotyping, and an androgynous worldview.

Equality of Opportunity: This means that everybody has an equal chance, especially for equal access. In other words, equality of opportunity means that there is no structural discrimination standing in the way of any individual or social group. Equality of opportunity for women would mean ending all gender discrimination.

Equality of Outcome: This is sometimes also referred to as "substantive equality", and refers to the insight that equality of opportunity may not be enough to redress the historical oppression and disadvantage of women. Because of their different positions in society, women and men may not be able to take advantage of equal opportunities to the same extent. In some cases, equal opportunities can harm women's well-being, if women exert time and energy to take advantage of them with no result. To ensure that development interventions result in inequality of outcome for women and men, it is necessary to design them based on gender analysis. "Equal" treatment, therefore, does not mean "the same" treatment.

Equality vs. Equity: Within the global women's movement, there has been a long-running debate about whether we should use the term "equality," "equity," or both. From a human rights perspective, the term "equality" is essential as this is the language of all international human rights treaties, including the Convention on the Elimination of All Forms of Discrimination Against Women (CEDAW). Furthermore, "equality" is a measurable objective that states have a legal obligation to ensure to all citizens. Most importantly, equality obligates states to eliminate all forms of discrimination, as any form of discrimination would result in some individuals being denied equal enjoyment of their rights. In human rights terms, equality is characterized by "equality of results," so, for example, since states must achieve the full and equal participation of women in politics, not only must they remove all barriers to participation, they may also have to undertake "temporary special measures," such as quotas or preferential treatment, to eliminate established patterns of inequality that privilege male participation while discriminating against women. This understanding of equality, referred to as *substantive equality*, has not yet been implemented by states, but this does not mean that they are not legally obligated to do so. To achieve substantive equality, states usually have to enact different laws and policies related to men and women or to different groups of women to level the playing field and ensure that both men and all women enjoy their human rights on an equal basis. For example, *for most women to have equal rights to work with may need different policies and laws from those that other women or men in need. They need maternity leave and extra* *safety conditions when pregnant and as long as they remain principally responsible for reproductive labour, most women need workplace nurseries and assistance to free them from household labour to enter the labour market equally. Furthermore, in human rights terms, states are obligated to take into consideration that not all women are equal either. Women of different ages, classes, caste, ethnicity, race, ability, or other conditions have different social positions and power, and therefore different needs* (Mukhopadhyay, 2004). Because "equality" in the western liberal tradition has been interpreted by states to mean formal equality, i.e. that men and women must be treated identically in the eyes of the laws, some feminists use the term "equity" to emphasise the notion of substantive equality and equality of impact or equality of results and to emphasise that "equality" has too often been translated into "equality of opportunity", which is only sufficient if everyone is starting from a level playing field. For these feminists, "equity" implies that men and women may need different laws and policies to exercise their rights on an equal basis. The critique of "gender equity" stems in part from how the term has been used in political negotiations to undermine women's rights, and because it does not require the elimination of discrimination. During the negotiation of the Beijing Platform for Action, ultra-conservative governments sought to replace "equality" with "equity" throughout the document. By doing so, they would be able to justify the discriminatory treatment of women based on a government's subjective determination of what is fair or just (i.e. equitable). For example, it may be considered "equitable" to prohibit women from inheriting property because local customs or norms require men to provide for the family. In addition, within human rights law, "equality" is clearly defined and has the power of enforcement, whereas "equity" does not provide any legal requirements for states to eliminate discrimination and achieve substantive equality between men and women. Because language is political, there is a risk that using "equity" and "equality" interchangeably can slowly unravel longstanding legal protections enshrined in numerous human rights treaties and agreements. (Facio and Morgan).

Equality: Refers to a revised term for 'Equal Opportunities'. It is based on the legal obligation to comply with anti-discrimination legislation. Equality protects people from minority groups from being discriminated against on the grounds of group membership, i.e. sex, race, disability, sexual orientation, religion or belief, or age. The quest for justice distributed *uniformly/equally* to the resources available in private and public sector.

Equity (and Sustainable Development): Equity derives from a concept of social justice. It represents a belief that there are some things that people should have, that there are basic needs that should be fulfilled, that burdens and rewards should not be spread too divergently across the community, and that policies should be directed with impartiality, fairness, and justice towards these ends. Equity means that there should be a minimum level of income and environmental quality below which nobody falls. The central ethical principle behind sustainable development is equity and particularly intergenerational equity defined as a development that meets the needs of the present without compromising the ability of future generations to meet their own needs. (See also **Gender Equity).**

Equity Feminism (Conservative Feminism): Christina Hoff Sommers, a resident scholar at the conservative American Enterprise Institute, is a champion of what she calls "equity feminism." In her view, "equity feminism" is focused on legal equality between men and women, while "gender feminism" focuses on disempowering women by portraying them as perpetual victims of the patriarchy. In the words of President Trump's advisor Kellyanne Conway: "I look at myself as a product of my choices, not a victim of my circumstances, and that's really to me what conservative feminism if you will, is all about".

Equity: Means fairness and justice in the distribution of benefits and responsibilities. There has been a debate as to whether equality or equity should be the goals of empowerment and change. Equity also means "having a stake in" or "having a share of". It is, therefore, an important component of equality. Technically equality before the law could and often does exist without those deemed to be "equal" really "having a stake in". However, because its meaning of equity has been seen to depend on the definition of fairness and justice it is often said to be a lesser term than equality. In addition, in its legal sense, the term equity may suggest a limited notion of the concept of justice, since equity refers to justice within the existing law, rather than justice by changing the law. By contrast, the Women's Equality & Empowerment Framework follows the 1979 Women's Convention in defining justice for women in terms of gender equality. The lack of definition in the term equity has led to the word being used in quite different ways. It can be used as a "stronger" word than equality, by those who recognize that women must demand more than equality with men in a man's world, and that gender equality must also entail the transformation to a different and more just society. On the other hand, equity can sometimes be used as a weak euphemism for equality by those who wish to avoid awkward issues or direct questions about equal rights for women. The term "gender equity", as we see below, has come to have a more precise meaning.

Essentialism: The assumption that people or things have a fixed "nature," as well as the generalizations that grow from such assumptions (e.g. the old shtick that "women are intuitive and emotional; men are rational and reflective"). Examples of slut-shaming include being criticized or punished for violating dress code policies by dressing in perceived sexually provocative ways, requesting access to birth control, having premarital, casual, or promiscuous sex, engaging in prostitution, or when being victim-blamed for being raped or otherwise sexually assaulted.

Ethnicity: A social construct that groups people based on a common language, history, religion, culture, or background. It is melded with the concept of race, which refers solely to physical characteristics. For example, within the "Asian" racial category, ethnic groups include Japanese, Thai, Cambodian, and Pacific Islander. See race and racism.

Eve Teasing: Refers to the temptress nature of Eve, placing responsibility on the woman as a tease. Teasing the girls, passing comments on them, harassing them, troubling them purposely is called 'eve-teasing.'

Exoticisation: The process of sexualizing a group and reducing it and its members to "Other." The exoticisation of women happens in many ways.

Extractive Industries: Industries that mine natural resources, such as petroleum, coal, gas, and minerals that are sold for profit and/or used for the production of other saleable goods, such as oil, jewelry, or computer chips. These industries are usually run by private foreign or national companies that accumulate huge amounts of wealth, rarely returning or re-investing their profits in the communities from which the natural resources came. Extractive industries are notorious for displacing indigenous populations, wreaking environmental havoc, and exploiting local labour, often enabled by local and national governments eager for private and foreign investment.

Family Planning: Services or programs that allow couples or individuals to make conscious efforts to plan their families and conceive the number of children they want. Family planning programs often offer contraceptives to prevent fertility and advocate child-spacing methods to help protect both mothers' and infants' health. Family planning is often mistakenly used as a synonym for contraceptives, which are only one component of family planning services. In this context, 'family' has been generally understood to refer to heterosexual married couples, thereby leaving out unmarried women and men, lesbians, gay men, and teenagers from both programme policy design and service provision. The word 'planning' may have a negative connotation in cases where family planning programmes are used coercively to control the population through centrally planned and controlled policies and services. Family planning is not a synonym for reproductive healthcare. (See also **Contraceptive**; **Family**; **Reproductive Health**)

Family: The family is defined by a set of relationships created by birth, adoption, lineage, marriage, common-law partnership, or other social commitments. These relationships usually extend beyond a single household to other households and groups. The family promotes social attitudes and values that influence the nature of the state, civil society, and the market. In the neoliberal paradigm, the family is considered a private realm; however, there are usually laws to regulate some aspects of family relationships. (VeneKlasen and Miller, 2002)

Fat Feminism: Fat feminism is a social movement that incorporates feminist themes of equality, social justice, and cultural analysis based on the weight of a woman or a non-binary feminine person. This branch of feminism intersects misogyny and sexism with anti-fat bias. Fat feminists advocate body-positive acceptance for women, regardless of their weight. There is also a focus on eliminating biases experienced directly or indirectly by overweight people. Fat feminism originated during second-wave feminism and is aligned with the fat acceptance movement.

Fatphobia: Hatred or dislike of fat folk.

Fat-Shaming: Unkind and usually public criticism of someone for being overweight.

Female–to–Male (FTM): Someone who was assigned female at birth, but who identifies as a male.

Female: Refers to biologically based references to sex. The word 'female' derives from the Latin 'femella', which is a diminutive of 'femina' or woman. It is often mistakenly assumed to have been derived from 'male', a word that comes through Old French from the Latin 'masculus', which is a diminutive of 'mas' (male, masculine). (See also **Girl; Woman**.).

Female Gaze: How popular visual culture attempts to appeal to a given audience by highlighting the perspectives or attitudes of women.

Female Genital Mutilation (FGM): Female genital mutilation comprises all procedures that involve partial or total removal of the external female genitalia, or other injuries to the female genital organs for non-medical reasons. The practice is mostly carried out by traditional circumcisers, who often play other central roles in communities, such as attending childbirths. Increasingly, however, FGM is being performed by medically trained personnel. FGM is recognised internationally as a violation of the human rights of girls and women. It reflects deep-rooted inequality between the sexes and constitutes an extreme form of discrimination against women. It is nearly always carried out on minors and is a violation of the rights of children. The practice also violates a person's rights to health, security, and physical integrity, the right to be free from torture and cruel, inhuman, or degrading treatment, and the right to life when the procedure results in death.

Female Infanticide: Killing of a girl child within weeks of her birth.

Female vs. Woman: "Female" denotes biological sex, while "woman" denotes gender (expression).

Female-Headed Household: A household in which an adult female is the sole or main income producer and decision-maker. In most countries, women are not usually considered as heads of households unless no adult male is living permanently in the household. The assumptions that heads of households are always adult males; even if a woman's economic contribution to the household's maintenance is the same or greater than a man's, is a form of gender bias. In developing countries, there is a general trend of more and more women being the primary source of economic support for their families.

Femicide: The killings of women and girls because of their gender. The causes and risk factors of this type of violence are linked to gender inequality, discrimination, and economic disempowerment and are the result of a systematic disregard for women's human rights. It occurs in an environment where everyday acts of violence are accepted and impunity is facilitated by the government's refusal to deal with the problems.

Feminazi: A derogatory term for a radical feminist, often used in alt-right circles, for feminists who are perceived to be either sexist against men, or who speak out about topics not believed to be important or real (e.g. sexism in the media, rape culture).

Feminine Ecriture (écriture féminine): "A gendered woman's writing." In "The Laugh of the Medusa," Hélène Cixous claims that "a woman must write herself: must write about women and bring women to writing, from which they have been driven away as violently as from their bodies." *Feminine ecriture* explodes or evades "the discourse that regulates the phallocentric system" of representation.

Feminine Labour: It is also rendered invisible because largely it is work that can never be completed (dishes are always made dirty again and thus can never fully be "done") and/or it is work that is only recognised when it is not completed (There's no milk in the fridge; but the fact that milk had been in the fridge for weeks, even months prior, always ready to be used is not acknowledged). In this way, the work is only recognised when it is incomplete, but not when it is finished. This constructs a system that devalues recognition of the housework completed, potentially even naturalising it and making it an extension of a mother's or wife's love of her family. For example, when I walk into Grammy's house, everything feels so homey, all the cushions just so, and the smell of cookies wafting from the kitchen. What is ignored in these kinds of sentiments is the work that the woman must do to create that homey feel or cook the baked goods and so forth. It functions as a way to naturalise and render her labour and contributions to the home invisible. This is a key component to exploiting feminine domestic labour. If it were visible, it would be far more difficult to exploit it.

Feminine Mystique: First named and explored by Betty Friedan in her ground-breaking book of the same name, the feminine mystique socialises women to locate their identity and meaning of their lives through their husbands and children, and involves a loss of one's identity in the needs and wishes of one's spouse and family.

Feminine: Gender characteristics and roles usually associated with women that may differ across cultures and societies.

Femininity: The set of expectations about how women should behave, think and appear in a given culture.

Feminisation of Migration: The growing participation of women in migration. Women now move around more independently and no longer concerning their family position or under a man's authority (roughly 48 percent of all migrants are women).

Feminisation of Poverty: The majority of the 1.5 billion people living on 1 dollar a day or less are women. In addition, the gap between women and men caught in the cycle of poverty has continued to widen in the past decade, a phenomenon commonly referred to as "the feminisation of poverty". Worldwide, women earn on average slightly more than 50 percent of what men earn. Women living in poverty are often denied access to critical resources such as credit, land, and inheritance. Their labour goes unrewarded and unrecognised. Their healthcare and nutritional needs are not given priority, they lack sufficient access to education and support services, and their participation in decision-making at home and in the community is minimal. Caught in the cycle of poverty, women lack access to resources and services to change their situation. Although in general, women are not always poorer than men, because of the weaker and contingent basis of their entitlements, they are generally more vulnerable and, once poor, have fewer options, in terms of escape. This suggests that interventions address women's poverty requires a different set of policy responses.

Feminism: Feminism begins with the desire to have equal rights and treatment. If you believe that women should be equal and strongly feel that they deserve the same things that men receive then you are considered to be a feminist. If you spoke your mind and fought for rights you would be considered an active feminist. Feminism might often stem from years of experience of men being more dominant than women and a continuation of this into the present day. In her introduction to Changing Their World: Concepts and practices of women's movements (Association of Women's Rights in Development (AWID), 2008), Srilatha Batliwala describes feminism as: "... both an ideology and an analytical framework that is both broader and sharper than it was in the 60s and 70s. The past three decades of activism, advocacy and research, and changing global geopolitical context, have generated powerful insights and experiences about our gains, setbacks, and the challenges of the future. These have also enabled us to re-frame our philosophy and approach, and generate a broader vision for ourselves and the world we want to create. We now stand not only for gender equality, but for the transformation of all social relations of power that oppress, exploit, or marginalise any set of people, women, and men, based on their gender, age, sexual orientation, ability, race, religion, nationality, location, class, caste, or ethnicity. We do not seek simplistic parity with men that would give us the damaging privileges and power that men have enjoyed, and end in losing many of the so-called "feminine" strengths and capacities that women have been socialised to embody. But we seek a transformation that would create gender equality within an entirely new social order – one in which both men and women can individually and collectively live as human beings in societies built on social and economic equality, enjoy the full range of rights, live in harmony with the natural world, and are liberated from violence, conflict, and militarisation." In the current global crisis of rising food prices, exorbitant energy costs, and the nightmare of climate change, feminism stands for economic policies based upon food sovereignty, clean renewable energy, and ecological soundness, to ensure a sustainable future for the planet, all its species, and its natural resources. Given the experience of the gendered and inequitable impacts of neo-liberalism and globalisation, we also stand for economic transformation that creates greater social equity and human development, rather than mere economic growth. We stand for political transformation that guarantees full citizenship rights, the full body of human rights, and for secular, plural, democratic regimes that are transparent, accountable, and responsive to all their citizens, women and men. Escalating levels of war and civil conflict, the conflict-related displacement and subjugation of both women and men, and increasing use of sexual violence against women as a political tool, have led feminists to oppose the violence of any kind and to stand against wars and conflicts that displace, violate, subjugate, and impoverish both women and men. Conversely, we stand for peace and nonviolence – and peaceful resolution of disputes achieved through inclusive and participatory processes. We stand for responsible co-dependence rather than individualism but believe in the right to freedom of choice of individuals concerning their private lives. We oppose the rampant promotion of consumerism that continues to objectify both men and women, and which promotes the wasteful use of the planet's natural resources and devastates the environment. Feminism stands for the power to, not power over – we struggle to change the practice of power both within our structures and movements as well as in the social, economic, and political institutions we engage. We support the renewal of our organizations and movements through empowering new generations of actors and leaders and creating respectful spaces and roles for the beginners, the experienced, and the wise. Finally, we stand against all ideologies and all forms of fundamentalisms that advocate against women's equal rights, or the human rights of any people, be it based on economic, social, racial, ethnic, religious, political, or sexual identity. (Batliwala, 2008) (OR) Feminism is a movement for social, cultural, political, and economic equality of women and men. It is a campaign against gender inequalities and it strives for equal rights for women. Feminism can be also defined as the right to enough information available to every single woman so that she can choose to live a life that is not discriminatory and which works within the principles of social, cultural, political, and economic equality and independence. Feminism can be also defined as a global phenomenon that addresses various issues related to women across the world in a specific manner as applicable to a particular culture or society. Though the issues related to feminism may differ for different societies and cultures they are broadly tied together with the underlying philosophy of achieving equality of gender in every sphere of life. So feminism cannot be tied to any narrow definitions based on a particular class, race, or religion.

Feminism and Modern Architecture: Feminist theory as it relates to architecture has forged the way for the rediscovery of such female architects as Eileen Gray. These women imagined an architecture that challenged the way the traditional family would live. They practiced architecture with what they considered feminist theories or approaches. The rediscovery of architecture through feminist theory is not limited to female architects. Architects like Le Corbusier and Adolf Loos have also had their architecture reexamined through feminist theory.

Feminist: A woman or a man who believes in feminism.

Feminist Advocacy: Refers to strategies, skills, and tools used to influence decision-making processes in the public and social arenas to eliminate inequalities between women and men. It often challenges other forms of oppression and exclusion. Feminist advocacy seeks to achieve respect for diversity and difference and to contribute to cultural, social, and political change for women's full and active citizenship. (AGENDE, 2001)

Feminist Epistemology: The study or theory of how gender influences the production of knowledge. Epistemology is concerned with what constitutes knowledge, and who decides it to be so. A core assumption of feminist epistemology is that knowledge is produced. Who creates the knowledge (the "knower" or the "subject position"), and the multitude of social, economic, cultural, political, and personal factors at play in any given time and place have a distinct and profound influence on the knowledge that is produced. Therefore, knowledge is situated, i.e., it always reflects the assumptions, biases, values, and context of the person(s) who created it. As such, knowledge is political, and the power to create knowledge is a function of social relationships. (JASS, 2008)

Feminist Leadership: An evolving way of thinking about leadership in which power and positions of authority – among individuals, in organisations, and within movements – in the state and elsewhere – are used to create inclusive processes and structures that privilege people who have been traditionally excluded, foster democratic participation, and operate based on authenticity, legitimacy, and accountability to constituents or stakeholders. (Batliwala, 2011a)

Feminist Movement-Building: Political organising that is characterised by inclusive and egalitarian processes designed to foster both individual agency and a common agenda that can serve as the basis for collective political action. Feminist movement building is not limited to or solely defined by any single issue(s) (e.g. "women's issues" such as reproductive rights or equal pay), and can focus on bringing women from different social movements and agendas together. Feminist movement-building brings a feminist analysis and principles, and specifically, the equal role and voice of women, into other agendas and movements, including the environmental, human rights, peace, and labour movements. This is different than building feminist movements which are a process of mobilising women and women's organisations for struggles whose goals are specific to gender equality outcomes, such as sexual and reproductive rights or violence against women. (Srilatha Batliwala, 2008 and JASS, 2009)

Feminist Movements: Movements with (a) gendered political goals, privileging women's interests and seeking to transform both gender and social power relations; (b) gendered strategies – that build on women's strategies and capacities, and involve women members at every stage of the process; and (c) an agenda built from a gendered feminist analysis of the problem or situation they are seeking to change.

Feminist Popular Education: A political, collective learning process aimed at "consciousness-raising", based on facilitated dialogue that places the learners' voices and lived experiences at the heart of the learning and enables an analysis of power and patriarchy. Brazilian scholar-activist Paulo Freire originally developed popular education about 50 years ago. Freire's methods have been widely critiqued and adapted over the years, spawning many participatory and interactive learning processes. Feminist popular education incorporates gender and a class analysis of oppression and starts with the personal dimension as a site for consciousness-raising and change. In this way, it seeks to develop understanding and capacities to influence how power operates within the private realm: families, sexual partnerships, and marriage. Feminist popular education acknowledges how socialisation impacts a woman's sense of herself, her self-confidence, health, body image, psychology, and ability to seek fulfillment and pleasure in all areas of life. (Freire, 1970 and VeneKlasen, 2006).

Feminist Scholarship: In the area of women's studies during the 1970s produced the earliest academic studies of privilege. These studies began by examining barriers to equity between the sexes. In later decades, researchers began to focus on the intersectionality and overlapping nature of privileges relating to sex, race, social class, sexual orientation, and other forms of social classification. Male privilege is often examined alongside the concept of patriarchy within the feminist movement. The use of masculine pronouns to refer to both sexes in some languages is often cited as an example of the privileged position given to males, as is the preference for sons over daughters in many cultures.

Feminist Theory: An examination of women's positions in society, based on the belief that current positions are unequal and unjust, which also provides tactics and criteria for change.

Feminist Transgression: Individual or collective forms of resistance that challenge or subvert the norms and customs imposed on women by capitalist patriarchy and has as its goal the permanent eradication of all forms of oppression. Recognising and acting in solidarity with women who resist and push back against increasing oppression, fundamentalisms, and violence is an essential element of feminist movement building.

The Feminisation of Migration: The trend in international migration patterns have resulted in many more women moving from one country to another independently, often in search of jobs that make them key economic providers for their households. While women have always been part of international migration trends, they have in recent decades been migrating for work on their own instead of as dependents or joining families abroad. The net feminisation of migration has been stark in regions like parts of Asia, with women dominating sectors such as domestic work and caregiving. Other specifically female forms of migration include the migration and trafficking of women for the sex industry and marriage migration. The feminisation of migration goes beyond statistics and raises other issues such as the role of gender in migration processes, the social cost of migration, labour policies in sending and receiving countries that affect gender, and remittances sent by women migrant workers. Women account for almost half of all migrants, a proportion that the United Nations says has changed little in the last two decades. (See also **Marriage Migration**.).

Feminisation: Process of associating people and things with the stereotypically feminine (or) Social shifts toward emphasizing the feminine (e.g., feminisation of education).

First Wave Feminism: Kicked off with the 1848 Seneca Falls Convention to discuss the "social, civil, and religious condition of woman" and continued into the early twentieth century. It culminated in 1920 with the passage of the 19th amendment, which gave women the right to vote, though some states made it difficult for women of colour to exercise this right until well into the 1960s. The feminist movement encompassing the 19th and early 20th century, focussed primarily on women's right to vote.

Fluid: A term used in gender theory often to explain subjectivity and sexuality as "unstable, contingent, situational, and historical" (Jackson & Mazzei, 2012, p. 70) (OR) in gender theory, the notion that identity and sexuality are not fixed categories.

Foresister: A feminist of a previous generation.

Fourth-Wave Feminism: The most recent wave, beginning in about 2012 and concerned primarily with combatting cyberbullying, sexual harassment, and violence against women.

Free Trade: Refers to trading agreements and relationships between states and sub-state actors based on neoliberal, free-market principles. Free trade agreements, particularly those promoted by the US government, typically require the state to remove "barriers" to trade, such as labour standards, tariffs on incoming goods and supports to strategic sectors, under the assumption that the global flow of goods and services will be more efficient, for example, things like food will ultimately be produced in the cheapest place possible, thereby making it affordable for everyone involved. Other social values such as employment generation, social equity, sustainability, and sovereignty do not enter into this model.

Free-Market or Market Economies: Economies in which goods and services are reduced to saleable units (commodities) and bought and sold on a market "free" of state regulation or interference. Prices are theoretically determined by supply and demand, in a competitive system that enhances efficiency. In reality, speculation, monopoly control, and state subsidies to the large industry in the form of cash payments or assumption of many of the real costs of production (environmental and social costs) exert major influence over prices. Proponents of the free market claim that by exchanging everything on the market, ranging from consumer electronics to real estate to education and healthcare, the law of supply and demand will regulate prices in a way that everyone will be able to have access to everything they need to survive. The theory also argues that the market will create competition among sellers to offer the best product at the best price, thereby benefitting all consumers. In reality, there is no such thing as a "free" market; global economic policies, trade agreements, and politics apply rules that overwhelmingly favour sellers, for example, by removing "barriers" such as environmental and labour standards that would otherwise drive up the financial cost of production. A market economy also assumes that everyone has similar potential and opportunity (if they just work hard enough). But things like wage discrimination, racism, and unequal access to quality education mean that that just isn't true. Also, see solidarity economy.

Friedanian: Relating to American feminist writer and activist Betty Friedan (1921-2006).

FTM (Female-to-Male): Someone who was assigned female at birth, but who identifies as a male. Gender: (1) A socially constructed system of classification that ascribes qualities of masculinity and femininity to people. Gender characteristics can change over time and are different between cultures. (2) One's sense of self as masculine or feminine or anywhere in between regardless of genitalia or other sex characteristics.

Fundamentalisms: A global phenomenon based on strict adherence to a specific ideology—religious, political, economic, or otherwise—that is acted out through concerted efforts to impose this ideology on all social, political, and economic arrangements and structures. Fundamentalist tendencies are present within all religions, including Buddhism, Catholicism, Christianity, Hinduism, Judaism, Islam, and localised religious traditions such as the ethnoreligious Kenyan Mungiki movement, Mexican indigenous Tepehuan, and Nepali shamanism. Fundamentalisms are largely associated with religion, but should not be conflated with it. There are also economic fundamentalisms (e.g. market fundamentalism refers to the rejection of state intervention in economic activities whatsoever) and political fundamentalisms (e.g. extreme stances that reject all other points of view such as libertarian fundamentalism). Fundamentalisms vary in form and content but share common features including intolerance for all other points of view and suppression of dissent. Within fundamentalist discourses, women are viewed as the reproducers and symbols of a community's collective identity. This translates into an obsession with the control of women's bodies and autonomy, and the prescription of strictly defined gender roles. Although fundamentalist movements in different regions and religions may emphasize one or another issue more strongly, in all contexts, these campaigns seek to exercise strict control over women's bodies and autonomy, and actively deny the rights of lesbian, gay, bisexual, transgender, queer, and intersex (LGTBQI) persons and communities. Because their messages become strongly internalized as part of people's identities, religious fundamentalists can restrict the space for dissent much more than other patriarchal systems. They limit questioning and freedom of choice, erode people's sense of self and autonomy, and attack tolerance and pluralism. Fundamentalisms exert control in societies through ascendance to state power, overt or covert alliances with state power, control of mass media, and/or cultural/ideological campaigns that influence civil society. Fundamentalist movements in all regions and religions specifically target youth – appealing to their needs and subjectivities, and penetrating the education system to mold future generations. (AWID, 2009)

Gas Lighting: a form of psychological abuse wherein the perpetrator makes the victim believe that they are imagining things, when in fact the perpetrator is manipulating the situation to gain control. This occurs frequently among marginalised groups who are told that they are just "imagining" the oppression that they face. (Also see **Victim-Blaming**).

Gay: A term most often used to describe a man who is sexually and romantically attracted to other men. Colloquially, it is used as an umbrella term to include all lesbian, gay, and bisexual, transgender, and queer people. (See also **Homosexuality; Sexuality, Sexual Identity; Sexual Orientation; Transgender**.).

Gender - Nonconformity: Any number of practices that reject participation in the gender binary. Most genderqueer folks are gender-nonconforming, but not all gender-nonconforming folks identify as genderqueer. Similarly, the trans* umbrella is inclusive of any gender-nonconforming person, but that does not mean all gender-nonconforming people identify as transgender, trans, or trans*.

Gender (Expression) vs. Sex: Gender (expression) refers to how individuals perceive their sexuality and present themselves as women or men or nonbinary. Sex is biologically defined as female or male. For example, females and males have different genitalia and hormones. Many view sex as a binary (e.g., female/male); however, when genitalia or chromosome assignment does not fit the biological norm (e.g., a child born with different internal and external genitals), sex exists on a continuum.

Gender (or Sexual) Division of Labor: This is an important concept in basic gender analysis that helps deepen understanding about social relations as an entry point to sustainable change through development. The division of labour refers to the way each society divides work among men and women, boys and girls, according to socially-established gender roles or what is considered suitable and valuable for each sex. Anyone planning a community intervention needs to know and understand the division of labour and allocation of assets on a sex-and-age disaggregated basis for every community affected by development interventions. Within the division of labour, there are several types of roles.

Gender: Any conceptualization of the sociological and behavioural characteristics traditionally associated with a particular biological sex. This term may also refer to gender identity, gender expression, or gender role. "Woman" and "man" are the genders traditionally associated with the biological sexes of "female" and "male" respectively.

Gender Accommodating: Similar to the concept of gender sensitivity, gender accommodating means not only being aware of gender differences but also adjusting and adapting to those differences. However, gender accommodating does not address the inequalities generated by unequal norms, roles, and relations (i.e., no remedial or transformative action is developed).

Gender Action Plan (GAP): The UNICEF Gender Action Plan serves to reinforce the commitments to gender found in the organisation's periodic strategic plans. The first GAP covered the five years 2014-2017 and the second GAP will cover 2018-2021. The document specifies how UNICEF intends to promote gender equality across all of the organisation's work at global, regional, and country levels, in alignment with the UNICEF Strategic Plan. The 2018-2021 GAP also serves as UNICEF's roadmap for supporting the achievement of gender equality goals as outlined in Agenda 2030 and the Sustainable Development Goals (SDGs) during the period.

Gender Advisor: Responsibility for implementation of the gender mainstreaming strategy lies with the senior management in each United Nations entity, as clearly stated in the Letter from the Secretary-General to heads of all United Nations entities in October 1997. In many parts of the United Nations system Gender Advisor posts have been established to support management to undertake their roles in implementing gender mainstreaming. Gender advisors promote and support gender-sensitive approaches to policy and program work within a given mission, office, team, etc. They provide strategic advice in planning and policy-making processes, in coordination meetings and task forces, as well as through existing gender units or gender focal points. They may be responsible for strategies such as advocacy and awareness-raising; training and capacity building; monitoring and advising; evaluation and reporting; and technical advice and support. Their work often focuses as much on in-house operations as it does liaising with national and regional partners to ensure that gender issues are adequately addressed.

Gender Analysis: Gender analysis is a critical examination of how differences in gender roles, activities, needs, opportunities and rights/entitlements affect men, women, girls, and boys in certain situations or contexts. Gender analysis examines the relationships between females and males and their access to and control of resources and the constraints they face relative to each other. A gender analysis should be integrated into all sector assessments or situational analyses to ensure that gender-based injustices and inequalities are not exacerbated by interventions and that where possible, greater equality and justice in gender relations are promoted.

Gender Analytical Information: Gender analytical information is qualitative information on gender differences and inequalities. Gender analysis is about understanding culture, e.g. the patterns and norms of what men and women, boys and girls do and experience with the issue being examined and addressed. Where patterns of gender difference and inequality are revealed in sex-disaggregated data, gender analysis is the process of examining why the disparities are there, whether they are a matter of concern, and how they might be addressed.

Gender and Development (GAD): This approach shifts the focus from women as a group to the socially determined relations between women and men. A GAD approach focuses on the social, economic, political, and cultural forces that determine how men and women might participate in, benefit from, and control project resources and activities differently.

Gender Apartheid: Gender apartheid (also called **Sexual Apartheid** or **Sex Apartheid**) is the economic and social sexual discrimination against individuals because of their gender or sex. It is a system enforced by using either physical or legal practices to relegate individuals to subordinate positions. Feminist psychologist Phyllis Chesler defines the phenomenon as "practices which condemn girls and women to a separate and subordinate sub-existence and which turn boys and men into the permanent guardians of their female relatives' chastity". Instances of gender apartheid lead not only to the social and economic disempowerment of individuals but can also result in severe physical harm.

Gender as Cultural Construction: Gender is mainly determined by one's society and culture, not merely their biological composition. Gender is constructed before birth when the parents are preparing for the child's delivery. Some of their activities would include painting the room pink for a girl or blue for a boy and also making a future for their child by hoping they will become a "soccer player" if it's a boy or a "ballerina" if it's a girl. After the birth, the toys the child is given is also gender-based: girls are usually given dolls and kitchen sets (domestic toys) to play with, while boys are given trucks, sports, and toolsets. Some jobs are associated with specific genders: mainly, males assume thé "protective" roles (ie. firefighters, policemen, politicians) while females are assumed to take the nurturing roles (i.e. nursing, mother, teacher). Those who do not assume the "socially accepted" role, they are most often shunned.

Gender Audit: A participatory gender audit is a tool and a process based on a participatory methodology to promote organisational learning at the individual, work unit, and organisational levels on how to practically and effectively mainstream gender. A gender audit is essentially a "social audit", and belongs to the category of "quality audits", which distinguishes it from traditional "financial audits". It considers whether internal practices and related support systems for gender mainstreaming are effective and reinforce each other and whether they are being followed. It establishes a baseline; identifies critical gaps and challenges; and recommends ways of addressing them, suggesting possible improvements and innovations. It also documents good practices towards the achievement of gender equality. A gender audit enhances the collective capacity of the organisation to examine its activities from a gender perspective and identify strengths and weaknesses in promoting gender equality issues. It monitors and assesses the relative progress made in gender mainstreaming and helps to build organisational ownership for gender equality initiatives and sharpens organisational learning on gender. The International Training Centre of the ILO offers a certification process for gender auditors.

Gender Awareness: This means the ability to identify problems arising from gender inequality and discrimination, even if these are not very evident on the surface, or are "hidden" - i.e. are not part of the general or commonly accepted explanation of what and where the problem lies. In other words, gender awareness means a high level of gender conscientisation.

Gender Aware-Policies can be Subdivided into two Policy Types: Gender-neutral policies approaches use the knowledge of gender differences in a given context to target and meet the practical needs of both women and men. Gender-neutral policies do not disturb existing gender relations. Gender-specific policies use the knowledge of gender differences in a given situation to respond to the practical gender needs of either women or men. These policies do not address the existing division of resources and responsibilities.

Gender Balance: This is a human resource issue calling for equal participation of women and men in all areas of work (international and national staff at all levels, including at senior positions) and in programs that agencies initiate or support (e.g. food distribution programs). Achieving a balance in staffing patterns and creating a working environment that is conducive to a diverse workforce improves the overall effectiveness of our policies and programs, and will enhance agencies' capacity to better serve the entire population.

Gender Bias: Making decisions based on gender that result in favouring one gender over the other which often results in contexts that are favouring men and/or boys over women and/or girls.

Gender Binary: The **gender binary**, also referred to as **gender binarism** (sometimes shortened to just **binarism**), is the classification of sex and gender into two distinct, opposite, and disconnected forms of masculine and feminine. The gender binary is one general type of a gender system. Sometimes in this binary model, "sex", "gender" and "sexuality" are assumed by default to align. For example, when a male is born, gender binarism assumes the male will be masculine in appearance, character traits, and behaviour, including having a heterosexual attraction to females.

Gender Blindness: This term refers to the failure to recognize that the roles and responsibilities of men/boys and women/girls are assigned to them in specific social, cultural, economic, and political contexts and backgrounds. Projects, programs, policies, and attitudes which are gender blind do not take into account these different roles and diverse needs. They maintain the status quo and will not help transform the unequal structure of gender relations.

Gender Budgeting: It means prepare budgets or to examine them from a gender perspective. Also referred to as gender-sensitive budgeting, this practice does not entail dividing budgets for women. It aims at dealing with budgetary gender inequality issues, including gender hierarchies and the discrepancies between women's and men's salaries. Gender budgeting allows governments to promote equality through fiscal policies by making analyses of a budget's differing impacts on the sexes as well as setting goals or targets for equality and allocating funds to support those goals. This practice does not always target intentional discrimination but rather forces an awareness of the effects of financial schemes on all genders.

Gender Characteristics: Refers to the primary and secondary sexual physical characteristics like height, weight, and body hair, over which the individual has no control and which do not constitute part of their expression or identification. Examples might include a man with a high voice, a woman with prominent facial hair, or a person with anomalous genitalia (more correctly referred to as "intersex").

Gender Conformity: When your gender identity and sex "match" (i.e. fit social norms). For example, a male who is masculine and identify himself that he is a man.

Gender- Critical: A political self-identifying euphemism used by trans-exclusionary radical feminists.

Gender Discrimination: Gender discrimination is defined as: "Any distinction, exclusion or restriction made based on sex which has the effect or purpose of impairing or nullifying the recognition, enjoyment or exercise by women, irrespective of their marital status, based on equality of men and women, of human rights and fundamental freedoms in the political, economic, social, cultural, civil or any other field." [United Nations, 1979. 'Convention on the Elimination of all Forms of Discrimination Against Women. Article 1] Discrimination can stem from both laws (de jure) or practice (de facto). The CEDAW Convention recognizes and addresses both forms of discrimination, whether contained in laws, policies, procedures, or practices.

Gender Disparities: Statistical differences (often referred to as "gaps") between men and women, boys and girls that reflect inequality in some quantity.

Gender Diversity: Gender diversity is a term that recognizes that many peoples' preferences and self-expression fall outside commonly understood gender norms.

Gender Division of Labour: This means an overall societal pattern where women are allotted one set of gender roles, and men allotted another set. Unequal gender division of labour refers to a gender division of labour where there is an unequal gender division of reward. Discrimination against women in this sense means that women get most of the burden of labour, and most of the unpaid labour, but men collect most of the income and rewards resulting from the labour. In many countries, the most obvious pattern in the gender division of labour is that women are mostly confined to unpaid domestic work and unpaid food production, whereas men dominate in cash crop production and wage employment.

Gender Effect: A term referring to the understanding of effect that a society invests in girls; the effects are deep for the girls, multiple for society, and a driver of sustainable development. According to an essay by the president of the Nike Foundation in UNICEF's, State of the World's Children

2011, "When a girl in the developing world receives seven or more years of education, she marries four years later. An extra year of primary school boosts girls' eventual wages by 10 to 20 percent. Studies in 2003 showed that when women and girls earn income, they reinvest 90 percent of it into their families, as compared to the 30 to 40 percent that men and boys contribute. Research has also shown that higher levels of schooling among mothers correlate with better infant and child health."

Gender Empowerment Measure (GEM): A measure of the empowerment of women in a country in three basic areas – economic participation and decision-making (the number of professional and managerial jobs held by women), political participation (the number of parliamentary seats held by women) and decision-making and power over economic resources. It is one of five indicators by which the UNDP ranks countries in its annual Human Development Report. Together with the Gender-related Development Index (GDI), it is one of two measures of human development of women first introduced in the Human Development Report 1995. The GEM and GDI are often used as advocacy and monitoring tools for gender-related analysis. (See also **Gender-related Development Index**.).

Gender Equality (Equality between Women and Men): This refers to the equal rights, responsibilities, and opportunities of women and men and girls and boys. Equality does not mean that women and men will become the same but that women's and men's rights, responsibilities, and opportunities will not depend on whether they are born male or female. Gender equality implies that the interests, needs, and priorities of both women and men are taken into consideration, recognising the diversity of different groups of women and men. Gender equality is not a women's issue but should concern and fully engage men as well as women. Equality between women and men is seen both as a human rights issue and as a precondition for, and indicator of, sustainable people-centered development.

Gender Equality as a Development Objective: "At the United Nation Fourth World Conference for Women held in Beijing 1995, both DAC members and their partner countries made commitments to gender equality and women's empowerment. The Beijing Declaration adopted at the Conference builds on the perspectives and strategies outlined at the previous United Nations conferences on education – Jomtien (1990), environment-Rio(1992), human rights Vienna (1993), population – Cairo (1994), and social development – Copenhagen (1995), including the Convention on the Elimination of all Forms of Discrimination against Women (CEDAW,

1979). It is based on the principles of human rights and social justice. It recognises that gender equality and women's empowerment are essential for addressing the central concerns of poverty and insecurity, and for achieving sustainable, people-centred development." The follow-up to the Fourth World Conference on Women in 1999 further recognises that gender mainstreaming is a tool for effective policy-making at all levels and not a substitute for targeted, women-specific policies and programs, equality legislation, national machinery for the advancement of women, and the establishment of gender focal points.

Gender Equality: Refers to the equal rights, responsibilities, and opportunities of women and men and girls and boys. Equality does not mean that women and men will become the same but that women's and men's rights, responsibilities, and opportunities will not depend on whether they are born male or female. Gender equality implies that the interests, needs, and priorities of both women and men are taken into consideration, recognising the diversity of different groups of women and men. Gender equality is not a 'women's issue but should concern and fully engage men as well as women. Equality between women and men is seen both as a human rights issue and as a precondition for, and indicator of, sustainable people-centered development. Gender equality is the preferred terminology within the United Nations, rather than gender equity. During the Beijing conference in 1995, it was agreed that the term equality would be utilized. In the context of international human rights, the legal concept of gender equality is enshrined in the 1948 Universal Declaration of Human Rights as well as in the 1979 United Nations Convention on the Elimination of All Forms of Discrimination against Women. The Convention which has been ratified by 100 countries, states clearly and unequivocally that "discrimination against women violates the principles of equality of rights and respect for human dignity." The governments of the world reaffirmed their commitment in 1995 to "the equal rights and inherent human dignity of all women and men" in the Beijing Declaration and Platform for Action.

Gender Equity: The preferred terminology within the United Nations is gender equality, rather than gender equity. Gender equity denotes an element of interpretation of social justice, usually based on tradition, custom, religion, or culture, which is most often to the detriment of women. Such use of equity with the advancement of women has been determined to be unacceptable. During the Beijing conference in 1995, it was agreed that the term equality would be utilised. This was later confirmed by the CEDAW Committee in its General Recommendation 28: "States parties are called upon to use exclusively the concepts of equality of women and men or gender equality and not to use the concept of gender equity in implementing their obligations under the Convention. The latter concept is used in some jurisdictions to refer to fair treatment of women and men, according to their respective needs. This may include equal treatment or treatment that is different but considered equivalent in terms of rights, benefits, obligations, and opportunities".

Gender Essentialism: Is the theory that there are certain universal, innate, biologically- or psychologically-based features of gender (different from sex) that are at the root of observed differences in the behaviour of men and women. In Western civilisation, it is suggested in writings going back to ancient Greece. With the advent of Christianity, the earlier Greek model was expressed in theological discussions as the doctrine that there are two distinct sexes, male and female created by God and that our nature is to be immutably one or the other. This view remained essentially unchanged until the middle of the 19th century until Darwin's publications on evolution. This changed the locus of the origin of the essential differences, in Sandra Bem's words, "from God's grand creation [to] its scientific equivalent: evolution's grand creation," but the belief in an immutable origin had not changed. It was not until the middle of the 20th century and the writings of second-wave feminism starting with Simone de Beauvoir that the first alternative theory for gender difference was proposed. This theory was developed by feminist theorists in the 1960s, 70s, and beyond, and described gender difference as being socially constructed, namely that the origin of gender difference is not in-born, but learned from interacting in society. Feminists are by no means unanimous in supporting theories of the social construction of gender. Many adhere more to gender essentialism, or to some intermediate viewpoint. The two theories of gender essentialism, and social constructionism, inform an active debate about the origins of gender differences in the fields of feminism, philosophy, and sociology which are sometimes acrimonious and break out into local and national politics.

Gender Expression/Gender Image: The way one presents oneself to the world, as either masculine or feminine, or both or neither. This can include dress, posture, vocal inflection, and other behaviour.

Gender Expression: The way a person's gender is expressed to the world: One's external physique and communication of masculine, feminine, or another gender through behaviour, dress, mannerisms, personality, etc.

Gender Fluid: A gender expression or identity is not fixed but changes across time or circumstances. Gender fluid people may present sometimes as men, sometimes as women, or sometimes as non-binary.

Gender Fluidity: Not identifying with a single, fixed gender.

Gender Focal Point: Gender focal points are change agents whose overriding role is one of advocating for increased attention to and integration of gender equality and women's empowerment in his or her agency's policy and programming and the related work of development partners. Gender focal points serve as a hub for new information on gender equality and as a conduit for information on what has worked well in the organisation. The role of gender focal points differs somewhat from country to country and agency to agency, depending on where she or he is placed within the organisation and what kind of gender architecture the organisation has in place. A gender focal point is not, however, intended to serve as a substitute for a full-time institutional gender specialist. The focal point's role is often more one of advocacy and facilitating communication and connections related to gender equality and women's empowerment, but may at times involve providing gender expertise or assisting colleagues and development partners to identify potential national or international consultants or organisations that have this expertise. Basic functions may include: coordinating the organisation/office/program gender mainstreaming strategy; contributing gender information and technical support for the inclusion of gender issues; supporting capacity development on gender equality within the organisation; knowledge management; and coordination on interagency initiatives, among others.

Gender Gap: The term gender gap refers to any disparity between women's and men's conditions or position in society. It is often used to refer to a difference in average earnings between women and men, e.g. "gender pay gap." However, gender gaps can be found in many areas, such as the four pillars that the World Economic Forum uses to calculate its Gender Gap Index, namely: economic participation and opportunity, educational attainment, health and survival, and political empowerment.

Gender Identity: Gender identity refers to a person's innate, deeply felt internal and individual experience of gender, which may or may not correspond to the person's physiology or designated sex at birth. It includes both the personal sense of the body, which may involve, if freely chosen, modification of bodily appearance or function by medical, surgical, or other means, and other expressions of gender, including dress, speech, and mannerisms.

Gender in Development (Condition and Position): Development projects generally aim to improve the condition of people's lives. From a gender and development perspective, a distinction is made between the day-to-day condition of women's lives and their position in society. In addition to the specific conditions which women share with men, differential access means women's position with men must also be assessed when interventions are planned and implemented. Condition: This refers to the material state in which women and men live, and relates to their responsibilities and work. Improvements in women's and men's condition can be made by providing, for example, safe water, credit, seeds, (i.e. practical gender needs). Position: Position refers to women's social and economic standing in society relative to men, for example, male/female disparities in wages and employment opportunities, unequal representation in the political process, unequal ownership of land and property, vulnerability to violence (i.e. strategic gender need/interests).

Gender in Development (GID): The GID or Gender in Development perspective emerged in the late 1980s as an alternative to the prevailing Women in Development or WID approach. Unlike WID, which focused on women only, and called for their integration into development as producers and workers, GID focuses on the interdependence of men and women in society and the unequal relations of power between them. The GID approach aims for a development process that transforms gender relations to enable women to participate on an equal basis with men in determining their common future. The GID approach emphasises the importance of women's collective organisation for self-empowerment. Note: There are two very similar terms in current usage – Gender in Development (GID): Gender and Development (GAD). There is no substantive difference in the meaning of these two terms, which may be used interchangeably. However, UNDP favours the use of the GID formulation, as it has a slightly more "integrated" connotation. Of course, if gender perspectives were fully mainstreamed into development thinking and action, there would be no need for either designation, as it would be understood that gender inequality is a fact of socioeconomic life, and therefore must be addressed as integral to all development initiatives.

Gender Indicators: Criteria used to assess gender-related change in a condition and to measure progress over time toward gender equality. Indicators used can be quantitative (data, facts, numbers) and qualitative (opinions, feelings, perceptions, experiences).

Gender Inequality Index (GII): In 2010, the UNDP developed a new index for measuring gender disparity, called the Gender Inequality Index (GII). This index is a composite measure that shows the loss in human development due to inequality between female and male achievements in three dimensions: (1) reproductive health, (2) empowerment, and (3) the labour market. The index ranges from zero, which indicates that women and men fare equally, to one, which indicates that women fare as poorly as possible in all measured dimensions. The new index was introduced in the 2010 Human Development Report as an experimental measure to remedy the shortcomings of the previous and no longer used, indicators, the Gender Development Index (GDI) and the Gender Empowerment Measure (GEM), both of which were introduced in the 1995 Human Development Report. According to the index, there is no country in the world where women are equal to their men. In other words, gender equality remains a distant reality still.

Gender Issues: Arise where an instance of gender inequality is recognised as undesirable, or unjust. There are three aspects of gender issues, namely: gender gap, discrimination, and women's oppression.

Gender Lens: Here are a few ways to use the gender lens to tell stories, for which this glossary can be a tool for using gender-sensitive and gender-aware terms does not mean removing all traces of sex or gender in nouns, and making stories gender-blind. Hiding sex or gender does not make for gender sensitivity. If the head of a committee is a woman, calling her chairwoman is by no means wrong or politically incorrect.

Gender Mainstreaming / Integrating: A strategy to accelerate progress on women's and girls' rights and equality about men and boys. This is the chosen approach of the United Nations system and international community toward implementation of women's and girls' rights, as a sub-set of human rights to which the United Nations dedicates itself. Gender equality is the goal. Gender mainstreaming is the process of assessing the implications for girls and boys and men and women of any planned action, including legislation, policies, and programs. It is a strategy for making girls' and women's, as well as boy's and men's, concerns and experiences an integral dimension of the design, implementation, monitoring, and evaluation of policies and programs so that girls and boys and women and men benefit equally, and inequality is not perpetuated.

Gender Mainstreaming: Are the chosen approach of the United Nations system and international community toward realising progress on women's and girl's rights, as a sub-set of human rights to which the United

Nations dedicates itself. It is not a goal or objective on its own. It is a strategy for implementing greater equality for women and girls with men and boys. Mainstreaming a gender perspective is the process of assessing the implications for women and men of any planned action, including legislation, policies, or programs, in all areas and at all levels. It is a way to make women's as well as men's concerns and experiences an integral dimension of the design, implementation, monitoring, and evaluation of policies and programs in all political, economic, and societal spheres so that women and men benefit equally and inequality is not perpetuated. The ultimate goal is to achieve gender equality.

Gender Needs/ Interests (Practical and Strategic): Women and men have different roles and responsibilities and therefore have different interests/needs. These are called gender interests/needs, practical and strategic. Practical and strategic gender interests/needs should not be seen as separate, but rather as a continuum. By consulting women on their practical gender interests/needs an entry point to address gender inequalities in the longer term (strategic gender interests/needs) can be created. (*Source:* C. Moser (1993) Gender Planning & Development, Routledge, London).

Gender Needs: Leading on from the fact that women and men have different roles based on their gender, they will also have different gender needs. These needs can be classified as either strategic or practical needs.

Gender-Neutral Language: Gender-neutral language or gender-inclusive language is a language that avoids bias toward a particular sex or social gender. In English, this includes the use of nouns that are not gender-specific to refer to roles or professions, as well as avoidance of the pronouns *he*, *him,* and *his* to refer to people of unknown or indeterminate gender. For example, the words *policeman* and *stewardess* are gender-specific job titles; the corresponding gender-neutral terms are *a police officer* and *flight attendant*. Other gender-specific terms, such as *actor* and *actress*, may be replaced by the originally male term; for example, *the actor* used regardless of gender. Some terms, such as *chairman*, that contain the component -*man* but have traditionally been used to refer to persons regardless of sex are now seen by some as gender-specific. When the gender of the person referred to is unknown or indeterminate, the third-person pronoun *he* may be avoided by using gender-neutral alternatives – possibilities in English include singular *they*, *he or she*, or *s/he*.

Gender Neutral: A concept, an entity, a style of language– that is unassociated with either the male or female gender. The nature of systemic and embedded or internalised bias is such that, unfortunately often, what is perceived to be gender-neutral is in fact gender blind.

Gender Neutrality: Gender neutrality (adjective form: **gender-neutral**), also known as **gender-neutralism** or the **gender neutrality movement**, describes the idea that policies, language, and other social institutions should avoid distinguishing roles according to people's sex or gender, to avoid discrimination arising from the impression that there are social roles for which one gender is more suited than another.

Gender Norms: Accepted attributes and characteristics of male and female gendered identity at a particular point in time for a specific society or community. They are the standards and expectations to which gender identity generally conforms, within a range that defines a particular society, culture, and community now. Gender norms are ideas about how men and women should be and act. Internalised early in life, gender norms can establish a life cycle of gender socialisation and stereotype.

Gender Parity: Gender parity is another term for equal representation of women and men in a given area, for example, gender parity in organisational leadership or higher education. Working toward gender parity (equal representation) is a key part of achieving gender equality, and one of the twin strategies, alongside gender mainstreaming.

Gender Parity Index (GPI): It is a socioeconomic indicator that assesses gender differences by looking at the ratio of girls to boys in the area of access to education. The GPI is the value of an indicator for girls divided by that for boys. A value of less than one indicates differences in favour of boys and a value near one indicates that parity has more or less been achieved; gender parity is often considered to have been attained when the GPI lies in between. Parity is also used in looking at the participation of women in politics, including their presence in parliament. (See also **Gender Equity; Gender Equality; Gender Mainstreaming; Gender Parity**.).

Gender Pay Gap: This is the average difference between the remuneration for men and women who are working. Women are generally paid less than men. There are two distinct numbers regarding the pay gap: *unadjusted* versus *adjusted* pay gap. The latter takes into account differences in hours worked, occupations chosen, education, and job experience. For example, someone who takes time off (e.g. maternity leave) will likely not earn as much as someone who does not take time off from work. Factors like this contribute to lower yearly earnings for women; while the pay gap has narrowed over time, a gender pay gap still exists, even when controlling for these external factors. [*not in citation given*] *Unadjusted* pay gaps are much higher. In the United States, for example, the unadjusted average female's annual salary has commonly been cited as being 78% of the average male salary, compared to 88-93% for the adjusted average salary for college graduates. The reasons for lower pay include both individual choice and other innate and external factors. An example of a voluntary choice is choosing to work part-time when full-time employment is available. An example of an involuntary choice is working a low-skill job because of an inability to access higher education. The gender pay gap can be a problem from a public policy perspective even when the reason for the gap is entirely voluntary because it reduces economic output and means that women are more likely to be dependent upon welfare payments, especially in old age.

Gender Performativity: A theory produced by feminist Judith Butler, holding that people construct and alter gender roles by causing the actions they perform to become associated with their gender.

Gender Perspective: The investigation of how men and women affect and are affected by economic, political, social, legal, and cultural events and processes in different ways. In news writing, the simplest form of a gender perspective is the inclusion of women's and girls' voices, which are not always heard in stories.

Gender Planning: Refers to the process of planning developmental programs and projects that are gender-sensitive and which take into account the impact of different gender roles and gender needs of women and men in the target community or sector. It involves the selection of appropriate approaches to address not only women's and men's practical needs but also identifies entry points for challenging unequal relations (i.e. strategic needs) and to enhance the gender responsiveness of policy dialogue.

Gender Policies: Gender policies are divided into three categories depending on the extent to which they recognise and address gender issues

• Gender-aware policies: Gender-aware policies recognise that women, as well as men, are actors in development and that they are often constrained in a different way to 15 men. Their needs, interests, and priorities may differ and at times conflict.

Gender Presentation: how a person dresses, looks, and acts; the presentation of one's sense of gender through behaviour and dress.

Genderqueer / Gender Non-conforming / Gender Non-binary: A gender-variant person whose gender identity does not conform to the gender binary of male or female. They may identify as neither male nor female, between or beyond genders, nor some combination of genders.

Gender Queer: Gender queer, also known as **non-binary**, is a catch-all category for gender identities that are not exclusively masculine or feminine—identities that are outside the gender binary and cisnormativity. Gender queer people may express a combination of masculinity and femininity, or neither, in their gender expression. Gender queer people may identify as either having an overlap of, or indefinite lines between, gender identity; having two or more genders (being bigender, trigender, or pangender); having no gender (being agender, nongendered, genderless, genderfree, or neutral); moving between genders or having a fluctuating gender identity (genderfluid); or being third gender or other-gendered, a category which includes those who do not place a name to their gender.

Gender Relations (Transforming): Changes in gender relations transform long-standing patterns; one change is acknowledged to bring others, and the nature and the degree of changes that occur in women's and men's lives as a result of successful interventions, explain why "transform" is the active construct chosen in this model. Transformation of this kind requires an understanding and parallel or concurrent attention to practical needs and strategic interests. The choice is not "one or the other"; the challenge is how to work with both — strategically, and practically. (See also Gender Relations).

Gender Relations and Gender Identity (Changes): Gender roles and characteristics in almost all societies have undergone many recent adjustments and changes in response to technological change, which has led to massive economic and social changes in all parts of the world. Changes in gender roles and relations often meet resistance, in particular from cultural forces of tradition. Anticipating and preparing for most likely forms of resistance to change in activities or the status and position of women is a valuable part of a project's gender strategy. Gender analysis can demonstrate that change in certain aspects of social roles and relations between women and men can improve the quality and conditions of life for everyone.

Gender Relations: These are the social relationships between women and men. Gender relations are simultaneously relations of co-operation, connection, and mutual support, and conflict, separation, and competition, of difference and inequality. Gender relations are concerned with how power is distributed between the sexes. They create and reproduce systemic differences in men's and women's positions in a given society. They define how responsibilities and claims are allocated and how each is given a value. The term "gender relations" also refers to the relationships between people and their broader community, if these relationships vary with the sex of the people concerned. For example, the relationship between members of a village community and their local government entity is a gender relationship if men and women experience different benefits and controls from it. (See also **Transforming Gender Relations**).

Gender Role Stereotyping: This is the constant portrayal, such as in the media or books, of women and men occupying social roles according to the traditional gender division of labour in a particular society. Such gender role, stereotyping works to support and reinforce the traditional gender division of labour by portraying it as "normal" and "natural".

Gender Role: Gender roles are socially and historically constructed norms that are deemed acceptable and appropriate for individuals based upon their assigned sex (or) A **gender role**, also known as a **sex role**, is a social role encompassing a range of behaviours and attitudes that are generally considered acceptable, appropriate, or desirable for people based on their actual or perceived sex or sexuality. Gender roles are usually centered on conceptions of femininity and masculinity, although there are exceptions and variations. The specifics regarding these gendered expectations may vary substantially among cultures, while other characteristics may be common throughout a range of cultures. There is ongoing debate as to what extent gender roles and their variations are biologically determined, and to what extent they are socially constructed.

Gender Roles and Responsibilities: This is another term for the gendered division of labour. It tends to be used most frequently in those analytic frameworks, especially the Harvard Framework and its derivatives such as the POP Framework which emerged before the use of the term "gender relations" became widespread during the 90s.

Gender Sensitivity and Gender Awareness: The ability to recognise gender issues and especially the ability to recognise women's different perceptions and interests arising from their different social locations and different gender roles. Gender sensitivity is considered the beginning stage of gender awareness. The latter is more analytical, more critical, and more "questioning" of gender disparities. Gender awareness is the ability to identify problems arising from gender inequality and discrimination, even if these are not very evident on the surface or are "hidden" (i.e., not part of the general or commonly accepted explanation of what and where the problem lies). Gender-Blind Person, policy, or institution that does not recognise that gender is an essential determinant of the life choices available to us in society.

Gender Sensitivity: It is the ability to recognise gender issues, and especially the ability to recognise women's different perceptions and interests arising from their different social location and different gender roles. Gender sensitivity is often used to mean the same as gender awareness, although gender awareness can also mean the extra ability to recognise gender issues that remain "hidden" from those with a more conventional point of view. But here we define gender sensitivity as the beginning of gender awareness, where the latter is more analytical, more critical, and more "questioning" of gender disparities.

Gender Sensitisation: Gender sensitisation presides over gender sensitivity which refers to the modification of behaviour by raising awareness of gender equality concerns. This can be achieved by conducting various sensitisation campaigns, training centers, workshops, programs, etc. Sensitisation in the domain of Humanities and Social Sciences is seen as an awareness informed propensity or disposition which aims at changing behaviour so that it is sensitive to certain issues. Gender sensitisation may be seen as "the awareness informed disposition or propensity to behave in a manner which is sensitive to gender justice and gender equality issues." It is interlinked with gender empowerment. Gender sensitisation theories claim that modification of the behaviour of teachers and parents (etc.) towards children can have a causal effect on gender equality. Gender sensitising "is about changing behaviour and instilling empathy into the views that we hold about our own and the other genders." It helps people in "examining their attitudes and beliefs and questioning the 'realities' they thought they know. Gender Sensitisation is one basic requirement for the normal development of an individual. Without being sensitive to the needs of a particular gender, an individual may refrain from understanding the opposite gender and in some acute cases even him or herself. The need for this sensitivity has been felt and realised through times immemorial and in almost all kinds of human existence, across the globe.

Gender Socialisation: Gender socialisation refers to the learning of behaviour and attitudes considered appropriate for a given sex. Boys learn to be boys and girls learn to be girls. This "learning" happens by way of many different agents of socialisation. The behaviour that is seen to be appropriate for each gender is largely determined by societal, cultural and economic values in a given society. Gender socialisation can therefore vary considerably among societies with different values. The family is certainly important in reinforcing gender roles, but so are groups including friends, peers, school, work, and the mass media. Gender roles are reinforced through "countless subtle and not so subtle ways" (1999:76). In peer group activities, stereotypic gender roles may also be rejected, renegotiated, or artfully exploited for a variety of purposes. Carol Gilligan compared the moral development of girls and boys in her theory of gender and moral development. She claimed (1982, 1990) that boys have a justice perspective meaning that they rely on formal rules to define right and wrong. Girls, on the other hand, have a care and responsibility perspective where personal relationships are considered when judging a situation. Gilligan also studied the effect of gender on self-esteem. She claimed that society's socialisation of females is the reason why girls' self-esteem diminishes as they grow older. Girls struggle to regain their strength when moving through adolescence as they have fewer female teachers and most authority figures are men. As parents are present in a child's life from the beginning, their influence in a child's early socialisation is very important, especially in regards to gender roles. Sociologists have identified four ways in which parents socialise gender roles in their children: Shaping gender-related attributes through toys and activities, differing their interaction with children based on the sex of the child, serving as primary gender models, and communicating gender ideals and expectations. Sociologist of gender R.W. Connell contends that socialisation theory is "inadequate" for explaining gender, because it presumes a largely consensual process except for a few "deviants," when most children revolt against pressures to be conventionally gendered; because it cannot explain contradictory "scripts" that come from different socialisation agents in the same society, and because it does not account for conflict between the different levels of an individual's gender (and general) identity.

Gender Stereotypes: Gender stereotypes are simplistic generalisations about the gender attributes, differences, and roles of women and men. Stereotypical characteristics of men are that they are competitive, acquisitive, autonomous, independent, confrontational, concerned about private goods. Parallel stereotypes of women hold that they are cooperative, nurturing, caring, connecting, group-oriented, concerned about public goods. Stereotypes are often used to justify gender discrimination more broadly and can be reflected and reinforced by traditional and modern theories, laws, and institutional practices. Messages reinforcing gender stereotypes and the idea that women are inferior come in a variety of "packages" – from songs and advertising to traditional proverbs.

Gender Stratification: It refers to the unequal distribution of wealth power and privilege across gender take for example the right to vote to deny. Gender stratification refers to the social ranking, where men typically inhabit higher statuses than women. Often the terms gender inequality and gender stratification are used interchangeably. There are a variety of approaches to the study of gender stratification. Most of the research in this area focuses on differences between men's and women's life circumstances, broadly defined. Scholarly debates focus on which dimensions of inequalities are most relevant and the level at which inequalities are generated and maintained (i.e., individual, couple, family, group, or societal level). Researchers have been challenged to explore gender, race, and class inequalities from an intersectional perspective, rather than treating gender as independent of race and class. There is little acknowledgment of the heteronormativity that is present in gender stratification research. Perhaps that will change once data regarding sexual orientation, gender identity, and gender expression becomes more widely available. In this section, we present key areas of gender stratification research. Gender stratification can be examined at the level of individual outcomes and interactions or with a macro perspective that compares indexes of gender inequalities across countries. Although welfare states research examines many aspects within and across societies, it provides important insights into how state policies can shape patterns of gender stratification. Gender inequality in the area of education, economic resources, and family are closely linked in individuals' lives, but distinct strands of research have emerged and will be discussed separately. Although we provide examples of research noting gendered health disparities are outcomes of gender inequalities within societies, not all health research makes this connection. Research on crime as well as migration and citizenship has traditionally focused on men. Yet a recent shift to include women more explicitly and gender more broadly have great potential to inform other areas of research on gender stratification.

Gender Studies: It is a fields for interdisciplinary study devoted to gender identity and gendered representation as central categories of analysis. It includes Women's Studies (concerning women feminism, gender and politics), men's studies and LGBT studies. Some times GS is offered together with study of sexuality. These disciplines study gender and sexuality in the field of literature, language, geography, history, political science, sociology, anthropology, cinema, media studies, human development, law and medicine.It also analyzes how to race, ethnicity, location, class, nationality and disability intersect with the categories of gender and sexuality. (See **Women's Studies**).

Gender Training: A facilitated process of developing awareness and capacity on gender issues to bring about personal or organizational change for gender equality. "The generic aim of gender training...is to consciously introduce gender as a category of analysis (as opposed to description), to point to the differing needs and interests of women and men and their unequal representation, and to increase awareness and reduce the gender-bias which informs the actions of individuals and institutions." This kind of gender training commonly involves: Raising participants' awareness of the different and unequal roles and responsibilities of women and men in any particular context. Looking at ways that development interventions affect, and are affected by, differences and inequalities between women and men. Equipping participants with knowledge and skills to understand gender differences and inequalities in the context of their work and to plan and implement policies, programs, and projects to promote gender equality.

Gender Violence: Any act or threat by men or male-dominated institutions that inflicts physical, sexual or psychological harm on a woman or girl because of their gender. There is, however, no single definition of gender violence accepted internationally and there is much debate over the breadth of inclusion. Commonly, the acts or threats of such included in the definition are rape, sexual harassment, wife-battering, sexual abuse of girls, dowry-related violence, and non-spousal violence within the home. Other definitions extend to marital rape, acts such as female genital mutilation, female infanticide, and sex-selective abortion. In addition, certain definitions include 'sexual exploitation such as enforced prostitution, trafficking of women and girls, and pornography.

Gender, Institutions, and Development Data Base (GID-DB): The Gender, Institutions, and Development Data Base (GID-DB) represent a new tool for researchers and policymakers to determine and analyze obstacles to women's economic development. It covers a total of 161 countries and comprises an array of 60 indicators on gender discrimination. The database has been compiled from various sources and combines systematically and coherently the current empirical evidence that exists on the socio-economic status of women. Its true innovation is the inclusion of institutional variables that range from intrahousehold behaviour to social norms. Information on cultural and traditional practices that impact women's economic development is coded to measure the level of discrimination. Such a comprehensive overview of gender-related variables and the database's specific focus on social institutions make the GID-DB unique, providing a toolbox for a wide range of analytical queries and allowing case-by-case adaptation to specific research or policy questions.

Gender: The concept of gender needs to be understood clearly as a cross-cutting socio-cultural variable. It is an overarching variable in the sense that gender can also be applied to all other cross-cutting variables such as race, class, age, ethnic group, etc. Gender systems are established in different socio-cultural contexts which determine what is expected, allowed, and valued in a woman/man and girl/boy in these specific contexts. Gender roles are learned through socialisation processes; they are not fixed but are changeable. Gender systems are institutionalised through education systems, political and economic systems, legislation, and culture and traditions. In utilising a gender approach the focus is not on individual women and men but on the system which determines gender roles/ responsibilities, access to and control over resources, and decision-making potentials. It is also important to emphasise that the concept of gender is not interchangeable with women. Gender refers to both, women and men, and the relations between them. The promotion of gender equality should concern and engage men as well as women. In recent years there has been a much stronger direct focus on men in research on gender perspectives. There are three main approaches taken in the increased focus on men. Firstly, the need to identify men as allies for gender equality and involve them more actively in this work. Secondly, the recognition that gender equality is not possible unless men change their attitudes and behaviour in many areas, for example, concerning reproductive rights and health. And thirdly, that gender systems in place in many contexts are negative for men as well as for women – creating unrealistic demands on men and requiring men to behave in narrowly defined ways. A considerable amount of interesting research is being undertaken, by both women and men, on male identities and masculinity. The increased focus on men will have a significant impact on future strategies for working with gender perspectives in development.

Gender-Based Constraints: Constraints that women or men face that are a result of their gender. An example of constraints women farmers face might be not having title to their land, male-dominated cooperative membership, is more tied to their homes preventing access to extension services. Constraints that are not based on gender are referred to as general constraints.

Gender-Based Violence (GBV): Violence that is directed at an individual based on his or her biological sex, gender identity, or his or her perceived adherence to socially defined norms of masculinity and femininity. It includes physical, sexual, and psychological abuse; threats; coercion; arbitrary deprivation of liberty; and economic deprivation, whether occurring in public or private life. GBV takes on many forms and can occur throughout the lifecycle, from the prenatal phase through childhood and adolescence, the reproductive years, and old age (Moreno, 2005). Types of GBV include female infanticide; harmful traditional practices such as early and forced marriage, honour killings, and female genital cutting; child sexual abuse and slavery; trafficking in persons; sexual coercion and abuse; neglect; domestic violence; and elder abuse. Women and girls are the most at risk and most affected by GBV. Consequently, the terms "violence against women" and "gender-based violence" are often used interchangeably. However, boys and men can also experience GBV, as can sexual and gender minorities such as men who have sex with men and transgender persons. Regardless of the target, GBV is rooted in structural inequalities between men and women and is characterised by the use and abuse of physical, emotional, or financial power and control. (Khan, 2011)

Gender-Based Violence in Emergencies (GBViE): In emergencies, such as conflict or natural disasters, the risk of violence, exploitation, and abuse is heightened, particularly for women.

Gender-Biased Sex Selection: "Sex selection can take place before a pregnancy is established, during pregnancy through prenatal sex detection and selective abortion, or following birth through infanticide or child neglect. Sex selection is sometimes used for family balancing purposes but far more typically occurs because of a systematic preference for boys. The biologically normal sex ratio at birth ranges from 102 to 106 males per 100 females. However, ratios higher than normal – sometimes as high as 130 – have been observed. This is now causing increasing concern in some South Asian, East Asian and Central Asian countries." (See: **Son Preference**.).

Gender-Blind Policies: Gender-blind Policies fail to distinguish between the different needs of women and men in their formulation and implementation. Thus, such policies are biased in favour of existing gender relations and therefore are likely to exclude women or exacerbate existing inequalities between women and men.

Gender-Blind: A **gender-blind** (or **unisex**) person is someone who adheres to not distinguishing people by gender. Gender blind people generally advocate gender neutrality in society, such as activities undertaken and services provided without regard to the gender of those who participate. Those who identify as pansexual may also refer to themselves as 'gender-blind': however, pansexuality emphasises gender-blindness in sexuality.

Gender-Blindness: This is the failure to recognise that gender is an essential determinant of social outcomes impacting projects and policies. A gender blind approach assumes gender is not an influencing factor in projects, programs, or policy.

Gender-Differentiated Impact: The effects of policies, programmes, projects, or measures, which have different impacts on men and women based on the different roles that they play in society and their differential access to resources. (See also **Gender Analysis**.).

Gender-Disaggregated Data: Data that is collected and analysed by sex. This kind of information distinguishes activities, aspirations, needs, and interests of men and women as well as their access to resources. Sex-disaggregated data is broken down only by sex, where sex is one of the independent variables.

Gender-Dominated Occupations: Jobs and occupations were one of the sexes –either male or female–predominates based on the gender-based division of labour. (See also **The Gender-Based Division Of Labour**.).

Gender-Neutral Programming and Policies: Programming and policies that do not center gender concerns or distinguish between genders in their design, interventions, and monitoring.

Gender-Responsive Programming and Policies: Intentionally employing gender considerations to affect the design, implementation, and results of programs and policies. Gender-responsive programs and policies reflect girls' and women's realities and needs, in components such as site selection, project staff, content, monitoring, etc. Gender- responsiveness means paying attention to the unique needs of females, valuing their perspectives, respecting their experiences, understanding developmental differences between girls and boys, women and men and ultimately empowering girls and women.

Gender-Neutral Pronouns: Pronouns that do not have female or male implications. Examples include the singular they (e.g., If *a person* sleeps late, *they* could be tardy for school) and abbreviated pronouns (e.g., *e* for s/he, *em* for her/him, *e ir* for her/his).

Gender-Neutral, Gender-Sensitive, and Gender Transformative: The primary objective behind gender mainstreaming is to design and implement development projects, programs, and policies that:

Gender-Nonconformity: Any number of practices that reject participation in the gender binary. Most genderqueer folks are gender-nonconforming, but not all gender-nonconforming folks identify as genderqueer. Similarly, the trans* umbrella is inclusive of any gender-nonconforming person, but that does not mean all gender-nonconforming people identify as transgender, trans, or trans*.

Genderqueer/Genderfuck: An identifying label for someone who redefines or plays with gender, or who refuses gender altogether. It is a label for people who bend/break the rules of gender and/or blur the boundaries.

Gender-Redistributive Policies: It aim to transform the existing distribution of resources and responsibilities to create a more equal relationship between women and men. Women and men may be targeted or one group alone may be targeted by the intervention. Gender-redistributive policies focus mainly on strategic gender interests but can plan to meet practical gender needs in a way which have transformative potential (provide a supportive environment for women's self-empowerment).

Gender-related Development Index (GDI): A measure of achievement in the same basic capabilities as the Human Development Index (HDI) of the United Nations Human Development Report, but factors in inequality in achievement between women and men in terms of a long and healthy life, knowledge and a decent standard of living. UNDP describes it as "simply the HDI discounted, or adjusted downwards, for gender inequality". The World Economic Forum also has an annual Global Gender Gap Report that measures how well countries are dividing their resources and opportunities among their male and female populations, regardless of the overall levels of these resources and opportunities. (See also **Gender Empowerment Measure**.).

Gender-Responsive Budgeting (GRB): Gender-responsive budgeting or GRB is a method of determining the extent to which government expenditure has detracted from or come nearer to the goal of gender equality. A gender-responsive budget is not a separate budget for women, but rather a tool that analyzes budget allocations, public spending, and taxation from a gender perspective and can be subsequently used to advocate for reallocation of budget line items to better respond to women's priorities as well as men's, making them, as the name suggests, gender-responsive. Government planning, programming, and budgeting contribute to the advancement of gender equality and the fulfillment of women's rights. It entails identifying and reflecting needed interventions to address gender gaps in the sector and local government policies, plans, and budgets. GRB also aims to analyze the gender-differentiated impact of revenue-raising policies and the allocation of domestic resources and Official Development Assistance.

Gender-Sensitive Budgets: Gender-Sensitive Budgets or 'women's budgets,' refers to a variety of processes and tools, which attempt to assess the impact of government budgets, mainly at the national level, on different groups of men and women, through recognising how gender relations underpin society and the economy. Gender or women's budget initiatives are not separate budgets for women. They include analysis of gender-targeted allocations (e.g. special programs targeting women); they disaggregate by gender the impact of mainstream expenditures across all sectors and services, and they review equal opportunities policies and allocations within government services.

Gender-Sensitive Programming and Policies: Programs and policies that are aware of and address gender differences.

Gender-Sensitivity: Encompasses the ability to acknowledge and highlight existing gender differences, issues, and inequalities and incorporate these into strategies and actions.

Gender-Socialization: The process of girls and boys, women and men learning social roles based on their sex, which leads to different behaviours and creates differing expectations and attitudes by gender. An example is the concept that girls and women do more household chores, such as cooking and cleaning, while boys and men do more work out of the home. Gender roles often lead to inequality.

Gender-Specific Torture and Ill-Treatment: Gender often has a considerable impact on the form of torture that takes place, the circumstances in which it occurs, its consequences, and the availability of and access to remedies for its victims. Rape, the threat of rape, electro-shock to the genitals, and strip-searching of women detainees by male guards are frequently the forms that such gender-specific torture. In societies where a woman's sexuality is a reflection of family "honour", these forms of torture and ill-treatment are rarely reported.

Gender-Transformative Programming and Policies: Programming and policies that transform gender relations to achieve gender equity.

Geographic Location: When referred to as a factor of discrimination or difference, the meaning has to do with the location where one lives, which often determines choices, opportunities, and access to resources. For example, rural residents are usually discriminated against in comparison to urban residents because they have less access to resources, services, and decision-makers. For many decades, another important geographic cleavage has existed between the "global north" and the "global south," referring to the north's access, exploitation, and control of resources over decades of colonialism and imperialism. While the "global north/global south" discourse remains relevant, an overly simplistic, dichotomic (to use a popular feminist concept) interpretation has been critiqued, given that there is also a 'south' (i.e. poor and socially-excluded groups) in the global north as well as privileged actors in the south.

Gilmanian: Relating to American feminist writer and sociologist Charlotte Perkins Gilman (1860-1935).

Girl: A female child. 'Girl child' is the term used by the United Nations to refer to a female child below the age of 18. The United Nations Convention on the Rights of the Child defines a child as a person below the age of 18. **A girl** is a young female, usually human, usually a child or an adolescent. When she becomes an adult, she is described as a woman. The term girl may also be used to mean a young woman and is sometimes used as a synonym for daughter. A girl may also be a term of endearment used by an adult, usually, a woman, to designate adult female friends. The treatment and status of girls in any society are usually closely related to the status of women in that culture. In cultures where women have a low societal position, girls may be unwanted by their parents, and the state may invest less in services for girls. Girls' upbringing ranges from being relatively the same as that of boys to complete sex segregation and completely different gender roles.

Glass Ceiling: A **glass ceiling** is a metaphor used to represent an invisible barrier that keeps a given demographic (typically applied to minorities) from rising beyond a certain level in a hierarchy. A metaphor to describe barriers: that stops even the most high-achieving women from rising to the level of power enjoyed by their male counterparts. The metaphor was first coined by feminists about barriers in the careers of high-achieving women. In the US, the concept is sometimes extended to refer to obstacles hindering the advancement of minority women, as well as minority men. Minority women often find the most difficulty in "breaking the glass ceiling" because they lie at the intersection of two historically marginalised groups: women and people of colour. Asian and Asian American news outlets have coined the term "bamboo ceiling" to refer to the obstacles that all Asian Americans face in advancing their careers. Within the same concepts of the other terms surrounding the workplace, there are similar terms for restrictions and barriers concerning women and their roles within organisations and how they coincide with their maternal duties. These "Invisible Barriers" function as metaphors to describe the extra circumstances, that, women undergo, usually when trying to advance within areas of their careers and often while trying to advance within their lives outside their workspaces.

Glass Escalator: The phenomenon of men who enter traditionally female-dominated fields of work being quickly promoted over the women.

Global Care Chains: This is a concept used to describe how to care responsibilities are transferred from one household to another, across national borders, forming chains. As individuals move, work in the care sector is internationalised. Through these chains, households in different places around the world are interconnected, as they transfer caregiving tasks from one household to another based on power hierarchies such as gender, ethnicity, social class, and place of origin. Global care chains are a phenomenon that is taking place within the context of globalisation, feminisation of migration, and the transformation of social welfare states. Chains are formed when women migrate to work in the care sector (domestic work, personal healthcare services, etc.) while transferring care work in their households in origin and sometimes in destination to other women.

Global Gender Gap Index: At the top of the Global Gender Gap Index is Iceland. The country has closed nearly 88% of its gap. It has been the world's most gender-equal country for nine years. Others in the top 10 include Norway (2nd), Finland (3rd), Rwanda (4) and Sweden (5), Nicaragua (6) and Slovenia (7), Ireland (8), New Zealand (9), and the Philippines (10). India's greatest challenges lie in the economic participation and opportunity pillar where the country is ranked 139 as well as the health and survival pillar where the country is ranked 141, the WEF said. The report attributed much of India's decline in position on the overall Global Gender Gap Index to a widening of its gender gaps in political empowerment as well as healthy life expectancy and basic literacy. "With more than 50 years having passed since the inauguration of the nation's first female prime minister in 1966, maintaining its global top 20 rankings on the political empowerment sub-index will require India to make progress on this dimension with a new generation of female political leadership," the report said. Moreover, the scale of India's gender gap in women's share among legislators, senior officials, and managers as well as professional and technical workers highlights that continued efforts will be needed to achieve parity in economic opportunity and participation. In India, the workplace gender gap is reinforced by extremely low participation of women in the economy (136 out of the total 144 countries covered) and low wages for those who work (136th ranking for estimated earned income), the WEF said, adding that "on average, 66% of women's work in India is unpaid, compared to 12% of men's". On a positive note, India succeeded in fully closing its primary and secondary education enrolment gender gaps for the second year running and for the first time has nearly closed its tertiary education gender gap. However, it continues to rank fourth-lowest in the world on health and survival, remaining the world's least improved country on this sub-index over the past decade, the WEF stated. "Competitiveness on a national and a business level will be decided more than ever before by the innovative capacity of a country or a company. Those will succeed best who understand to integrate women as an important force into their talent pool," said Klaus Schwab, founder, and Executive Chairman, World Economic Forum (WEF).

Globalisation: A highly contested term. As a technical process, globalisation can be understood as the increasing ease and speed at which people, commerce, culture, media, and ideologies move across political and geographic borders, thanks to increasing access to various technologies, not the least, internet communications technologies. As a political process, globalisation refers to how states and multinational actors (such as corporations) have used these new technologies to restructure political and economic arrangements based on neoliberal principles, eliminating trade barriers to expand their influence and reach. Critics see globalisation as the current model of world development that seeks to reorganize the distribution and use of natural resources in favour of companies and profit generation in which the global North plays a dominant role in coordination with elites in the Global South. The globalisation of production has forced free trade agreements and has led countries to try to compete for investment by offering ever-cheaper labour, state benefits, and access to natural resources to increase the profit margins of transnational corporations, dismantling labour and environmental regulations in the process. (Kerr and Sweetman, 2003)

Governance: This is the capacity and the quality of governing. In its broadest terms, governance refers to the relationships between people and different institutions; it is the mechanism that allows for information owes decision-making, and accountability. This might be between a government and its citizens, between an NGO and the people with whom they work, or it could be the internal management structure of any organisation and applies to international organisations, such as the World Trade Organisation, national government or grassroots organisations. Each level has relevance in the right for justice and equity for poor and marginalised people. Moreover, different people will conceptualise and experience governance differently due to their power and position in society. Over the last few years, governance has become a buzzword in development, referred to frequently by organisations such as the World Bank and international and national NGOs. "Good governance" is heralded as a prerequisite for positive change by strengthening government accountability, decreasing corruption and abuse of power, and increasing citizens' voices in decision-making. A major critique of the "good governance" discourse is that it is focused on making power more efficient, not redistributing it. (Newman, 2004)

Guerrilla Girls: The Guerrilla Girls are a group of masked feminists and artists who have been working anonymously to expose and disrupt "sexism, racism, and corruption in politics" (Guerrilla Girls, 2016, para.1) and popular visual culture for over 30 years.

Gynocriticism: Gynocriticism or gynocritics is the term coined in the seventies by Elaine Showalter to describe a new literary project intended to construct "a female framework for the analysis of women's literature". By expanding the historical study of women writers as a distinct literary tradition, gynocritics sought to develop new models based on the study of female experience to replace male models of literary creation, and so "map the territory" left unexplored in earlier literary criticisms.

Hegemonic Masculinity: Socially and the historically constructed idea of what men ought to be, in a way a structure that links power to masculinity.

Hegemony: The process through which the world view of dominant groups comes to be accepted as "common sense" or the "natural" order of things. Italian activist and theorist Antonio Gramsci developed the concept of cultural hegemony to explain how a dominant group generates ideas and consensus about those ideas to maintain popular support and legitimacy. Hegemony can be expressed through language, culture, patriarchy, political and economic systems, etc…and is designed to maintain the status quo in the interest of those in power (OR) One group's domination and suppression of another through social, cultural, political, and/or economic influence (Grand Rapids Community College, 2012, para. 23).

Herstory: Feminist effort to revise "history" so that it includes women and their importance in the shared temporal narrative of events; some feminists find the term frivolous.

Heteronormative: A perspective that privileges heterosexuality and marginalises nonheterosexuality. For example, heteronormativity supports normative views about sexual and marital relations between women and men. Heteronormative views also place stable, binary understandings upon both gender (expression) and sex. In sum, "[t]he heteronormative view is that physical sex, gender identity, and gender roles should, in any given person, align to either all male or all female cultural norms" (Feminish, 2012, para. 10).

Heteronormativity: Heteronormativity is the belief that people fall into distinct and complementary genders (male and female) with natural roles in life. It assumes that heterosexuality is the only sexual orientation or the only norm and that sexual and marital relation are most (or only) fitting between people of the opposite sex. A "heteronormative" view, therefore, involves alignment of biological sex, sexuality, gender identity, and gender roles.

Heteropatriarchy: Related to patriarchy; the organisation of society in such a way that heterosexuality and cisgender men are favoured and given more institutional power than women and LGBT demographics.

Heterosexism/Heterosexual Privilege: The assumption that people are heterosexual, or the attitude that people should be heterosexual because heterosexuality is the only valid sexual orientation. It often takes the form of ignoring bisexuals, gay men, and lesbians. Heterosexual privilege refers to the benefits granted automatically to heterosexual people that are denied to bisexuals, gay men, and lesbians.

Heterosexism: Belief in the inherent superiority of heterosexuality. The concept refers to power used over the other based on an ideology dictating both compulsory heterosexuality and certain types of masculinities as the ideal forms. Heterosexism situates other types of masculinities - and more commonly femininities - in less valued positions, and pressurizes individuals to conform to binary gender roles, positions, and to adopt traits associated with heterosexuality. Thus, heterosexism is about power rather than sexual orientation.

Heterosexual: The dictionary definition of this would be "a sexual orientation in which a person is romantically and sexually attracted to a person of the opposite gender." This definition should be problematised because there are not only two genders. Perhaps a better, more accurate definition of this descriptor would be "a person who is attracted to primary people of other genders, as opposed to their same gender."

Heterosexuality (Compulsory): The assumption that women and men are innately attracted to each other emotionally and sexually and that heterosexuality is normal and universal. This institutionalisation of heterosexuality in our society leads to an institutionalised inequality of power not only between heterosexuals and non-heterosexuals but also between men and women, with far-reaching consequences.

Hidden Sexuality Curriculum (Hidden Hetero gender Curriculum): The terms refer to the invisibility of the curriculum we use while dealing with issues related to sexuality. They also tell us that, in addition to invisibility, the curriculum can be unconscious. Heterogender further tells us about the close connection between sexuality constructions and gendering.

Hierarchical: Means arranged as a hierarchy - ranked one above the other, with the one above is more important than the one below. The five levels of the Women's Equality and Empowerment Framework are described as "hierarchical" because in some ways each "higher level is more important than the one below. For example, gender inequality in welfare is caused by gender inequality in access, which then raises the discussion to a more important and quite different level of discussion. These are five levels of analysis and not five stages of the development process. Any development problem has these five dimensions within it, and a project must address gender issues progressively at these levels if women's development is to make progress.

Hierarchy: Value system of ordering people's roles as "above" and "superior" in descending order to "below" and "inferior." Hierarchies establish relatively fixed positions within a social system.

HIV: Human Immunodeficiency Virus, or the virus that causes AIDS. The virus is transmitted through unprotected sexual contact, through blood, and from mother to child. As the virus damages the immune system of a person, some opportunistic infections such as diarrhea, fever, tuberculosis, pneumonia, and lymphoma begin to develop, becoming progressively severe.

Homonormativity: A way of privileging a type of homosexuality that encourages assimilation to dominant, mainstream, heterosexual norms (i.e. marriage) and marginalizes other sexualities and identities.

Homophobia: A fear of homosexuality. A phobia is an irrational fear that runs contrary to cultural norms, but homophobia is most often used to designate a prejudicial hatred of homosexuality comparable to racism. Homophobia can be and often is institutionalised in antigay laws, policies, and the pronouncements of church and state. It also manifests itself in individuals, where its effects can range from verbal abuse to gay-bashing and even murder. One of its most unfortunate manifestations is in homosexuals who have been convinced by society that their affections and desires are monstrous and deserving of punishment.

Homosexual: An individual who is romantically and/or sexually attracted to others of their sex.

Homosociality: In simple terms, homosociality means that a certain social context is limited to, or is strongly dominated by, same-sex individuals. The concept was developed in the field of gender research to explain how men identify with, are drawn to, and understand their social position to other men. Women are excluded from these social contexts, partly to keep them from interfering with the often fairly intimate culture and partly because, based on established power structures, they do not possess the economic, social, and political resources that would otherwise make it worthwhile to include them. Jokes about decisions being made in the sauna or on the golf course refer to homosocial contexts in real life, where men by tradition meet in informal environments to which women are not invited or explicitly welcome. The concept of male homosocial desire points to how the homosocial groupings that the superordination of men rests upon often exhibit a split attitude to sexuality. At the same time as the single-sex social environments can be very intimate, it can be part of the jargon to express homophobic attitudes (see also heteronormativity). Examples of this can be found in both ice hockey locker rooms and exclusive gentlemen's clubs. Homosociality can have an impact in both recruitment and nomination processes, for example, when boards are appointed (see also quotas and quota systems). Men benefit from approaching and mimicking other men and tend to select more men than women to their group or context. Organisational research shows how the presence of a few women in a male homosocial context becomes very noticeable, and that this leads to a strong emphasis on women's 'non-standard' traits and features. For women who want to reach important positions, the logical strategy instead becomes to stress that they can make unique contributions.

Honour Killings: Acts of violence, usually murder, committed by male family members against female family members who are perceived to have brought dishonour upon the family.

Hooksian: Relating to American feminist writer Bell Hooks (b. 1952).

Hostile Sexism: The one most people think about, i.e., openly insulting, objectifying, and degrading women.

Household Maintenance: All domestic and people-related activities carried out by household members, such as the collection of fuelwood and water, meal preparation, child care, repair services, financial services, banking and legal services. All of these activities are taken into consideration in a country's satellite account.

Housewife: A woman whose principal occupation is managing a household and who does not receive remuneration or profit from her activities. The preferred gender-sensitive term to use in news and writing is 'homemaker'. (See also reproductive labour.).

Human Papilloma Virus (HPV): Human Papilloma Virus (HPV) is the most common sexually transmitted infection (STI). HPV is so common that nearly all sexually active people get it at some point in their lives. HPV is spread by vaginal, anal, or oral sex with someone who has the virus and can be transmitted even when an infected person has no signs or symptoms. Symptoms can also develop years after having sex with someone infected. In most cases, HPV goes away on its own and does not cause any health problems. However, there are many different types of HPV; some types can cause health problems including genital warts and 18 cervical and other cancers. HPV types - 16 are responsible for about 70% of all cervical cancer cases worldwide. The U.S. Centers for Disease Control recommend that all boys and girls ages 11 or 12 years get vaccinated. By March 2017, 71 countries (37%) had introduced HPV vaccine in their national immunisation program for girls and in 11 countries (6%) also for boys.

Human Rights with a Gender Perspective: This perspective recognises that differences in life experiences based on gender often result in social, economic, political, and other inequities for women and girls. This view, when applied to policy development and service delivery, promotes positive change in the lives of women and girls. For example, home-based English as a Second Language programme would allow immigrant mothers who care for their children at home to learn English and function in their new surroundings. See rights and women's human rights.

Human Rights: Human rights are commonly understood as being those rights that are inherent to the human being. The concept of human rights acknowledges that every single human being is entitled to enjoy his or her human rights without distinction as to race, colour, sex, language, religion, political or other opinions, national or social origin, property, birth, or other status. Human rights are legally guaranteed by human rights law, protecting individuals and groups against actions that interfere with fundamental freedoms and human dignity. They are expressed in treaties, customary international law, bodies of principles, and other sources of law. Human rights law places an obligation on States to act in a particular way and prohibits States from engaging in specified activities. All human rights and instruments that concern them apply equally to men and women. In addition, the CEDAW has specified and complemented some of them from the perspective of women's rights.

Human Rights-Based Approach (HRBA): A human rights-based approach entails consciously and systematically paying attention to human rights in all aspects of programme development. An HRBA is a conceptual framework for the process of human development that is normatively based on international human rights standards and operationally directed to promoting and protecting human rights. The objective of the HRBA is to empower people (rights-holders) to realise their rights and strengthen the State (duty-bearers) to comply with their human rights obligations and duties. States' obligations to human rights require them to respect, protect and fulfill women's and girls' rights, along with the rights of men and boys. When they fail to do so, the United Nations has a responsibility to work with partners to strengthen their capacity to more effectively realise that duty. A human rights-based approach (HRBA) to gender issues uncovers how human rights issues affect women and men differently and how power relations and gender-based discriminations affect the effective enjoyment of rights by all human beings. HRBA and gender mainstreaming are two of the five UN programming principles (the others are results-based management, environmental sustainability, and capacity development). As such, every UN staff member should use them in their programming work.

Human Security: A people-centered approach to security that responds to authentic causes of vulnerability by expanding human rights, basic economic justice, access to food and healthcare, protection from the ravages of environmental disasters and degradation, personal freedom from violence, including domestic abuse, and protection from ethnic and sectarian violence. Also see security militarism A broad analytical framework for describing the collective impacts of the use of military force and violence on everyday life and on the social, economic, and political institutions that shape it. This analysis identifies a military logic in the organisation of society, beginning with the violent oppression of colonialism and its legacies, vis-à-vis militaristic post-colonial regimes; proxy wars during the Cold War that propped up authoritarian dictators and led to arms proliferation; and current-day military rule and violent civil and political conflicts. It also encompasses the role and effects of US military bases on communities and the impact of the US-led "wars" on terror and drugs that have led to massive flows of resources to law enforcement and defense sectors in the name of "national security." (Mama and Okazawa Ray, 2008)

Human Smuggling: The movement and importation of people into a country through the deliberate evasion of immigration laws, usually for financial or other material benefits. People who are smuggled can range from those seeking better employment and financial opportunities in another country where they are not nationals or residents of, asylum seekers, refugees, and others fleeing conflict or persecution. While people who are smuggled usually pay fees to get them to their destinations, this is not always the case when it comes to families and friends who get others to join them. Smuggling, including that by organised networks in different parts of the world, is usually differentiated from trafficking by the elements of coercion and deception that go with the latter. (See also **Trafficking of Persons**.).

Hypermasculinity: Exaggerated image of hegemonic masculinity, mainly in media. It overemphasizes the ideals set out for men hence reinforcing them.

Identity Politics: In many societies, sexual and racial or ethnic minorities are systematically excluded. Vibrant social movements such as the Dalit movement in South Asia, the US civil rights movement, and the global movement for lesbian, gay, and transgender rights focus on bringing people together to build pride, reclaim dignity and identify common interests based on a collective identity, and to make political demands and fight discrimination. These movements have built solidarity and active citizenship among many formerly socially and politically excluded groups. The risk of identity politics is that the complexity of human identity is reduced to labels that exclude or marginalise people, such as "HIV positive" or "migrant worker," even as every individual has multiple identities defined by race, gender, class, religion, sexual orientation, ethnicity, age, and the like. Identity politics can also lead to discriminatory forms of politics that focus narrowly on the self-interest of a particular group, rather than building alliances with others around common interests to advance rights and build inclusive societies.

Identity vs. Subjectivity: Humanist theorists generally view identity as dictated by an internal, essential nature (Jackson & Mazzei, 2012; Jagger, 2008). Post theorists (poststructural, postmodern, posthuman) understand subjectivity as constituted and regulated in historical, cultural, and political contexts (Jagger, 2008). In brief, identity is understood as stable, while subjectivity is seen as fluid.

Ideology: A system of ideas or beliefs or ways of perceiving and analyzing social reality. Ideologies can justify, support, or challenge the power and interests of the dominant group. Ideologies are disseminated and enforced through social, economic, political, and religious institutions and structures such as the family, education system, media, economy, or legal system. These institutions and structures are set up and mediated by the state and tend to reinforce the dominant ideology and the power of the dominant groups within it. Alternative ideologies, such as feminism, are created in a continuous process of resistance by the less powerful and marginalised sections of society, resulting in various degrees of change in power dynamics, including transformation.

Impairment: An injury, illness, or congenital condition that causes or is likely to cause a loss or difference of physiological or psychological function.

In the Closet: Keeping one's sexual orientation and/or gender or sex identity a secret.

Incest: Sexual contact between closely related individuals that violate socio-cultural or religious norms or laws. The types of kinship within which sex is forbidden vary widely among cultures.

Indigenous Feminism: Feminism combined with concerns about indigenous sovereignty, focussed on decolonization and the empowering of indigenous women.

Individualist Feminism: Feminism holding that gender equality can be achieved through equal rights for all individuals without respect to gender. More often than not, this is a euphemism for libertarian anti-feminists who want to co-opt the label to prop up their oftentimes reactionary criticisms of feminism.

Inequalities in Economic Participation and Opportunities: In most countries, women and men are distributed differently across sectors. Women are receiving lower wages for similar work, are more likely to be in low-paid jobs and unsecured work (part-time, temporary, home-based) and are likely to have less access than men to productive assets such as education, skills, property, and credit.

Inequalities in Political Power and Representation: Women are often underrepresented informal decision-making structures, including governments, community councils, and policy-making institutions.

Informal Economy: Not one but many economies or parts of the economy in which goods and services are bought and sold outside of the formal market, without state regulation or taxation, and in some cases, based on non-monetary exchanges. Informal economies and the people in them are often invisible within "official" data on economic growth and labour. The informal sector creates opportunities for people to earn income, for example by selling food, caring for children, or providing labour, when jobs aren't available in the formal sector. Because the informal sector operates with little or no government oversight or regulation, workers do not receive benefits or protections in labour law. Participants can establish and enforce their own rules of exchange to protect themselves. Alternatively, informal economies can be highly exploitative and violent, particular where the goods and services exchanged are highly restricted or illegal, like weapons or illicit drugs. Due to discrimination that presents barriers to women's participation in the formal labour market, women's labour is concentrated in the informal economy in many countries; as a result of neo-liberal policies to avoid labour rights, the informal economy is the fastest-growing economic sector in many developing countries. In many developing countries around the world, women are disproportionately represented in the informal sector.

Informal Labour: Informal labour refers to income-producing work that happens part or partially outside the formal employment system that is regulated and taxed by the state.

Informal Sector: The term informal sector refers to employment and production that takes place in small and/or unregistered enterprises. It includes self-employment in informal enterprises (small and unregistered enterprises) and wage employment in informal jobs (unregulated and unprotected jobs) for informal enterprises, formal enterprises, households, or for no fixed employer.

Inheritance: The right to receive goods and property through transfer entitlements upon the death of the owner of goods or property. Traditionally, inheritance rights concern the transfer of goods and property between biological family members. Women in some cultures do not have the legal right to inheritance or to share equally with male heirs.

Institutional Power: Means control, access, and influence. In U.S. society, power means having *control* of and *access* to ruling institutions; freedom from the threat of being questioned or reprimanded for wrongdoing; and the ability to define standards and norms.

Institutional Racism: Societal patterns that have the net effect of imposing oppressive or otherwise negative conditions against identifiable groups based on race or ethnicity; in the United States, institutional racism results from the social caste system that sustained, and was sustained by, slavery and racial segregation.

Institutionalised Oppression: A specific arrangement of society that benefits one group at the expense of another through cultural and social institutions such as language, media, religion, economics, education system, etc.

Institutionalised Sexism: Sexism against women, upheld by society and its institutions.

Intention/Intentionality: In essence, refers to clarity and determination of purpose. It was applied as a planning term by Maria Suarez to describe the aim of social or political change efforts among feminists in Mesoamerica. The term was conceived as an alternative to linear goal- and outcome-oriented planning and evaluation frameworks that have contributed to the depoliticization of social change efforts. The prevalent technical approach to planning emphasises qualitative and cause-and-effect thinking that does not accurately capture the dynamic patterns of feminist organising and often does not account for the underlying structural drivers (i.e. power) of inequality. The term seeks to recover the dynamism and uncertainty in political work and to ensure flexibility while simultaneously communicating clear political meaning, particularly with existing and potential financial donors. (Also, see **NGO'isation**).

Inter-Agency Network on Women and Gender Equality (IANWGE): The Inter-Agency Network on Women and Gender Equality (IANWGE) is a network of Gender Focal Points in United Nations offices, specialised agencies, funds, and programmes and is chaired by UN Women. UN Women also serves as the Secretariat for the Network. All UN member entities are represented in the Network. The network supports and monitors the implementation of the Beijing Platform for Action adopted at the Fourth World Conference on Women and the outcome of the twenty-third United Nations General Assembly special session "Women 2000: Gender equality, development and peace for the twenty-first century" (Beijing+5); and gender-related recommendations emanating from other recent UN General Assembly special sessions, conferences, and summits, especially by ensuring effective co-operation and coordination throughout the UN system. The Network also monitors and oversees the mainstreaming of a gender perspective in the programmatic, normative, and operational work of the UN system. IANWGE's work follows guidelines recommended by the United Nations System Chief Executives Board (CEB) for Coordination, and its two high-level committees, the High-Level Committee on Programmes (HLCP) and the High-Level Committee on Management (HLCM).

Intermediate Barriers/Causes: Intermediate barriers and causes of gender inequality, also commonly referred to as 'gender bottlenecks', determine options and opportunities available to persons according to their gender. These might include girls' and women's greater concerns for safety and mobility when using washrooms or collecting water, or heavier burdens and responsibilities in the household.

Internalised Misogyny: Misogynic attitudes and behaviours displayed by a woman (OR) the involuntary internalisation by women of the sexist messages that are present in their societies and culture; how women reinforce sexism by utilising and relaying sexist messages that they've internalised.

Internalised Oppression: The process through which a marginalised person or group comes to believe, accept, or live out inaccurate stereotypes and misinformation about their group because of the pervasive degree to which they have been steeped in prejudice and discrimination against their identity group.

Internalised Racism: The process by which people of colour, reproduce dominant narratives about their local ethnic communities/groups to justify their low socioeconomic positions.

Internalised Sexism: Sexist attitudes toward women as internalised by a woman, manifesting as part of her self-concept (OR) When the belief in women's inferiority becomes part of one's worldview and self-concept.

International Conference on Population and Development (ICPD): A United Nations conference that focused on the linkages among population, human rights (including reproductive health), sustained economic growth, and balanced development. Also called the 'Cairo Conference', the ICPD was held in the Egyptian capital in September 1994. In the 20-year Programme of Action they adopted in Cairo, 170 governments confirmed as cornerstones of population and development policies the advancement of gender equality, elimination of violence against women, and women's ability to control their fertility. Discussions on population had tended to focus on demographic targets and population control, until the Cairo consensus introduced a new concept of reproductive health by focusing on the rights of individuals and couples to decide the number, spacing, and timing of their children, as a key part of social development. At the same time, discussions about reproductive health as a right, as well as contraception and reproductive health services for adolescents, ignited debates in many countries before and after the conference.

International Day of the Girl Child: On 19 December 2011, United Nations General Assembly adopted resolution 66/170 declaring 11 October the International Day of the Girl Child to recognize girls' rights and the unique challenges girls face around the world and to promote girls' empowerment and the fulfillment of their human rights.

International Financial Institutions (IFIs): These institutions provide loans to cash-strapped countries to cover funding shortfalls or to finance development projects, for example, to build roads, improve sanitation, or fund education and healthcare services. Although they are "multinational" institutions, their lending policies are driven and determined by wealthy Western countries and private enterprises that have a long history of promoting large loans to low-income countries accompanied by conditions that require economic reforms to support neo-liberalism. IFIs have issued massive loans, particularly in the 1970s, to prop up dictators, buy small arms, repay other loans, or cover the artificially high cost of oil. Today, low-income countries still carry huge amounts of this "illegitimate debt," along with other loans that force poor countries to adopt neo-liberal "conditionalities" imposed by the IFIs that service these loans. (Jubilee USA Network)

Interpersonal Racism: Any experience or incident in which race functions as a catalyst for disparate treatment.

Intersectional Analysis: Exploration of the ways race, class, sexual orientation, gender identity, etc. may impact an individual and one's treatment in society.

Intersectional Feminism: If feminism is advocating for women's rights and equality between the sexes, intersectional feminism is the understanding of how women's overlapping identities — including race, class, ethnicity, religion, sexual orientation, and disability status — impact the way they experience oppression and discrimination.

Intersectionality: A concept often used in critical theories to describe how oppressive institutions (racism, sexism, homophobia, transphobia, ableism, xenophobia, classism, etc.) are interconnected and cannot be examined separately from one another. Tool for analysis, advocacy, and policy development, that addresses multiple discriminations and helps understand how different sets of identities impact access to rights and opportunities. Intersectionality is an analytical tool for studying, understanding and responding to how gender intersects with other identities and how these intersections contribute to unique experiences of oppression and privilege. It starts from the premise that people live multiple, layered identities derived from social relations, history, and the operation of structures of power. The intersectional analysis aims to reveal multiple identities, exposing the different types of discrimination and disadvantage that occur as a consequence of the combination of identities. It aims to address how racism, patriarchy, class oppression, and other systems of discrimination create inequalities that structure the relative positions of women. Intersectional analysis posits that we should not understand the combining of identities as additively increasing one's burden but instead as producing substantively distinct experiences. It is therefore an indispensable methodology for development and human rights work.

Intersex: A set of medical conditions that feature congenital anomalies of the reproductive and sexual system. That is, intersex people are born with "sex chromosomes," external genitalia, or internal reproductive systems that are not considered "standard" for either male or female. The existence of intersex people shows that there are not just two sexes and that our ways of thinking about sex (trying to force everyone to fit into either the mail box or the female box) are socially constructed. About 1 in 2000 infants born is at risk for intersex genital mutilation (meaning a decision is made at birth by parent, a doctor, or both, to alter the infant's genitalia to be either fully male or female). An even higher proportion of the population is intersex in some way. This word replaces "hermaphrodite," which is generally considered rude, not politically correct, and/or derogatory.

The invisibility of Feminine Labour: Is the term used for the idea that women's work in the home is devalued in society. In other words, domestic labour is not as important or valuable as other types of paid labour. This creates a society in which women don't want to be associated with domestic labour or would choose to not stay in the home/associate themselves with unpaid work.

Invisible Minority: A group whose minority status is not always immediately visible, such as some disabled people and LGBTIQ people. This lack of visibility may make organising for rights difficult.

Kyriarchy: A concept first created by Elisabeth Schüssler Fiorenza in 1992 to describe her theory of interconnected, interacting, and self-extending systems of domination and submission, in which a single individual might be oppressed in some relationships and privileged in others.

The Labour Force: the currently active population, comprises all persons who fulfill the requirements for inclusion among the employed (civilian employment plus the armed forces) or the unemployed. The employed are defined as those who work for pay or profit for at least one hour a week, or who have a job but are temporarily not at work due to illness, leave or industrial action. The armed forces cover personnel from the metropolitan territory drawn from the total available labour force who served in the armed forces during the period under consideration, whether stationed in the metropolitan territory or elsewhere. The unemployed are defined as people without work but actively seeking employment and currently available to start work. This indicator is seasonally adjusted and it is measured in persons.

Lactivism: Women's activism to remove the stigma from breastfeeding in public.

Lambda: The Gay Activist Alliance originally chose the lambda, the Greek letter "L", as a symbol in 1970. Organisers chose the letter "L" to signify liberation. The word has become a way of expressing the concept "lesbian and gay male" in a minimum of syllables and has been adopted by such organisations as Lambda Legal Defence and Education Fund.

Lateral Violence: This is displaced violence directed against one's peers rather than adversaries. This construct is one way of explaining minority-on-minority violence in developed nations. Those who experiencing and those committing lateral violence are more likely to be involved in crime in the United States, the United Kingdom, and elsewhere. In Australia and Canada, lateral violence is widely seen as an intergenerational learned pattern and a major social problem in indigenous communities. In Australia, surveys have reported that up to 95% of Aboriginal youth had witnessed lateral violence in the home and that 95% of the bullying experienced by Aboriginals was perpetrated by other Aboriginals. Lateral Violence occurs within marginalised groups where members strike out at each other as a result of being oppressed. The oppressed become the oppressors of themselves and each other. Common behaviours that prevent positive change from occurring include gossiping, bullying, finger-pointing, backstabbing, and shunning.

Latinx(s) (pronounced "latinexx"): A gender-neutral way of describing people from Latin America. "Hispanic" is a term that ties folks back to their Spanish colonizers, can feel oppressive, and also does not include Brazil, Haiti, etc. Latin@ to capture a/o is sometimes used but creates a problematic gender binary. It makes the word gender-neutral since latin@ is the only o/a, it only encompasses masculinity and femininity. Latinx includes non-binary identifying people. It is pronounced Latinexx.

Lesbian Feminism: A current of feminism advocating that women direct their energies toward other women rather than men, seeing lesbianism as the practical application of feminism.

Lesbian: Female for whom her sexual orientation is predominantly or exclusively directed to a person of the same sex. Lesbian is used interchangeably with homosexual and gay when referring to females. Lesbian is usually the preferred word of the gay and lesbian community when referring to homosexual females.

LGBTQ: The acronym for "lesbian, gay, bisexual, transgender, and queer." Some people also use the Q to stand for "questioning," meaning people who are figuring out their sexual or gender identity. (also see LGBTQIA). I stands for intersex and A for asexual/aromantic/ agender.

LGBTQ+: Umbrella term for all persons who have a non-normative gender or sexuality. LGBTQ stands for lesbian, gay, bisexual, transgender, and queer, questioning. Sometimes a + at the end is added to be more inclusive. A UNICEF position paper, "Eliminating Discrimination Against Children and Parents Based on Sexual Orientation and/or Sexual Identity (November 2014)," states all children, irrespective of their actual or perceived sexual orientation or gender identity, have the right to a safe and healthy childhood that is free from discrimination.

Liberal Feminism: Feminism encouraging women to achieve and maintain their equality through their actions and through campaigning for political and legal reform, in a sense, the polar opposite of radical feminism.

Libfem: Liberal feminism or a liberal feminist.

Lipstick Feminism: Lipstick feminism can be seen as a reaction to the common prejudice that feminists are ugly and hate sex. They embrace, among other things, the idea that wearing make-up and suggestive clothing can be empowering for women.

Livelihood: A person's or community's livelihood is a productive activity that sustains life and supports themselves and their families.

Logocentrism: The assumption that there is truth in the sign system (language, etc.) we accept, to the exclusion of historical context, the marginalised and the absent.

Mainstream Feminism: Feminism is promoted to and accepted by relatively large numbers of people. In recent years, it has come to mean fourth-wave feminism is promoted through celebrities and popular feminist blogs like Everyday Feminism or Feminising.

Mainstreaming: Of women's development entails addressing gender issues in all development projects and programmes, irrespective of the sector or type of project. Mainstreaming is therefore the very opposite of a strategy of segregating gender issues into separate "women's projects". The term "mainstreaming" is currently used in two rather different ways, depending on the user's perspective on women's development. For those who interpret women's development as being merely concerned with improving women's access to resources and productivity, the strategy of mainstreaming may be interpreted in the minimum or weaker sense of integrating gender issues by adding gender objectives to existing programmes. This involves some adaptation, but not the transformation of the development process. By contrast, a stronger sense of the term mainstreaming is used by those who see women's development as being essentially concerned with women's participation and empowerment, to address issues of gender inequality. From this perspective, the mainstreaming of gender issues entails the transformation of the development process. UNICEF has an explicit policy on mainstreaming which embraces this stronger meaning of mainstreaming.

Mako Mori Test: A variation on the Bechdel test, gauging the proportion of works that feature a named woman who has her narrative arc that does not exist to support the narrative arc of a male character.

Male as Norm: In feminist theory, the principle of **male-as-norm** holds that "language referring to females, such as the suffix -ess (as in actress), the use of man to mean "human", and other such devices, strengthens the perceptions that the male category is the norm and that the corresponding female category is a derivation and thus less important. Sexist terms such as chairman, anchorman, etc., are cited as examples of how the English language mirrors social gender biases. The idea was first clearly expressed by 19th-century thinkers who began deconstructing the English language to expose the products and footings of patriarchy. The principle of male-as-norm and the relation between gendered grammar and how its respective speakers conceptualise their world has received attention in varying fields from philosophy to psychology and anthropology and has fueled debates over linguistic determinism and gender inequality. The underlying message of this principle is that women speak a less legitimate language that both sustains and is defined by the subordination of the female gender as secondary to the accepted male-biased normative language. By regarding women's language as deficient to that of men it has been assumed that something is wrong with women's language. Subsequently, research in the social sciences, particularly in discourse analysis, has maintained and qualified systemic male bias. In practice, grammatical gender exhibits a systematic structural bias that has made masculine forms the default for generic, non-gender-specific contexts. According to the male-as-norm principle, the male linguistic bias works to exclude and ignore women, diminish the female experience, and rule that all that is not male is deviant and unfit to represent many social categories.

Male Chauvinism: The attitude that men are categorically superior to women, as held by a man.

Male Gaze: In feminist theory, the **male gaze** is the act of depicting women and the world, in the visual arts and literature, from a masculine, heterosexual perspective that presents and represents women as sexual objects for the pleasure of the male viewer. The male gaze has three perspectives: (i) that of the person behind the camera, (ii) that of the characters within the representation, and (iii) that of the spectator. The film critic Laura Mulvey coined the term *male gaze*, which is contrasted with the concept of the female gaze; as such, the male gaze is comparable to scopophilia, which is sexual pleasure derived from observing the passive female as an object.

Male Privilege: Male privilege is a concept within sociology for examining social, economic, and political advantages or rights that are available to men solely based on their sex. A man's access to these benefits may vary depending on how closely they match their society's ideal masculine norm.

Male Supremacy: A system of oppression that gives power to men and values masculinity, at the expense of women and femininity.

Male-Dominated Society: Organisation or area of activity is one in which men have most of the power and influence.

Malestream: The idea that mainstream social science findings are biased towards a masculine perspective, which is assumed to apply to women as well.

Male-to-Female (MTF): Someone assigned male at birth that identifies as female.

Malnutrition: Is a condition that results from eating a diet in which one or more nutrients are either not enough or are too much such that the diet causes health problems. It may involve calories, protein, carbohydrates, vitamins or minerals. Not enough nutrients are called under nutrition or undernourishment while too much is called over nutrition. Malnutrition is often used to specifically refer to undernutrition where an individual is not getting enough calories, protein, or micronutrients. If undernutrition occurs during pregnancy, or before two years of age, it may result in permanent problems with physical and mental development. Extreme undernourishment, known as starvation, may have symptoms that include: a short height, a thin body, very poor energy levels, and swollen legs and abdomen. People also often get infections and are frequently cold. The symptoms of micronutrient deficiencies depend on the micronutrient that is lacking.

Man: Man is a male human. The term man is usually reserved for an adult male, with the term boy being the usual term for a male child or adolescent. However, the term man is also sometimes used to identify a male human, regardless of age, as in phrases such as "men's basketball". Like most other male mammals, a man's genome typically inherits an X chromosome from his mother and a Y chromosome from his father. The male fetus produces larger amounts of androgens and smaller amounts of estrogens than a female fetus. This difference in the relative amounts of these sex steroids is largely responsible for the physiological differences that distinguish men from women. During puberty, hormones that stimulate androgen production result in the development of secondary sexual characteristics, thus exhibiting greater differences between the sexes. However, there are exceptions to the above for some transgender and intersex men.

Mansplain (verb) Mansplainy (adjective): When a man explains something to a woman in a condescending way when he either (1) doesn't know anything about it or (2) knows far less than the woman he is talking to. Sorry, if you already knew that.

Mansplaining: (Of a man) Explaining to a woman something related to her own direct experiences in a way that condescendingly assumes superior knowledge.

Manspreading: Manspreading or **Man-Sitting** or **Ballrooms** is the practice of men sitting in public transport with legs wide apart, thereby covering more than one seat. Both this posture and the use of the neologism "manspreading" have occasioned some internet criticism and debates in the US, UK, Turkey, and Canada. The public debate began when an anti-manspreading campaign started on the social media website Tumblr in 2013; the term appeared a year later. Oxford Dictionaries.com added the word "manspreading" in August 2015. The use of the term has been criticised as "a caricature of feminism" and the practice has been juxtaposed with examples of women taking up excessive space in public spaces with bags.

Manterrupting: When a man interrupts a woman, especially excessively. Examples: During the 2009 MTV Video Music Awards when Kanye West grabbed the mic from Taylor Swift, who had just won an award and was trying her best to accept it, to let everyone know "Imma let you finish, but Beyoncé had one of the best videos of all time." Or, during September's presidential debate when Donald Trump interrupted Hillary Clinton 22 times in the first 26 minutes. Or when Senate majority leader Mitch McConnell interrupted Elizabeth Warren's recitation of Coretta Scott King's 1986 letter against Jeff Sessions but allowed Bernie Sanders to read it the next day.

Marginalisation: The act of placing at the margins or edges or assigning lesser importance to those not considered as important to a society, culture, or text.

Marginalise: To assign lesser importance or an "absent presence," to objectify or place "at the margins" those not considered important to a society, culture, or text.

Marginalised Group: Any group of people who do not hold power and privilege in a particular social category and are therefore disadvantaged and/or excluded. Misogyny: A cultural attitude of hatred or dislike of women that manifests itself in a myriad of ways, usually some form of social disadvantage, oppression, and/or violence.

Marginalised: Excluded, ignored, or relegated to the outer edge of a group/society/community.

Market: Arena where the exchange of goods and services occurs and where business, industry, trade, and consumption happen.

Marxist Feminism: It is an interpretation based on the ideology of Karl Marx and Friedrich Engels. In Marxist feminism, the men in society exploit women for their services to benefit themselves socially. This demonstrates a social ladder/hierarchy in which men are at a place of privilege.

Masculinity: A gender perspective, or way of analyzing the impact of gender on people's opportunities, social roles, and interactions, allows us to see that there is pressure on men and boys to perform and conform to specific roles. Thus, the term masculinity refers to the social meaning of manhood, which is constructed and defined socially, historically, and politically, rather than being biologically driven. There are many socially constructed definitions for being a man and these can change over time and from place to place. The term relates to perceived notions and ideas about how men should or are expected to behave in a given setting. Masculinities are not just about men; women perform and produce the meaning and practices of the masculine as well.

Matriarchy: It is a social system organised around the principle of mother- rule in which mothers, or females, are at the top of the power structure. There is no solid evidence that a matriarchal society has ever existed. Even in societies with matrilineal descent, the power structure is either egalitarian or dominated formally by the father or some other male figure. For a social system to be considered a matriarchy, it would need the support of a culture that defined women's dominance as desirable and legitimate. So, even though women are the authority figures in single-parent families, they are not considered matriarchies.

Matrilineal / Matrilocal: Kinship, ancestry, and descent from the mother.

Matrix of Domination: The **matrix of domination** or **matrix of oppression** is a sociological paradigm that explains issues of oppression that deal with race, class, and gender, which, though recognised as different social classifications, are all interconnected. Other forms of classification, such as sexual orientation, religion, or age, apply to this theory as well. Patricia Hill Collins is credited with introducing the theory in her work entitled *Black Feminist Thought: Knowledge, Consciousness, and the Politics of Empowerment*. As the term implies, there are many different ways one might experience domination, facing many different challenges in which one obstacle, such as race, may overlap with other sociological features. Characteristics such as race, age, and sex, may affect an individual in extremely different ways, in such simple cases as varying geography, socioeconomic status, or simply throughout time. Other scholars such as Kimberle Crenshaw's *Mapping the Margins: Intersectionality, Identity Politics, and Violence against Women of Colour* are credited with expanding Collins' work. The matrix of domination is a way for people to acknowledge their privileges in society. How one can interact, what social groups are in, and the networks one establishes are all based on different interconnected classifications.

Measures: The term "measures" encompasses a wide variety of legislative, executive, administrative, and other regulatory instruments, policies, and practices, such as outreach or support programmes; allocation and/or reallocation of resources; preferential treatment; targeted recruitment, hiring, and promotion; numerical goals connected with time frames; and quota systems. The choice of a particular "measure" will depend on the context in which article 4, paragraph 1, is applied and on the specific goal it aims to achieve. Time use: Time use is an important measure of women's and men's activities in their productive, reproductive, and community roles. Time use can be measured through surveys which are carried out on the activities people perform during a given period (usually a day or a week). While time use surveys can and have been used for a wide variety of purposes, the most common reason for carrying out such surveys in developing countries is to provide better information about the work performed by men and women and to highlight the time spent on unpaid activities, which are often invisible in ordinary census data. This unpaid work, which includes work for others, is considered a major contributing factor to gender inequality and women's poverty (Mohammed, 2009). Despite the changes that have occurred in women's participation in the labour market, women continue to bear most of the responsibilities for the home: caring for children and other dependent household members, preparing meals, and doing other housework. In all regions, women spend at least twice as much time as men on unpaid domestic work. When unpaid work is taken into account, women's total work hours are longer than men's in all regions (UN, 2010). In many ways, the 24 hour day time use analysis signaled the end of the Women-In-Development (WID) approach and the desire to "put" women in development as if they were not already involved, and the beginning of a gender approach that more systematically analyzed the differences between women's and men's lives and reality.

Men who have Sex with Men (MSM): Men who engage in same-sex behaviour, but who may not necessarily self-identify as gay.

Men's Rights Activists (MRAs): People who believe that social, legal, and economic discrimination against males is present in society to the extent that fighting it deserves an organised effort mirroring feminism; generally have asserted since the 80s that women and feminism "went too far," and have harmed men in the process.

Menopause: It is defined as the point in time when menstrual cycles permanently cease due to the natural depletion of ovarian oocytes from aging. The diagnosis is typically made retrospectively after the woman has missed menses for 12 consecutive months. It marks the permanent end of fertility and the average age of menopause is 51 years.

Men's Rights Movement: An antifeminist movement based on the belief that men, not women, are the real victims of societal discrimination and oppression. Adherents usually assert that feminism has overshot its mark and harmed men.

Menstrual Hygiene Management (MHM): Programming that helps girls and women manage their monthly periods safely and with dignity, focusing on the fact that menstruation is a normal biological process and an important facet of reproductive health. To improve girls' and women's access to knowledge about menstruation. Systematizing the proper and hygienic-sanitary facilities and materials in schools and homes. Programmes may include addressing cultural taboos, increasing access to affordable and hygienic-sanitary materials, facilitating disposal options, access to safe and private toilets, and provision of clean water and soap for personal hygiene. Some practitioners are calling for MHM to be a separate SDG and considered a human right.

Menstruation: Menstruation or period, is normal vaginal bleeding that occurs as part of a woman's monthly cycle. Every month, your body prepares for pregnancy. If no pregnancy occurs, the uterus, or womb, sheds its lining. The menstrual blood is partly blood and partly tissue from inside the uterus. It passes out of the body through the vagina.

Mentalism/Sanism: A form of discrimination and oppression because of a mental trait or condition a person has or is judged to have.

Metanarrative / Master Narrative: The notion of one historical narrative as being central, involving the exclusion or marginalisation of oppressed groups.

Method: Techniques used for gathering information in the process of research. For example interviews, surveys, desk-review, focus groups, community mapping exercises, etc. (See also quantitative methods and qualitative method).

Methodology: Refers to the theoretical analysis of the methods appropriate to a field of study or the body of methods and principles particular to a branch of knowledge. The methodology is a theory and analysis of how research should be conducted.

Microaggression: Small, ambiguous behaviours toward minority group members that repeat or affirm stereotypes and subtly devalue.

Millennium Development Goals (MDGs): Set for the year 2015, the MDGs are an agreed set of goals designed to respond to the world's main development challenges and to the calls of civil society. The MDGs represent a global partnership that grew out of the commitments and targets established at the world summits of the 1990s. The eight MDGs seek to promote poverty reduction, education, maternal health, and gender equality and aim at combating child mortality, AIDS, and other diseases. As 2015 approaches, consultations are underway to establish the Post-2015 Development Framework or Agenda, which will succeed the MDGs.

Misandry: Hatred of men.

Misogynoir: Hatred of and discrimination against black women; an intersection of misogyny and racism.

Misogyny: The hatred of women. It is a psychological manifestation of sexism that is expressed socially in discrimination, denigration, and humiliation of women, violence against women and sexual objectification of women (or) **Misogyny** is the hatred of, contempt for, or prejudice against women or girls. Misogyny can be manifested in numerous ways, including social exclusion, sex discrimination, hostility, androcentrism, patriarchy, male privilege, belittling of women, violence against women, and sexual objectification. Misogyny can occasionally be found within sacred texts of religions and mythologies, and various influential Western philosophers and thinkers have been described as misogynistic.

Missing Women: The number of women missing from global population data, as their potential existence had been eliminated through foeticide, infanticide, sex-selective abortion, selective malnourishment, denial of healthcare, and various forms of gender violence. The term was coined by Indian economist Amartya Sen, who wrote an article in 1990 that referred to the estimated 100 million women who were missing as a result of various forms of gender inequality. (See also **Pre-Natal Sex Selection; Son Preference**)

Mobilise: To engage people as political activists through actions that build and use the strength of organised numbers and other resources to make demands known, influence those in power, and ultimately bring about a particular political objective. All too often, people find themselves "mobilised" or "turned out" in the service of an agenda that they had no voice in shaping. This can weaken linkages and leave people feeling hostile and alienated. In contrast, movement-building approaches to mobilisation engage people as political protagonists, educating and building new leadership in addition to activating their support. Also, see constituency building. (VeneKlasen and Miller, 2002).

Monogamy: is a form of relationship in which an individual has only one partner during their lifetime — alternately, only one partner at any one time (serial monogamy) — as compared to non-monogamy (e.g., polygamy or polyamory). The term is also applied to the social behaviour of some animals, referring to the state of having only one mate at any one time.

Monosexism: Used to refer to beliefs, structures, and actions that promote monosexuality (either exclusive heterosexuality or homosexuality) as the only legitimate or right sexual orientation, excluding bisexual or other non-monosexual orientations.

Movement: Characteristics include: (a) an organised set of constituents pursuing a common political agenda of change through collective action; (b) a membership or constituency base – the individuals or communities most vested in the change; (c) some degree of formal or informal organisation – networks, member collectives, etc. – are part of the organised core of a movement; (d) a clear political agenda – common analysis, goals, targets for change; (e) leadership from the constituency at multiple levels– i.e. not entirely dependent on external leadership; (f) collective or joint actions in pursuit of common goals – movements are not based on providing services alone (though they may do so, for their members) but on acting for change; (g) Some continuity over time (movements are not a "campaign," though they may use campaigns as a strategy, nor are they a one-time struggle over a specific issue); and (h) strategies that combine contestation (e.g. marches, protests) and critical cooperation (advocacy and lobbying) forms – i.e. the strategies manifest visible political struggle.

Movement-Building: A process of organising and mobilising communities and/or constituencies to respond to common problems and concerns; the organising process involves developing a shared analysis of why the problem exists, a common vision and agenda for change, and short and long-term strategies; movement-building also requires that those involved define shared principles and mechanisms for communication, roles, responsibilities, and all of the internal governance of the movement itself.

MTF (Male-to-Female): Someone assigned male at birth who identifies as female. Passing: An arguably problematic term that refers to a trans*, homosexual, etc. person being read by the world as part of the dominant group. In other words, a homosexual man being read by the world as heterosexual, or a trans* person being read as cisgender, specifically the gender they identify with. The idea of "passing" is fairly innocuous when about some things, but when about transgender people the definition betrays the transphobic and transmisogynistic belief that the gender identity of a trans person is not their real gender, and that they are somehow deceiving people in being perceived the way they identify. Click here to hear transgender activist and author Janet Mock explain the complexities around "passing."

Multiple Discrimination: Concept used to describe the complexity of discrimination implicating more than one ground, also known as "additive," "accumulative," "compound," "intersectional," "complex bias" or "multi-dimensional inequalities." Though the terminology may seem confusing, it tends to describe two situations: (1) situation where an individual is faced with more than one form of grounds-based discrimination (i.e. sex plus disability discrimination, or gender plus sexual orientation). In such circumstances, all women and all persons with disabilities (both male and female) are potentially subject to discrimination. (2) Situation where discrimination affects only those who are members of more than one group (i.e. only women with disabilities and not men with disabilities), also known as intersectional discrimination.

Naturalisation: The social construction of gender and other roles as "natural" or innate to a given group. In social practice, the construction of these roles is obscured once the naturalisation process becomes a social "given".

Nature/Culture: Binary hierarchy that values the "civilised," cultured and refined over the "natural," barbaric, or uncivilised; cultural prejudice.

Neo-liberalism: A set of economic and political theories that posit the centrality of a "free-market" system under which market forces, rather than governments, determine key aspects of the economy, with governments acting to support globalised markets, market-oriented processes, and the interests of capital Neo-liberal economic reforms over the past three decades have expanded and deepened the influence of capitalism, especially consumerism and the use of credit, on social and political institutions and culture. This agenda includes free trade, privatisation, reduced government spending on social programmes, huge increases in spending on subsidies to business and security, deregulation of businesses, no curbs on foreign investors, low taxes on the wealthy and corporations, minimal labour and environmental protections, no subsidies or supports for poor people and sectors, etc. Neo-liberalism has accelerated the accumulation of capital and the taking of huge profits by the "big capitalists." As a result, the crisis of overproduction and over-accumulation by a few has persisted at a rapid and worse rate. These big capitalists have resorted to tricks of finance capitalism and have spawned a financial oligarchy in an attempt to override the recurrent crisis of overproduction and the tendency of the profit rate to fall. These big capitalists have repeatedly expanded the money supply and credit, generated derivatives in astronomical amounts, and made one financial bubble after another to raise their profits and overvalue their assets.

Neurodiversity: The idea that neurological differences like autism and ADHD are the result of normal, natural variation in the human genome.

NGO (Non-Governmental Organisation) : A phrase to critique the dominance of NGOs within social justice organising efforts. It also refers to a trend toward the professionalisation and institutionalisation of civil society and a shift in accountability from communities and constituencies to financial donors. Although NGOs take on many forms and are not inherently problematic, the critique holds that NGO-isation often weakens social justice efforts by de-politicizing them, replacing grassroots organisation that challenges power with technocratic institutions that soak up donor funds even as they become increasingly removed from the needs, experiences, and priorities of grassroots organising Deliberate action intended to bring people together to develop leadership strategies and the collective capacity needed to confront a common issue or push an alternative justice agenda. For justice organising, the people involved are often those who are disadvantaged by the system or excluded from decision-making venues and their allies. Ideally, people gradually take on greater leadership in addressing problems and build organisations and movements bound by mutual respect, trust, and common purpose. Also, see constituency building.

NGO-isation: A phrase to critique the dominance of NGOs within social justice organising efforts. It also refers to a trend toward the professionalisation and institutionalisation of civil society and a shift in accountability from communities and constituencies to financial donors. Although NGOs take on many forms and are not inherently problematic, the critique holds that NGO-isation often weakens social justice efforts by de-politicising them, replacing grassroots organisation that challenges power with technocratic institutions that soak up donor funds even as they become increasingly removed from the needs, experiences, and priorities of grassroots "the debate about NGOisation was, to put it mildly, particularly heated and often acerbic. In fact, in the eyes of their staunchest critics, NGOs were traitors to feminist ethical principles. [NGOs] depoliticised feminist agendas and collaborated with neoliberal ones. But those kinds of blanket assessments of feminist NGOs as handmaidens of a global neoliberal patriarchy failed to capture the ambiguities and variations in and among NGOs in particular countries, and regions, and even the same neighborhoods. The good NGOs/bad NGOs binary simply doesn't do justice to the dual or hybrid identity of feminist NGOs: technical organisations that are, at the same time, some of them, intricate parts of what we call "the movement."

Nice Guy (TM): Men who view themselves as prototypical "nice guys," but whose "nice deeds" are in reality only motivated by attempts to passively please women into a relationship and/or sex. *Brita's Note: If I ever refer to someone as a nice guy, without capital letters, I genuinely mean he's a good man. The capital letters refer to the above Nice Guy.*

Nineteenth Amendment: The 19th amendment to the United States Constitution, granting women's suffrage in 1920.

No Means No: An anti-rape slogan emphasising consent.

Non-Binary: An umbrella term for people who don't identify as female/male or woman/man.

Non-Op: Refers to transsexuals who seek sex reassignment through hormones and who cross life, but stop just short of surgery. Some have concerns about major surgery, which is not always successful, others are unable to pay for the expensive procedures surgery would entail, and still, others feel that they are complete without the surgery.

Non-Productive Activities: Refer to personal and recreational activities such as learning, leisure, and personal hygiene. Activities falling in this category are not part of the economy.

Not All Men: A defensive response based on a misinterpretation of complaints about sexism as generalisations of all men. The phrase has become a popular feminist hashtag.

Objectification: In literature, the reduction of character to behaviour and public speech, refusing the character her/his psychology and inner subjectivity. In society, objectification (and specifically sexual objectification) occurs when a person is defined by her/his sexual attributes and the rest of her/his personality and existence are ignored; objectification involves the reduction of a person to an object for one's gaze or pleasure.

Occupational Segregation: Occupational segregation is the distribution of workers across and within occupations, based upon demographic characteristics, most often gender. Occupational segregation levels differ on a basis of perfect segregation and integration. Perfect segregation occurs where any given occupation employs only one group.

Perfect integration, on the other hand, occurs where each group holds the same proportion of positions in an occupation as it holds in the labour force. Many scholars, such as Biblarz et al., argue that occupational segregation is most likely caused by gender-based discrimination that often occurs in patterns, either horizontally (across occupations) or vertically (within the hierarchy of occupations). Both of these contribute to the gender pay gap.

On T: When an FTM takes the hormone testosterone.

Oppression: A systemic social phenomenon based on the perceived and real differences among social groups that involves ideological domination, institutional control, and the promulgation of the oppressor's ideology, logic system, and culture to the oppressed group. The result is the exploitation of one social group by another for the benefit of the oppressor group. (Goodman and Schapiro, 1997) See *power*.

Other: Term used by Simone de Beauvoir to describe the marginalisation of a group or individual as "not-Self"; the objectification of a subject/self, which makes it possible for those in the "center" to define their subject/selves against those which are different ("the margin constitutes the center").

Othering: The process by which social exclusion occurs, where a dominant group claims normative status, and everyone outside of that group is defined about the dominant group. "Othering" is also described as what happens when a person, group, or category is treated as an object by another.

Out or **Out of the Closet:** Refers to varying degrees of being open about one's sexual orientation.

Outreach (for organising): A wide variety of strategies – participatory planning and organising, media, education, mobilisation, and direct recruitment – that aim to gain the support and direct involvement of constituencies and to build their capacity as active citizens.

Paglian: Relating to American feminist social critic Camille Paglia (b. 1947).

Paid Labour: Refers to time spent on productive activities for which the individual receives payment in exchange for labour.

Pansexual: A person who is fluid in sexual orientation and/or gender or sex identity.

Paradigm: A pattern of thought that gives people a way of understanding and valuing their world; a worldview providing a basis for customs, explanations, perceptions, institutions, and behaviour. The "dominant paradigm" refers to the attitudes, values, ideologies, and systems of thought in a particular society at a given moment in time. Currently, the dominant paradigm is patriarchy in a phase of globalised capitalism.

Parity in Education: Refers to equivalent percentages of males and females in an education system (relative to the population per age group). Parity is essential but not sufficient for achieving gender equality.

Participant Observer: One of the most commonly-used methods for conducting participatory research, the participant-observer method was established in the field of anthropology. The method is based on observing actions (rather than surveys or interviews) to gain insight into a community's values, dynamics, internal relationships, structures and conflicts. The participant-observer attempts immersion, to the extent permitted, in local life to understand and document how things work. However, the participant-observer method is the least "objective" of all methods, relying heavily on the intellectual honesty of the researcher, whose experiences cannot be replicated. It is also the most time-consuming.

Participation: In the general sense, means having a share, or taking part. The Women's Equality & Empowerment Framework uses this word to denote having a share and taking part in decision-making. We are therefore here defining the term "participation" in this active sense of having a say in how things are done, and in how resources are allocated. Merely to have a share in resources is not in itself participation in the sense that it is used to denote an empowerment level in the Framework. The Framework sees gender equality in decision-making as one of the essential aspects of women's empowerment and uses the word "participation" to denote this aspect of empowerment.

Participatory Action Research (PAR): PAR is the most activist-based method of the several commonly-used participatory research methods. With roots in the work of Paulo Freire and other South American social scientists, PAR focuses on the empowerment of local communities and works directly with local political/development organisations to bring about sustainable change. The methods used emphasise participation, capacity-building, ownership of knowledge, and empowerment.

Participatory Development: Implies a partnership which is built on dialogue among the various actors (stakeholders), during which the 'agenda' is set jointly and a variety of local views and indigenous knowledge are deliberately sought and respected. Participatory development implies negotiation rather than the dominance of an externally set project agenda.

Participatory Poverty Assessments (PPA): A commonly-used participatory research method referring to a variety of qualitative methods used to assess the multi-dimensional nature of poverty, highlighting how different aspects of poverty are connected. Methods include focus groups, in-depth discussions, and various techniques such as mapping transects and Venn diagrams. It is particularly useful for gauging the gendered aspects of poverty, such as the specific disadvantages faced by poor women, connections between reproduction and production, women's lack of access to resources, and gender differences in priorities. It has its origins in Participatory Rural Appraisal (PRA) approaches.

Participatory Rural Appraisal (PRA): A commonly-used method for conducting participatory research on poverty. Building on Rapid Rural Appraisal (RRA), PRA's emerged in the 1980s, and use local graphic representations created by the community that legitimizes local knowledge and promotes empowerment. Five concepts are central to PRA: empowerment, respect, localisation, enjoyment, and inclusiveness.

Pass: Means to be in your preferred gender image and to be able to do so convincingly in the eyes of those around you, for example, an FTM or crossdresser or drag king who looks like a man and not like a woman.

Passing: An arguably problematic term that refers to a trans*, homosexual, etc. person being read by the world as part of the dominant group. In other words, a homosexual man being read by the world as heterosexual, or a trans* person being read as cisgender, specifically the gender they identify with. The idea of "passing" is fairly innocuous when about some things, but when about transgender people the definition betrays the transphobic and transmisogynistic belief that the gender identity of a trans person is not their real gender, and that they are somehow deceiving people into being perceived the way they identify.

Patriarchal Resistance: It is the present context, means the various ways patriarchal government or authority may try to stop women's collective action for an equal share in decision making, and equal control over the distribution of resources.

Patriarchy/Patriarchal: Social organisation favouring males on every level; rule by men.

Patriarchy: Patriarchy is a social system in which males hold primary power and predominate in roles of political leadership, moral authority, social privilege, and control of the property. Patriarchy is associated with a set of ideas, a patriarchal ideology that acts to explain and justify this dominance and attributes it to inherent natural differences between men and women. Sociologists tend to see patriarchy as a social product and not as an outcome of innate differences between the sexes and they focus attention on the way that gender roles in a society affect power differentials between men and women. Some patriarchal societies are also patrilineal, meaning that property and title are inherited by the male lineage. Historically, patriarchy has manifested itself in the social, legal, political, religious, and economic organisation of a range of different cultures. Even if not explicitly defined to be by their constitutions and laws, most contemporary societies are, in practice, patriarchal.

Patrilineal/Patrilocal: Kinship, ancestry, and descent from the father.

Pay Equity: Compensation based on education, skills, effort, training, and responsibility rather than classifications of sex, age, race, ethnic background, or other discriminatory classifications. Pay inequalities are differences in remuneration for the same work when performed by men and women. (See also discrimination.).

Penis Envy: Term developed by Freud as a primary characteristic in the psychology of girls; Freud's perceptions of women distorted gendered perceptions in the field of psychology for generations.

Performative: Term used by Judith Butler to describe gendered behaviour as a performance.

Performativity: A term originated by Butler (1993) concerning the assimilation to the dominant culture to remake selected norms. Also considered is the capacity of speech and communication to act, construct, and perform an identity.

Performativity: It is a language that affects change in the world and functions as a form of social action. The concept has multiple applications in diverse fields, such as linguistics, philosophy, anthropology, law, gender studies, performance studies, and economics. Performativity was first defined by philosopher of language John L. Austin as the capacity of speech and communication to act or to consummate an action. Common examples of performative language are making promises, betting, performing a wedding ceremony, an umpire calling a strike, or a judge pronouncing a verdict. Austin differentiated this from constative language, which he defined as descriptive language that can be "evaluated as true or false". Influenced by Austin, philosopher and gender theorist Judith Butler argued that gender is socially constructed through commonplace speech acts and nonverbal communication that are performative, in that they serve to define and maintain identities. This view of performativity reverses the idea that a person's identity is the source of their secondary actions (speech, gestures). Instead, it views actions, behaviours, and gestures as both the result of an individual's identity as well as a source that contributes to the formation of one's identity which is continuously being redefined through speech acts and symbolic communication. This view was also influenced by philosophers such as Michel Foucault and Louis Althusser.

Petro-Sexual Politics: Petro-Sexual Politics is a lens used to better understand the relationships between petroleum and gender violence and the role colonial powers possess. The underlying theme of petro-sexual politics is that gender violence is part of a larger political economy of violence. Petro-sexual politics can yield new methods of theorising global politics, particularly as explained here for the Nigerian case of the "natural resource curse".

Phallocentric: The term refers to the cultural and social organisation of the world fostered by the patriarchy.

Phallocentrism: Phallocentrism is the ideology that the phallus, or male sexual organ, is the central element in the organisation of the social world. Phallocentrism has been analyzed in literary criticism, psychoanalysis and psychology, linguistics, medicine and healthcare, and philosophy.

Phallogocentrism: "A combination of phallocentrism and logocentrism, resulting in a historical and non-contextualized view of male dominance, thus limiting and restricting knowledge while also forming the roots of women's oppression" (from the Women's Studies Sparkchart). In critical theory and deconstruction, **phallogocentrism** is a neologism coined by Jacques Derrida to refer to the privileging of the masculine (phallus) in the construction of meaning. The word is a portmanteau of the older terms *phallocentrism* (focusing on the masculine point of view) and *logocentrism* (focusing on language in assigning meaning to the world). Derrida and others identified phonocentrism, or the prioritising of speech over writing, as an integral part of phallogocentrism. Derrida explored this idea in his essay "Plato's Pharmacy".

Physical Autonomy: The freedom to make decisions regarding sexuality, reproduction, and the right to live a life free from violence.

Physical Violence: Physical violence is an act attempting to or resulting in pain and/or physical injury. It includes beating, burning, kicking, punching, biting, maiming, the use of objects or weapons, or tearing out hair. At its most extreme, physical violence may lead to femicide or the gender-based killing of a woman. Some classifications also include trafficking and slavery in the category of physical violence because initial coercion is often experienced, and the young women and men involved end up becoming victims of further violence as a result of their enslavement. Physical, sexual, and psychological violence perpetrated or condoned by the State, wherever it occurs.

Pink-Collar Worker: In the United States and (at least some) other English-speaking countries, a pink-collar worker refers to someone working in the care-oriented career field or jobs historically considered to be "women's work." This may include jobs in nursing, teaching, secretarial work, waitressing, or childcare. While these jobs may be filled by men, they are typically female-dominated and may pay significantly less than white-collar or blue-collar jobs.

Planned Parenthood: The desire and ability to determine the number and spacing of births. (See also **Family Planning**.).

Political: This refers to relationships of power that exist within and among all organisations, institutions, and people. "Politics" tends to refer to governments and the organisations competing for and using state power, and are often characterised by unequal power relationships conferred by wealth, social status, gender, education, etc. The feminist phrase "the personal is political," reflects the belief that families and relationships have their politics as well because power dynamics are operating everywhere. While many people have a negative view of all things political, in JASS we use the phrase "political with a small p" to motivate women to think and act politically. In this way, the word political refers to the process of resisting and challenging different kinds of control and oppression while negotiating differences – different interests, different opinions, different needs, and priorities – between and among individuals and groups of individuals to be able to work together for change.

Politics of Location: A research perspective that grew out of feminist methodology, primarily through the critiques of women of colour in both the global north and global south who viewed the majority of early gender research as stemming from a generic white, Northern, middle-class perspective. The politics of location suggests that the personal backgrounds and experiences of researchers (whether chosen or imposed by society) have political and theoretical implications that must be articulated throughout the research process.

Politics: The process of negotiating difference – different interests, different opinions, different needs, and priorities – between and among individuals and groups of individuals. At its core, politics is about power – it's about whose interests and voices count and prevail in decision-making. Politics is often associated exclusively with formal decision-making bodies, such as legislatures and national assemblies, but politics occurs across all social relationships, from the home to the corridors of government institutions. (VeneKlasen and Miller, 2002).

Polyamory: The practice of having multiple open, honest love relationships.

Polyandry: is a form of polygamy in which a woman takes two or more husbands at the same time. Polyandry is contrasted with polygyny, involving one male and two or more females. If a marriage involves a plural number of "husbands and wives" participants of each gender, then it can be called polygamy, group, or conjoint marriage. In its broadest use, polyandry refers to sexual relations with multiple males within or without marriage.

Polygamy: A man marrying more than one wife or temporary wife leading to the insecurity of women and facilitating the spread of HIV/AIDS. It is illegal in most countries but persists.

Positive Parenting: Educating parents on children's rights and development to improve parenting practices, to end violence, abuse, and exploitation of children. Helping parents improve their skills to manage their children's behaviour. Positive parenting is the foundation for curbing violence at home and in the community. It encourages the engagement of fathers and men and considers the various stages of a child's life cycle.

Postfeminism: Any movement reacting to any of the waves of feminism, working to build on it, address perceived shortcomings, or oppose its continuation.

Post-2015 Development Agenda: The Post-2015 Development Agenda refers to an UN-led process that aims to help define the future global development framework that will succeed the Millennium Development Goals (MDGs), which expire in 2015. Secretary-General Ban Ki-moon has established a UN System Task Team to support system-wide preparations for the Post-2015 UN Development Agenda. It comprises 60 agencies, as well as the World Bank and the International Monetary Fund. In June 2012, it published the report "Realising the Future We Want for All" which serves as an input to the work of the High-Level Panel.

Consultations are underway regionally, nationally, and thematically with a broad range of actors. Regarding gender equality, debates center principally on whether to have a separate goal on gender equality, to ensure that gender is mainstreamed throughout all the goals or both.

Postcolonialism: The postcolonial school of thought is based on the understanding that colonialism did not end when the areas that were colonized by the Europeans in the 1700s-1900s became autonomous. The effects of colonialism keep influencing how the world and unequal power relations are constructed today (see also **Power**). The questions asked by the postcolonial theory are which role the colonial past plays in today's world and how it is recreated both locally and globally in contemporary societies. The notions of a modern, civilized and rational 'West' are closely interlinked with the construction of an irrational, pre-modern and mystical 'East' (see also dichotomy). This view legitimises super- and subordination, where the Western culture and model of society are placed at the very front of the colonial hierarchical development model. The notion of the global North and South relates to this East/West distinction, where the North is portrayed as modern, rich, civilised, and developed compared with the undeveloped, outdated and uncivilised South. Sweden participated not only in the trans-Atlantic slave trade and colonisation, since the colonisation of Lapland, home to the Sami, follows the same pattern. In the latter case, it is the Swedish state that is portrayed as civilised and modern while the Sami people are conveyed as the opposite (see also **Othering**). This colonisation can be understood as continuing today, and postcolonial theories can offer an understanding of how and why this is possible. Feminist theories and postcolonial theory have influenced each other in many ways. Although feminist theory and postcolonial theory are two different fields, they join forces in what can be described as a search for alternative knowledge where critical perspectives on knowledge production, universalism, power, and dominant worldviews meet. Postcolonial feminism has emerged, describing how sexism, racism, and homophobia can be connected to questioning of global forms of domination, where the colonial past plays a central role. Knowledge production and the possibility to create space for new subjects of knowledge are the central theme´s in postcolonial feminism. Which stories and people have or are given space in the development and production of knowledge? (see also **Situated Knowledge**) What can be called white feminism have in many ways subscribed, and contributed, to a colonial ideology (see also **whiteness**). 'Other women', 'third-world women', 'brown women' and these people's knowledge, experiences, and needs have been both silenced and ignored. Postcolonial feminism asks questions about power and knowledge that challenge the Western notion of superiority, related to ideas about, for example, gender, sexuality, racialisation, and exploitation.

Postmodern Feminism: Feminism intertwined with postmodern theory and ideals, usually seeing gender and ideas of the feminine as constructs of language. A conscious departure from what is perceived as the "modernist" polarity of liberal vs. radical feminism.

Postmodernism: A set of theories that argues that there is no absolute truth and that one's view of reality is relative and subjective, dependent on interests and perspective. It emphasises the role of language, power relations, and motivations in the formation of ideas and beliefs. In particular, it challenges the use of sharp categories of analysis such as male versus female, straight versus gay, white versus black, and imperial versus colonial. This is in contrast to the masculinised dichotomic (binary or black and white – you're either with us or against us) way of thinking and analyzing. Writers and philosophers associated with the development of post-modern thought include Martin Heidegger and Michel Foucault as well as feminists Judith Butler, Hélène Cixous, and Luce Irigaray.

Post-Op: A transsexual who has had their sex-change operation and now has the physical anatomy which mimics that of the sex they have transitioned to.

Power: Power involves the ability, skill, or capacity to make decisions and take action; physical force or strength. The exercise of power is an important aspect of relationships. The more power a person has, the more choices are available to that person. People who have less power have fewer choices and are therefore more vulnerable to abuse. When women's movements, feminist groups, and development organisations help people acquire "power" individually and collectively, they do not necessarily understand the power in its traditional sense of domination or "power over." Instead, they have agreed that there are several kinds of power involved in the empowerment process. These four dimensions are called: power over, power to, power with, and power from within.

Power With: Social or political power which highlights the notion of common purpose or understanding, as well as the ability to get together to negotiate and defend a common goal (individual and collective rights, political ideas such as lobbying, etc.). Collectively, people feel they have power when they can get together and unite in search of a common objective, or when they share the same vision.

The Power Within: This notion of power refers to self-awareness, self-esteem, identity, and assertiveness (knowing how to be). It refers to how individuals, through self-analysis and internal power, can influence their lives and make changes.

Practical Gender Needs (PGN): These are gender needs that women and men can easily identify, as they relate to living conditions. PGNs do not challenge, although they arise out of, gender divisions of labour and women's subordinate position in society. PGNs are a response to an immediate and perceived necessity, identified within a specific context. They are practical and often concern inadequacies in living conditions such as water provision, healthcare, and employment. Needs are identified by women within their socially constructed roles in society. Although they often arise from gendered divisions of labour and women's subordinate position in society, practical gender needs do not challenge these norms. Practical gender needs are a response to an immediate perceived necessity identified within a specific context, such as access to clean water or adequate housing. They are practical and often concern inadequacies in living conditions. (See also **Strategic Gender Interests**).

Practical Gender Needs and Strategic Gender Interests: A two-part typology developed by Caroline Moser (1993) with Practical Gender Needs (PGNs) and Strategic Gender Interests (SGIs). PGNs are those needs that have been identified by women within their socially defined roles as a response to an immediate perceived necessity (e.g., inadequacies in living conditions such as water provision, healthcare, and employment). They do not challenge gender divisions of labour and women's subordinate position in society. In contrast, Strategic Gender Interests (SGIs) vary by context and are identified by women as a result of their subordinate social status. They tend to challenge gender divisions of labor-power and control, as well as traditionally defined norms and roles (e.g., legal rights, domestic violence, equal wages, and women's control over their bodies).

Practical Needs: Maxine Molyneux defines two types of "women's interest": practical interests and strategic interests. The term needs, rather than interests, is often used. Practical needs are those needs which do not challenge the unequal structure of gender relations, divisions of labour, or traditional balances of power but relate to the spheres in which women have primary responsibilities. These differ from women's special needs but may sometimes arise from them. Practical needs may differ according to the women's or group of women's social class, age, and situation. They can vary from the need for income to send children to school, weeding tools for agricultural work to pumps for water.

Prejudice: Is made up of unfavourable or discriminatory attitudes (not actions) towards persons of different categories. Racial, sexual, and other types of discrimination can exist at the level of personal relations and individual behaviour as well as be institutionalised as legal or administrative policy.

Pre-Natal Sex Selection: Abortion is performed because the sex of the fetus is judged to be undesirable to one or both parents. This usually happens in societies where there is a strong son preference and usually refers to the abortion of female fetuses. It is also called sex-selective abortion. (See also **Missing Women; Son Preference**)

Pre-Op: A transsexual who has not yet had their sex-change operation(s) but who plans on having it/them.

Present: Refers to gender expression and the process of reflecting one's gender to others; someone who is bi-gendered may present as female one day and male the next.

Private and Public Spheres: The traditional areas into which society is divided, into those regarded as being for women and those for men. Women's activities have been associated with the private and domestic spheres of life, usually regarded as non-economic; and men to the public ones – usually regarded as economic and political.

Privatisation: When the state or other collective entity sells off goods or services to the private sector. The shorthand term for a complex web of policies, processes, and a core component of neoliberal ideology in which responsibility for distributing public resources and essential services is shifted from the government to the private sector (for-profit and non-profit entities). Privatisation is based on the market model and is often proposed as a response to dysfunctional or under-performing government programs. It assumes that market forces will promote consumer choice and healthy competition, thereby creating an incentive to improve services. Privatisation emphasises individualistic and competitive values and focuses on economic returns. This is in contrast to concepts such as mutual responsibility or community solidarity and downplays the notion of public services as a right or public good. (Reilly and Marphatia, 2006).

Privilege: An unearned resource or state of being that is only readily available to some people because of their social status, such as being male, white, certain nationalities, heterosexual, or wealthy. Privilege confers benefits concerning access to resources, social rewards, and the power to shape the norms and values of society. People with privilege become the norm against which others are defined, hence, those with privilege are considered "individuals," while those without are defined by their socially constructed categories such as race, nationality, or gender. (Wijeyesinghe, Griffin and Love, 1997)

Problematise: looking at a concept or an idea that has typically been taken for granted as just the way things are, without question. Problematising it is making it into a problem - not necessarily saying it's a bad idea/term/concept, but questioning it by doing 3 things: (1) figuring out the history of the idea, (2) figuring out WHY it is the way it is, and looking at what and (3) consequences that have for anyone it affects. So a critical scholar will always work to problematise issues - even ones they agree with - to make sure they're seeing all sides of something.

Pro-Choice: The stance advocating for a woman's right to terminate her pregnancy if she chooses.

Production: The creation or manufacture for the sale of goods and services. Production results in rewards, benefits, privileges, or power deriving from an individual's production while using her/his own or hired resources. A distinction is usually made between productive or economic activities, which are usually remunerated and socially recognised, and reproductive or human maintenance activities, which are carried out to reproduce and care for the household, its members, and the community at large, including fuel and water collection, crop cultivation and livestock production, food preparation, childcare, education, healthcare, and home maintenance. Reproductive activities, including many done by women, are generally viewed as non-economic and thus often carry no monetary compensation, leading them to be excluded from the national income accounts. (See also domestic responsibilities; household maintenance; labour; national accounts; reproductive labour.).

Productive Roles: Refer to the activities carried out by men and women to produce goods and services either for sale, exchange, or to meet the subsistence needs of the family. For example, in agriculture, productive activities include plating, animal husbandry, and gardening that refers to farmers themselves, or for other people at employees.

Productive Work: This is work that produces goods and services for exchange in the marketplace (for income). Some analysts, especially those working on questions of equality between men and women, include the production of items for consumption by the household under this definition, even though they never reach the marketplace, regarding this as consumption of a form of non-monetary income. Both men and women contribute to family income with various forms of productive work, although men predominate in productive work, especially at the higher echelons of remuneration. Historically, in most societies, changes in economic structure, and hence in the structure of productive activities, have led to changes in the sexual division of labour and gender relations.

Profeminism: Support of feminism by people who are not deemed to be or do not identify as part of feminism; this term is sometimes used for men.

Programme: In these reading is used differently from "project", to mean a collection of projects with a larger developmental purpose than an individual project.

Project: This is here used to mean an organisation of people and resources over time, used to bring about planned and pre-determined change by the end of the project period, for the benefit of a well-defined target group. A project provides a planned developmental intervention to meet a need or to overcome a problem. A project is also concerned with women's development if it recognises gender issues as part of the problem, and addresses these issues as part of the overall project purpose.

Prostitute: A man, woman, or transgender who engages in sex acts or sexual intercourse for money or goods. The term 'sex worker' is also used frequently and many activists use the term 'people in prostitution and sex work'. The debate has continued around the use of the words 'commercial sex worker' and 'prostitute'. Some women's rights advocates say prostitution is work that a person can enter into voluntarily and enjoy benefits and legal protection for, while others say that the room for choice in it is inherently limited and necessarily involves exploitation or is immoral and/or illegal.

Prostitution: Is the business or practice of engaging in sexual activity in exchange for payment. Prostitution is sometimes described as sexual services, commercial sex, or, colloquially, hooking. It is sometimes referred to euphemistically as "the world's oldest profession" in the English-speaking world. A person who works in this field is called a prostitute and is a type of sex worker.

Protofeminism: Fundamentally feminist ideas appearing in a period before the onset of the feminist movement.

Psychoanalysis: Method of understanding individual psychology via free association, testimonies, dreams, fantasies, etc., with the idea of removing a person's defenses to get at hidden problems, thus freeing the "analysand" of impediments to her/his psychological health.

Psychological Violence: Psychological violence can include, for example, threatening behaviours that do not necessarily involve physical violence or even verbal abuse. It can include actions that refer to former acts of violence, or purposeful ignorance and neglect of the other. Psychological violence may also be perpetrated through isolation or confinement, withholding information, disinformation, etc.

Public/Private Spheres: Distinction is important to feminism because the private, or domestic, sphere has historically been labeled as feminine while the public sector has been labeled as male or masculine. Also refers to the notion that the only things that matter happen in public, while what happens in private is both unimportant and meant to be hidden from view (e.g., Women's Hygiene, Domestic Violence, Family Life).

Purity Culture: The view of any discussion of things of a sexual nature outside of the context of heterosexual marriage as taboo; adherence to a strict hetero normative lifestyle that forbids most physical contact with significant others, as well as engaging in self-pleasure, or holding lustful thoughts about another person that is not a spouse; includes an insistence on female modesty and responsibility to shield boys and men from sexual temptation.

Purple Washing: Presenting an idea or action as feminist while concealing its antifeminist aspects. It is used by critics of pornography and sex work as a means of calling out the more oppressive elements of sex positivity.

Qualitative Methods: Qualitative research involves an in-depth understanding of human behaviour and the reasons that govern human behaviour. Unlike quantitative research, qualitative research relies on the reasons behind various aspects of behaviour. Simply put, it investigates the why and how of decision-making, as compared to what, where, and when of quantitative research. Hence, the need is for smaller but focused samples rather than large and random samples.

Quantitative Methods: Quantitative research is the systematic scientific investigation of quantitative properties and phenomena and their relationships. Quantitative research is widely used in both the natural and social sciences, including physics, biology, psychology, sociology, geology, education, and journalism. The objective of quantitative research is to develop and employ mathematical models, theories, and hypotheses about natural phenomena. The process of measurement is central to quantitative research because it provides the fundamental connection between empirical observation and the mathematical expression of quantitative relationships.

Queer: Originally a synonym for "odd," this term became a derogatory epithet for gay men and lesbians in the twentieth century, especially in the United States, where it emphasised the alleged "unnaturalness" of homosexuality. Although many people still use "queer" as an anti-gay slur, there emerged a movement in the 1980s that sought to reclaim the term and rob it of its negative meaning. In this usage, "queer" is an inclusive umbrella term that designates all those who are sexually dissident, even if they are not strictly homosexual, and all "transgressive" forms of sexuality. Many lesbians and gay men, transsexuals, bisexuals, and even heterosexuals whose sexuality does not fit into the cultural standard of monogamous heterosexual marriage have adopted the "queer" label. Some gay men and lesbians, however, remembering the hurt caused by its pejorative meaning, dislike the term, even in its "reclaimed" usage, and feel that it has the effect of diluting the specificity of the narrower categories.

Quotas: Quota systems have been viewed as one of the most effective special measures or affirmative action's for increasing women's political participation. There are now 77 countries with constitutional, electoral, or political party quotas for women. In countries where women's issues had always been relegated to the lowest priority, increases in the number of women in decision-making positions help move women's agendas up to a higher priority level.

Race: Refers to the physical characteristics of people, but has been used as a social construct that goes beyond a biological or genetic characteristic in many countries. Racial categories typically exist in a dominant group and are based on relatively small external physical differences such as skin colour. For example, in the United States, Western Europe, and South Africa, "black," "coloured," "non-white," and "Asian," are understood in contrast to "white" people of Anglo/European/North American descent. Similarly, 'whiteness' or 'western-ness is constructed in contrast to stereotypes of black or "third world" women. Racial categories are typically created by the socially dominant group to reinforce their power or supremacy and to justify differential treatment for other groups of people. At the same time, racial categories have been used in more neutral or positive ways to establish group identity and solidarity.

Racialisation: Racialisation occurs when different people, with different experiences, opinions, and backgrounds are lumped into groups according to preconceptions based on, for example, external features (such as skin colour), culture, and religion. When racialisation is analysed, race and ethnicity are understood as social constructions where so-called racialisation processes generate different racial identities and groups. These processes occur in both state institutions and everyday life. Racialisation is not a new term in the academic world. However, it is rapidly gaining popularity also outside academia, where the term is often used as a description of a person as 'racialised'. There is a risk that this way of using and understanding the term may remove the attention from precisely the racialisation processes that generate uniform groups of people with different backgrounds. Being a racialised person then becomes synonymous with being 'an immigrant', 'non-white, or some other label that has been used at some point to signal differentness among minority groups in Sweden (see also othering). This can lead to a situation where 'white', majority of Swedes are not understood as racialised, which in turn hides the fact that racialisation processes result in systems and structures not only for oppression and discrimination but also for privileges and power positions. In other words, a situation in which people racialise each other is not characterised by symmetrical or equal relationships. The process and its consequences follow a racial hierarchy and whiteness norm (see also whiteness, norm/norm criticism). One way to understand how also whiteness is constructed through racialisation processes is to talk about marked and unmarked positions. All bodies are racialised, but some (whites) are unmarked while others (non-whites) are marked through racialisation.

Racism: Prejudice or discrimination is rooted in the idea that race or skin colour is a determinant of human traits or capacities, and that differences in skin colour confer or reflect inherent inferiority and superiority. Racism and racial discrimination can be overt, for example, in the form of discriminatory laws and policies. More often, racism is deeply embedded in social and political institutions and belief systems in ways that are unexamined or disguised.

Radfem: Radical feminism or a radical feminist.

Radical Feminism: Feminism is based on the idea that inherently patriarchal society and its institutions are the foundation of women's oppression and must be radically overhauled to achieve equality. To some extent, the term has been hijacked by nominally feminist groups and individuals with anti-sex work and anti-trans views, who use "radical feminist" as a political euphemism in a similar manner to "gender-critical".

Rainbow Flag: The Rainbow Freedom Flag was designed in 1978 by Gilbert Baker to designate the great diversity of the LGBTIQ community. It has been recognised by the International Flag Makers Association as the official flag of the LGBTIQ civil rights movement.

Rape (Date): Sexual intercourse that takes place against a person's will through the means of violence, coercion, or intimidation, either physical or psychological, by an acquaintance, friend, or a dating or intimate partner. Thus, date rape is a type of sexual assault, where the victim and the perpetrator are or have been, in some form of personal social relationship. Date rape victims are almost entirely women.

Rape (Marital): Marital rape is any unwanted sexual abuse - even after reaching an apparent place of safety. Internally displaced women often suffer similar experiences.

Rape Culture: This is a sociological concept for a setting in which rape is pervasive and normalised due to societal attitudes about gender and sexuality. Behaviours commonly associated with rape culture include victim-blaming, slut-shaming, sexual objectification, trivializing rape, denial of widespread rape, refusing to acknowledge the harm caused by some forms of sexual violence, or some combination of these. The notion of rape culture has been used to describe and explain behaviour within social groups, including prison rape and in conflict areas where war rape is used as psychological warfare. Entire societies have been alleged to be rape cultures group. This objectification allows dominant actors to rationalise or justify the subordination of individuals and groups of people based on arbitrarily defined characteristics. (GSDRC) Also, see social exclusion.

Rape Schedule: This is a concept in feminist theory used to describe the notion that women are conditioned to place restrictions on and/or make alterations to their daily lifestyles and behaviours as a result of constant fear of sexual assault. These altered behaviours may occur consciously or unconsciously.

Rape: Rape is the sexual penetration, however slight of any part of the body of the victim with a sexual organ, or the anal or genital opening of the victim with any object or any other part of the body. The invasion is committed by force, or by the threat of force or coercion, such as that caused by fear of violence, duress, detention, psychological oppression or abuse of power, against such person or another person, or by taking advantage of a coercive environment, or committed against a person incapable of giving genuine consent (if affected by natural induced or age-related incapacity). Since the rape is committed as part of a widespread or systematic attack directed against a civilian population, when the perpetrator knows that, it is a crime against humanity.

Repression: In psychoanalysis, the unconscious burying of painful experiences, memories, and desires.

Reproductive Age: The span of age at which individuals are capable of bearing children. Although the term can refer to both men and women, most frequently it refers only to women. For example, the phrase 'couples of reproductive age' almost always means a couple in which the woman is of childbearing age. The age range referred to is usually 15 to 49.

Reproductive Health: The state of complete physical, mental and social well-being –and not merely the absence of disease or infirmity– in all matters relating to the reproductive system and its functions and processes. It is also the ability to enjoy sexual relations without fear of infection, to avoid unwanted pregnancies or coercion; to regulate fertility without risk; to go safely through pregnancy and childbirth, and to bear and raise healthy children. Reproductive healthcare refers to the methods, techniques, and services that contribute to reproductive health and well-being by preventing and solving reproductive health problems, ranging from family-planning counseling and information, prenatal and post-natal care, complications of pregnancy, treatment of sexually transmitted diseases and infertility, and HIV and AIDS. (See also sexual health.).

Reproductive Justice: This is a concept that links reproductive rights with social justice. Abortion discourse in the United States is often explained in terms of being "pro-choice," i.e. in favour of abortion rights, or "pro-life," i.e. favouring fetal development and the unborn child, and generally being opposed to abortion. Reproductive justice challenges the pro-choice/ pro- life dichotomy. RJ understands "choice" as something that divides women in policy and practice because it assumes that all women have an equal ability to make the same choices. Therefore, "choice" ignores structural factors such as economic status, race, immigration state, etc. Some women's studies scholars like Greta Gaard argue that "choice" is a "scheme of omission" which means that it leaves many women out of the conversation, particular women of colour, immigrant women, queer women, transgender women, etc. Structurally, these identities do not have the same degrees of choice when it comes to accessing reproductive care. Guard argues that this further divides women according to class and race. This creates a need for a new frame that is more inclusive and reproductive justice is supposed to say frame. As a framework, reproductive justice is said to be more expansive and inclusive than "pro-choice." RJ includes community safety, violence, and the government's role in reproduction. The "go-to" or key example used to show how "reproductive justice" differs from "pro-choice," is police brutality. The reproductive justice framework addresses community issues including the right to safety and to parent in safe environments whereas pro-choice typically does not. Therefore, police brutality is seen as a reproductive justice issue. The water crisis in Flint, Michigan, would also be considered a reproductive justice issue because this issue shapes the well-being and health of children and members of that community. Reproductive justice advocates do not prefer choice as a term because it colloquially refers to a woman's right to choose abortion as guaranteed by *Roe v. Wade* (1973). RJ is about more than just abortion rights, which explains the need for new terminology. These advocates explain that reproductive health is about more than just abortion, especially for communities of colour who have faced a history of forced sterilisation and eugenic practices. A common misconception is that reproductive justice is meant to replace the terms "reproductive rights" and/or "reproductive health". For reproductive justice advocates, it is not that one term is better than another term, but they do refer to different things. Reproductive justice as both a phrase and a concept is based on black women's voices and lives. It is based on movement-building. Reproductive rights refer to legal issues and reproductive health refers to services about reproduction.

Reproductive Labour: Reproductive labour work is often associated with caregiving and domestic roles including cleaning, cooking, childcare, and the paid domestic labour force.[1] The term has taken on a role in feminist discourse and philosophy as a way of calling attention to how women in particular are assigned to the domestic sphere where the labour is reproductive and thus uncompensated and unrecognised in a capitalist system. These theories have evolved as a parallel of histories focusing on the entrance of women into the labour force in the 1970s, providing an intersectionalist approach that recognises that women have been a part of the labour force since before their incorporation into the mainstream industry if we consider reproductive labour. (See also **Domestic Responsibilities; Household Maintenance; Labour; National Accounts; Production**.).

Reproductive Rights and Sexual and Reproductive Health: Reproductive rights include the rights of all individuals and couples to decide freely and responsibly the number, spacing, and timing of their children, and to have the information and means to do so. Further, decisions concerning reproduction should be made free from discrimination, coercion, and violence. These services are essential for all people, married and unmarried, including adolescents and youth. For people to realize their reproductive rights, they need access to reproductive and sexual healthcare in the context of primary healthcare. This should include a range of family planning; obstetrical and gynecological care; prevention, care, and treatment of STIs and HIV/AIDs; education and counselling on human sexuality and reproductive health; prevention and surveillance of violence against women and elimination of traditional harmful practices.

Reproductive Rights: Reproductive rights embrace certain human rights that are already recognised in national laws, international human rights documents, and other consensus documents. These rights rest on the recognition of the basic right of all couples and individuals to decide freely and responsibly the number, spacing, and timing of their children and to have the information and means to do so, and the right to attain the highest standard of sexual and reproductive health. It also includes their right to make decisions concerning reproduction free of discrimination, coercion, and violence, as expressed in human rights documents. The promotion of the responsible exercise of these rights for all people should be the fundamental basis for government- and community-supported policies and programmes in the area of reproductive health, including family planning.

Reproductive Roles: Activities needed to ensure the reproduction of society's labour force. This includes housework like cleaning, cooking, childbearing, rearing, and caring for family members. These tasks are done mostly by women.

Reproductive Tax: Feminist economist Diane Elson coined this term to acknowledge the penalties that women male bias in the economy; wages participation in the labour market does not account for women's unpaid work – housework, child care… penalties women face in the workforce/ labour market; motherhood penalty.

Reproductive Work: This work involves all the tasks associated with supporting and servicing the current and future workforce – those who undertake or will undertake productive work. It includes child-bearing and nurture, but is not limited to these tasks. It has increasingly been referred to as "social reproduction" to indicate the broader scope of the term than the activities associated with biological reproduction. Socially reproductive activities include childcare, food preparation, care for the sick, socialisation of the young, attention to ritual and cultural activities through which the society's work ethic is transmitted, and community sharing and support which is essential to the survival of economic stress. The fact that reproductive work is the essential basis of productive work is the principal argument for the economic importance of reproductive work, even though most of it is unpaid, and therefore unrecorded in national accounts. Women and girls are mainly responsible for this work which is usually unpaid. The intersection of peoples' productive and reproductive responsibilities with policy priorities, which has repercussions at all levels of an economy and society, is the principal focus of gender analysis.

Resistance: The act of challenging the dominant power structure. There are everyday acts of resistance, for example, challenging rigid gender roles within the family or calling out discrimination within the workplace. Alternately, the organized and collective forms of resistance range from subtle, symbolic gestures, such as silent protests, to highly visible demonstrations such as marches, strikes, or boycotts. At its core, resistance is a dynamic, revolutionary, or radical action used in some instances after engagement with the established channels and formal institutions of power fail.

Resonance: The ability of people to see their own lives and experiences reflected in the lives, feelings, and struggles of others, built on empathy and solidarity, it can serve as a transformative political process that helps people analyze discrimination and inspires deeper relationships, visions of justice and action. (Suarez and Miller)

Resources: Resources are means and goods, including those that are economic (household income) or productive (land, equipment, tools, work, credit); political (capability for leadership, information and organisation); and time.

Resources: The potential wealth or means of a country or society. It refers to what people use to perform their activities, such as land, seeds, trees, credit, technology, labour, and services. Access to resources is the possibility to use resources readily, without necessarily having control over them. Control of resources includes decision-making power over the use and distribution of resources. (See also **Labour; Ownership; Production; Reproductive Labour**)

Respectability Politician: A feminist who criticises the critique of the cultural critic, and favours social assimilation.

Respectability Politics: originated as cultural, sexual, domestic, employment, and artistic "guidelines" or "rules" for racially marginalised groups to follow in the effort to be viewed as "human" in a White supremacist society and by individual Whites. The politics of respectability implies that recognition of Black humanity has to be "earned" by Black people by engaging in puritanical behaviour as approved by White supremacy...behaviours that Whites themselves don't have to engage in to "prove" humanity because of White privilege; they're always viewed as "the default human." Applicable to all other marginalised groups as well.

Richian: Relating to American radical feminist essayist Adrienne Rich (1929-2012).

Rights (Sexual): Women's sexual rights include the right to control their sexuality and the provision of sexual and reproductive health-related services. They include reproductive rights where the number and spacing of children can be chosen in a free, responsible, and informed way. Women's sexuality is not solely associated with issues of responsibility or risks concerning reproduction. Sexual activity is above all an integral part of a woman's life, of her private life and sexual enjoyment thereof. Women's sexual rights recognise the right to sexual well-being and the freedom of choice concerning partner(s), sexual orientation, sexual preferences, and the choice of each woman whether or not to have sexual relations.

Rights: Something to which a person has a just claim. Rights may be enshrined in law, defined by custom, and/or established as a social norm. Rights confer a certain degree of power and for this reason, what is recognised and protected as a right is a perpetual work in progress. The concept and international consecration of rights is a potent tool for reframing people's hopes and needs as legitimate political claims for which the state and/or other actors have the responsibility and can be held accountable. That said, for this conceptual approach to have practical meaning, definitions of citizenship (i.e. who has rights), the state's jurisdiction concerning the public and private spheres, and the indivisibility of social, economic, civil, and political rights must be addressed. See also women's human rights.

Role Conflict: Role Conflict occurs when there are incompatible demands placed upon a person such that compliance with both would be difficult.[1] Persons experience role conflict when they find themselves pulled in various directions as they try to respond to the many statuses they hold.[2] Role conflict can be something that can be for either a short period, or a long period, and it can also be connected to situational experiences.

Rosie the Riveter: Symbolic name was given to women who filled U.S. factories during the second world war, proving that women can do difficult labour as well as or better than their male counterparts.

Safe Motherhood: The concept of ensuring that women receive the appropriate care to be safe and healthy throughout pregnancy and childbirth with a low risk of death or ill health. This requires putting in place priorities at the country level such as the empowerment of women to ensure choices, delay in marriage and first birth, ensuring good-quality and skilled delivery, improvement in access to reproductive health services, and prevention of unwanted pregnancies.

Safe Sex: Sexual behaviour that does not pose risks for the transmission of sexually transmitted diseases (STDs), including HIV and AIDS. However, some reproductive health experts argue that, except for abstinence and solo masturbation, there are no safe sexual behaviours, and therefore the term 'safer sex' is more appropriate. In this context, safer sex refers to sexual behaviours that reduce – as against do not pose – any risks of transmission of STDs. The consistent use of condoms during sexual activity and non-penetrative sexual activities are some examples of safer sex techniques. Other definitions of safe sex might include relations that lower the risk not only of disease transmission but also of unintended pregnancy, violence, coercion, or abuse of power. In this case, safer sex also includes protected sex, which refers to any sexual behaviour that provides protection either from unwanted pregnancy or from STDs.

Safe Space (for Feminist Organising): A closed environment built based on trust where women can be open and honest in discussing their fears, risks and, if needed, recover from the physical and psychological effects of burnout and violence, and identify resources and pursue solutions. A safe space acknowledges differences among women and consciously works to avoid reproducing oppressive social hierarchies that both the privilege and silence individuals and groups of women. In some situations, physical, emotional, and psychological violence is used as a weapon to undermine women's political participation or to silence women. Sustainable feminist organising requires spaces to deal with the conflict or violence that women's resistance can generate and develop strategies for risk assessment and safety.

Sati or suttee: It is an obsolete funeral custom where a widow immolates herself (Anumarana) on her husband's pyre or takes her own life in another fashion shortly after her husband's death. Mention of the practice can be dated back to the 3rd century BC, while evidence of this by widows of kings only appears beginning between the 5th and 9th centuries CE. The practice is considered to have originated within the warrior aristocracy in the northern Indian subcontinent, gradually gaining in popularity from the 10th century CE and spreading to other groups from the 12th through 18th century CE. The practice was particularly prevalent among some Hindu communities, observed in aristocratic Hindu families, and has been attested to outside the Indian subcontinent in several localities in Southeast Asia, such as in Indonesia and Vietnam. The practice was never widespread throughout India, nor did it have the scriptural sanction. Old age refers to ages nearing or surpassing the life expectancy of human beings and is thus the end of the human life cycle. Terms and euphemisms include old people, the elderly (worldwide usage), seniors (American usage), senior citizens (British and American usages), older adults (in the social sciences), and the elders (in many cultures—including the cultures of aboriginal people). Old people often have limited regenerative abilities and are more susceptible to disease, syndromes, injuries, and sickness than younger adults. The organic process of aging is called senescence, the medical study of the aging process is called gerontology, and the study of diseases that afflict the elderly is called geriatrics. The elderly also face other social issues around retirement, loneliness, and ageism.

Second Shift: A synonym for the double day.

Second Wave Feminism: Began in the 1960s and bloomed in the 1970s with a push for greater equality. Think Gloria Steinem, Dorothy Pitman Hughes, Betty Friedan. It was marked by huge gains for women in legal and structural equality.

Security: The traditional understanding of security revolves around the security of states from external attacks, provided by governments through military means. The realities of the current historical moment, however, argue for a broader understanding of security that takes into account the dangers people confront from environmental degradation, violent conflict, human rights violations, the inability of states to deliver on basic human needs, and similar challenges. (Also, see **Human Security**).

Self-Identify: Refers to the process of people choosing with which identifying terms/groups they identify. (E.g. someone could self-identify as male, female or bi-gendered, multi-racial, etc.).

Self-Reliance: Is the ability of people to improve themselves out of their resources, by their efforts. But here the term is given the special - and common - meaning of people's advancement by their own efforts within the existing social structure. This meaning of self-reliance implies that development problems arise from inadequacies in people's present abilities and efforts, rather than from inadequacies in society, or structural inequality. This definition enables us to make a useful distinction between "self-reliance" and "empowerment", where the latter means taking power in both the individual and social plans. Where women's development involves overcoming a social system of discrimination against women, it is inadequate to discuss the development process purely in terms of women's self-improvement or increased self-reliance; we need also to discuss women's collective action for increased empowerment.

Separatist Feminism: A type of radical feminism holding that feminists should completely avoid all forms of contact with men, in a sense, the extreme endpoint of lesbian feminism.

Sex and Gender: Sex refers to the biological characteristics between men and women, which are universal and do not change. These sets of biological characteristics are not mutually exclusive as there are individuals who possess both, but these characteristics tend to differentiate humans as males and females. As race, class, age, ethnic group, etc the notion of gender needs to be understood clearly as a cross-cutting socio-cultural variable. Gender refers to social attributes that are learned or acquired during socialization as a member of a given community. Gender is therefore an acquired identity. Because these attributes are learned behaviours, they are context/ time-specific and changeable (with increasing rapidity as the rate of technological change intensifies) and vary across cultures. Gender, therefore, refers to the socially given attributes, roles, activities, responsibilities, and needs connected to being men (masculine) and women (feminine) in a given society at a given time, and as a member of a specific community within that society. Women and men's gender identity determines how they are perceived and how they are expected to think and act as men and women. Gender determines what is expected, allowed, and valued in a woman or a man in a given context. In most societies, there are differences and inequalities between women and men in responsibilities assigned, activities undertaken, access to and control over resources, as well as decision-making opportunities. Other important criteria for socio-cultural analysis include class, race, poverty level, ethnic group, and age. It is worth noting that when the word "gender" was first used in this way, to signify social rather than grammatical difference, at the Institute for Development Studies at the University of Brighton, in the mid-1970s, the intention was not so much as to distinguish men from women, but to find an analytic tool to disaggregate the category "women". In other words, the

the intention was to refine the analysis of the differing impacts of development on different groups of women, as well as differences between women and men.

Sex Identity: It denotes a person sees them as. This can include refusing to label oneself.

Sex Positive: An attitude that views sexual expression, sexual pleasure, if it's healthy and consensual, as a good thing.

Sex Role Stereotype: Shared and generally reductive gender beliefs about the nature of the sexes. Sex-role stereotypes are the grist for many commercials.

Sex Roles: This may, therefore, be contrasted with gender roles, since sex roles refer to an occupation or biological function for which a necessary qualification is to belong to one particular sex category. For example, pregnancy is a female sex role because only members of the female sex may bear children.

Sex Strike: A **sex strike**, sometimes called a **sex boycott**, is a strike, a method of non-violent resistances in which one or multiple persons refrain from sex with their partner(s) to achieve certain goals. It is a form of temporary sexual abstinence. Sex strikes have been used to protest many issues, from war to gang violence.

Sex Typing: Treating a person differently because of her/his biological sex.

Sex vs. Gender: Sex is the biological aspect of one's identity; gender is the social construction of.

Sex Worker-Exclusionary Radical Feminism: Radical feminism is hostile to and exclusionary of sex workers, seeing their work as colluding with the oppression of women. Adherents are called SWERFs for short.

Sex: Identifier related to a person's biological sex organs. A person's sex may or may not match their gender identity and/or expression.

Sexuality/Sexual Orientation: The direction of one's sexual attraction. It exists on a continuum and not a set of absolute categories; sometimes referred to as affection orientation or sexuality.

Sex-Disaggregated Data: Sex-disaggregated data is data that is cross-classified by sex, presenting information separately for men and women, boys and girls. Sex-disaggregated data reflect roles, real situations, general conditions of women and men, girls and boys in every aspect of society.

For instance, the literacy rate, education levels, business ownership, employment, wage differences, dependants, house and land ownership, loans and credit, debts, etc. When data is not disaggregated by sex, it is more difficult to identify real and potential inequalities. Sex-disaggregated data is necessary for effective gender analysis.

Sexism in Medicine: Sexism in medicine involves discriminating against patients, physicians, medical students, and medical-school staff based on gender. Most sexism is directed against women. The discrimination can involve comments on women's appearance; the imposition of an aggressive "macho" culture; verbal abuse; bullying; sexual assault; being passed over for promotion, and being denied treatment. Assessing the differences in pain treatment and the report of pain between men and women is complicated by the possibility that men and women perceive or experience pain differently. Men in nursing are often subjected to sexist treatment.

Sexism: Actions or attitudes that discriminate against people based solely on their gender. Sexism is linked to power in that those with power are typically treated with favour and those without power are typically discriminated against. Sexism is also related to stereotypes since the discriminatory actions or attitudes are frequently based on false beliefs or over generalisations about gender and on seeing gender as relevant when it is not (or) **Sexism** is prejudice or discrimination based on a person's sex or gender. Sexism can affect anyone, but it primarily affects women and girls. It has been linked to stereotypes and gender roles and may include the belief that one sex or gender is intrinsically superior to another. Extreme sexism may foster sexual harassment, rape, and other forms of sexual violence.

Gender Discrimination: It may encompass sexism and is discrimination toward people based on their gender identity or their gender or sex differences. Gender discrimination is especially defined in terms of workplace inequality.

Sexism: Discrimination against women that results from the male supremacy system of oppression.

Sex-Positivity: A positive attitude toward and valuing sexual freedom, sexual identities, and consent.

Sex-Reassignment Surgery (SRS): Sex change operation.

Sex-Shaming (f.k.a. "slut-shaming"): Shaming someone because of their sexual behaviours/desires.

Sexual and Domestic Violence: Women tend to be more often victims in a form of domestic violence by a woman's intimate partner, sexual exploitation through trafficking and sex trade, in wars by an enemy army as a weapon of attempted 'ethnic cleansing' etc.

Sexual and Reproductive Health and Rights (SRHR): Taken together, sexual and reproductive health and rights (SRHR) can be understood as the right for all, whether young or old, women, men or transgender, straight, gay, lesbian or bisexual, HIV positive or negative, to make choices regarding their sexuality and reproduction, providing they respect the rights of others to bodily integrity. This definition also includes the right to access information and services needed to support these choices and optimise health.

Sexual Assault: Non-consensual sexual contact that is obtained through coercion or the use or threat of force. Sexual assault is a deliberate act of gender-based violence and an expression of power, control, and domination over another. It is not a manifestation of uncontrolled desire, attraction, or arousal. Sexual assault occurs in every socioeconomic level of society and a variety of settings. Sexual assault may be perpetrated by non-state actors, such as acquaintances, dating partners, or intimate partners such as current or former husbands and boyfriends. Sexual assault may also be committed by state actors such as the police or military. In particular, women are vulnerable to particular forms of sexual abuse and assault when they are in state custody. Women are also sexually assaulted and abused during and after an armed conflict. During the conflict, rape is used as a weapon of war. Even when not used as a military strategy, however, rape and sexual assault are commonly perpetrated by military forces, and may even be perpetrated by peacekeepers after the cessation of hostilities. Whether the assault is perpetrated by an agent of the government or a family member, victims of sexual assault often face many obstacles in obtaining needed protection and assistance.

Sexual Consent: The expression of agreement to participate in sexual activity.

Sexual Division of Labour: The sexual division of labour is a phenomenon found in virtually all human societies. Due to its importance, economists have attempted to model the causes and implications of gender roles across societies. Economic theory suggests that occupational segregation by gender might be due to supply-side factors, demand-side factors, or a combination of both. For instance, the major supply-side theory consists of the human capital explanation which states that since women generally anticipate shorter and less continuous work lives than men, it will be in their interest to choose occupations that require smaller human capital investments and have lower wage penalties for time spent out of the labour market (The fact that women may face barriers to obtaining education and pre-job training in traditionally male fields is called "societal discrimination" and constitutes an alternative supply effect explanation). On the demand side, the sexual division of labour is supported by discrimination against women within the paid labour force.

Sexual Exploitation: Any abuse of a position of vulnerability, differential power, or trust for sexual purposes; this includes profiting momentarily, socially, or politically from the sexual exploitation of another.

Sexual Harassment / Gender Harassment: As defined by the Equal Employment Opportunity Commission, sexual harassment involves unwelcome sexual advances, requests for sexual favours, and other verbal or physical conduct of a sexual nature when submission to or rejection of this conduct explicitly or implicitly affects an individual's employment, unreasonably interferes with an individual's work performance, or creates an intimidating, hostile, or offensive work environment. There are two types: quid pro quo, a request for sexual favours that implies a trade (e.g. advancement on the job), and "hostile environment, a situation involving a sexually charged workplace in which the employee is subjected to sexualised behaviour and made to feel uncomfortable or threatened. Sexual harassment is a violation of Title VII of the 1964 Civil Rights Act (amended), and corporations and institutions of higher learning should all have and enforce policies prohibiting it. See the GRCC Women's Studies website (policies section) for examples. The forms of sexual harassment are usually divided into three different types: (1) verbal: e.g. remarks about figure/ looks, sexual and sexist jokes, verbal sexual advances, comments that implicate stereotypic and discriminative attitudes; (2) non-verbal and/or visual: e.g. staring at someone and whistling; and (3) physical: acts from unsolicited physical contact to assaults and rape.

Sexual Health: A state of physical, emotional, mental, and social well-being related to sexuality; it is not merely the absence of disease, dysfunction, or infirmity. Sexual health requires a positive and respectful approach to sexuality and sexual relationships, as well as the possibility of having pleasurable and safe sexual experiences, free of coercion, discrimination, and violence. For sexual health to be attained and maintained, the sexual rights of all persons must be respected, protected, and fulfilled.

Sexual Identity: One's gender orientation (heterosexual, homosexual, bisexual, transsexual). According to most gender theories, sexuality is fluid, not a fixed concept, so these categories may be unnecessarily rigid.

Sexual Minority: (1) Refers to members of sexual orientations or who engage in sexual activities that are not part of the mainstream. (2) Refers to members of sex groups that do not fall into the majority categories of male or female, such as intersexuals and transsexuals.

Sexual Objectification: Is the act of treating a person as a mere object of sexual desire. Objectification more broadly means treating a person as a commodity or an object without regard to their personality or dignity. Objectification is most commonly examined at the level of society, but can also refer to the behaviour of individuals and is a type of dehumanization.

Sexual Orientation: Sexual orientation refers to each person's capacity for profound emotional, affectional, and sexual attraction to, and intimate and sexual relations with, individuals of a different sex/gender or the same sex/ gender or more than one sex/gender. There are three predominant sexual orientations: towards the same sex/gender (homosexuality), towards the opposite sex/gender (heterosexuality), or both sexes/genders (bisexuality).

Sexual Orientation: The deep-seated direction of one's sexual (erotic) attraction. It is on a continuum and not a set of absolute categories, sometimes referred to as affection orientation or sexuality.

Sexual Reassignment Surgery (Sexual/Gender Confirmation Surgery): Any number of physical surgeries a transgender individual might undergo to match their physical appearance with the gender they identify with. Transgender: Transgender people are those whose gender identity differs from the social gender expectations connected to the biological sex they were born with. To understand this, one must understand the separation between biological sex (genitals, chromosomes, secondary sex characteristics, etc.), and social gender, which refers to levels of masculinity and femininity ascribed by society or perceived in the self. Often, society conflates sex and gender, viewing them as the same thing; they are not the same thing, and one does not inherently determine the other. It is also important to recognise that like gender in general, transgender identities operate on a spectrum. Similar to many identities, the way gender operates is exceptionally complex, and every person's experience with their particular gender identity will be specific and unique; there is no one way to necessarily describe someone's experience of being transgender.

Sexual Rights: Sexual rights embrace human rights that are already recognised in national laws, international human rights documents, and other consensus documents. These include the right of all persons, free of coercion, discrimination, and violence, to the highest attainable standard of health about sexuality, including access to sexual and reproductive healthcare services; seek, receive and impart information with sexuality; sexuality education; respect for bodily integrity; choice of partner; decide to be sexually active or not; consensual sexual relations; consensual marriage; decide whether or not, and when to have children; and pursue a satisfying, safe and pleasurable sexual life.

Sexual Violence: Sexual violence includes many actions that are equally hurtful to every victim and are used similarly in the public and private spheres. Examples include rape (sexual violence including some form of penetration of the victim's body), marital rape, and attempted rape. Other types of forced sexual activities include being forced to watch somebody, forcing somebody to in front of others, forced unsafe sex, sexual harassment, and, in the case of women, abuse related to reproduction (forced pregnancy, forced abortion, forced sterilization).

Sexuality: Human sexuality is how people experience and express themselves as sexual beings. Biologically, sexuality can encompass sexual intercourse and sexual contact in all its forms, as well as medical concerns about the physiological or even psychological aspects of sexual behaviour. Our behaviour and views about sex and sexuality are determined by cultural, social, political, and legal systems. Although sexuality is the most basic and normal part of being human, in most societies, sex and sexuality are taboo and the subject of great moral, ethical and religious debate. The control of sexuality is a critical feature of patriarchy in all societies, and this includes how women see themselves, definitions of rape, access to contraception, and abortion. Michel Foucault, a famous philosopher who wrote in **The History of Sexuality,** that "sexual meanings" – what different people think is erotic – are social and cultural constructs. He and many other writers highlight that sex is political. In other words, those in power define what is normal and not normal through institutions, such as education, religion, media, medicine, etc. To escape this type of control of "sexuality" Foucault recommended focusing on "bodies and pleasures."

Sexually Transmitted Infections (STIs): Infections are usually passed from person to person by sexual contact, although some can be passed on by other means (e.g., through needlestick injury). It is also called sexually transmitted diseases or STDs.

Shakespeare's Sister: A figure from Virginia Woolf's **A Room of One's Own,** Shakespeare's sister presents an example of the gifted young woman denied the opportunity to develop her talents; she illustrates the effects of untrammeled patriarchy and the denial of women's rights.

Showalterian: Relating to American feminist literary critic Elaine Showalter (b. 1941).

Single men: They are often called bachelors. Single women are sometimes called bachelorettes, especially in festive contexts in American English, but the historic term is a spinster. The connotations of the word spinster have changed over time so that it is now considered a derogatory term. In legal definitions for interpersonal status, a **single person** is someone unmarried, not in a relationship, and not part of a civil union. In common usage, the term 'single' is often used to refer to someone who is not involved in any type of serious romantic relationship, including long-term dating, engagement, marriage, or someone who is 'single by choice. Single people may participate in dating and other activities to find a long-term partner or spouse. People may remain single for a variety of reasons, including financial and emotional or physical health issues, the stress in the family, time constraints, education, career, personal preferences, advanced age or social fears, living in a society or locality where there are an insufficient number of people of the preferred sex for romantic or sexual attraction, or simply extreme bad luck with finding anyone who will reciprocate an interest in a relationship. In some cases, single people may be uninterested in marriage, domestic partnerships, or other types of committed relationships. Certain careers and positions require that people remain single. Sometimes, this is coupled with celibacy or chastity, either for secular or for religious reasons, such as priests, nuns, and monks in certain faiths. Loneliness can occur for some people who look for but cannot find anyone they might wish to date, especially for those suffering the loss of companionship following divorce or bereavement. Some single people, however, regard and appreciate solitude as an opportunity. In some countries, particular laws may directly or indirectly disadvantage single persons. In the United States, for example, Social Security widow(er) benefits are only available to those persons who have been previously married, and single people in the United States pay more income taxes than married people. In many countries tour and holiday, operators impose a penalty (often as much as 100%) on persons who travel alone.

Single Parent: A person who is bringing up a child or children without the assistance of a partner. (See, also parental rights; parenthood)

Sisterhood: Solidarity among women; the bonding of women who share the same goals, experiences, or points of view toward their empowerment and an important term in second-wave feminism.

Situated Knowledge: It is related to a criticism that pertaining to the idea of researchers as neutral observers of reality. The expression was coined in an analysis of how the establishing of modern science from the 1500s and onwards as part of the creation of a new form of masculinity: the scientist, who was assumed to be free from social and biological ties that could interfere with the ability to remain unbiased in the study of reality. In feminist theory, the assumed ability to act as a neutral observer, to be able to see everything from nowhere without being seen, is called God's trick. The seeing is always bodied; that is, you have to have a body to be able to see, and that body has a gender, a variation of functionality, and ethnicity, to name some of the many factors that shape a person's experience and understanding of the world. There is a relationship between knowledge production and power structures such as gender, class, ethnicity, functionality, and sexuality (see also **Heteronormativity**). The knowledge of one's social position, formed by the prevailing power structures, is a prerequisite for knowledge about society and human beings. There are no neutral positions that can give privileged persons the right of interpretation when it comes to other people's experiences. The concept of situated knowledge brings attention to the fact that our possibility to gain knowledge about reality is limited by what it is to be human. Researchers can never be completely neutral. However, their objectivity can be strengthened by making them – as well as their social and cultural understandings – visible in the research process. Interpretations of reality are always incomplete, and researchers take responsibility for making the knowledge more trustworthy by acknowledging this limitation. Since knowledge is produced in a specific social context, certain experiences, which vary with the topic, are particularly valuable in the generation process. It can be the ability to ask the right questions or see which experiences and perspectives are made invisible. For example, knowledge about oppressive social structures and relations becomes more trustworthy if it is produced from the perspective of the oppressed people's position and experiences. One current example is discrimination and oppression based on preconceptions about certain races, such as Afrophobia (see also **Racialisation**). When people who have personal experience of this are asked about it, new knowledge about the oppressive structures emerges, the knowledge that Whites do not have access to (see also **Whiteness).** This is called standpoint epistemology. Another example can be found in the field of history, where feminist researchers since the 1960s have brought attention to the observation that only men's experiences have been addressed and that the research therefore can only be considered to concern men's history. Thus, it has been important to conduct complementary research.

Slut-Shaming: Slut-shaming is the practice of criticising people, especially women and girls, who are perceived to violate expectations of behaviour and appearance regarding issues related to sexuality. The term is used to reclaim the word *slut* and empower women and girls to have agency over their sexuality. It may also be used about gay men, who may face disapproval for sexual behaviours considered promiscuous. Slut-shaming rarely happens to heterosexual men.

Slut Walk: An ongoing trans-national movement calling for an end to rape culture.

Social Capital: Perceived benefits associated with knowledge of and access to a network of individuals with privilege and in powerful advantageous positions.

Social Construction: The concept of social construction was first used in the mid-1960s as part of an ambition to explain how people perceive their social reality. Since then, the concept has been further developed within the critical theory to show that phenomena such as gender, race, and identity are not constant, inevitable, or given by nature, but are rather products of human interaction and collective actions (see also **Queer, Racialization**). They are characterised by historic and cultural variations. Even the production of knowledge itself is affected by such social norms (see also situated knowledge). If we have social norms that describe homosexuality as a disease and something deviant, a lot of the knowledge produced in the area will be shaped by these norms and therefore reinforce rather than challenge them (see also **Heteronormativity, Othering**). Social construction is sometimes used and understood incorrectly, to denote something as not existing in a physical or material sense. More correctly, however, social constructions should be understood as capturing the meanings, characteristics, and attributes that are assigned various phenomena giving it its meaning. For example, small children use attributes to describe people's gender; long hair, make-up and a purse mean woman, regardless of the person's physical and biological appearance. This is an example of how we can view attributes, traits, and behaviour as some of the building blocks of our perception of a person's gender, beyond biology. The discussion around social construction has been developed further for example through a questioning of the difference that is often made between biological sex and gender, or social sex. By pointing at how biological attributes are given a meaning in a social context, it can be said that people 'make' gender through their behaviour and actions. Others have discussed race as a social construction, where what is relevant is not whether race in a biological sense exists or does not exist but rather what social meaning skin colour, religion, cultural attributes, and other external features are assigned through racialisation processes.

Social Constructionism: "Sociological and psychological theories" of knowledge that consider how social phenomena develop in particular social contexts. Within constructionist thought, social construction is a concept or practice which may appear to be natural and obvious to those who accept it, but in reality, is an invention or artifact of a particular culture or society.

Social Exclusion: A framework that has been used and expanded upon by feminists and disability and queer rights activists to deepen analyses of poverty and inequality to address the multiple ways that people are excluded from full participation in society, based not only on material deprivation, but also on noneconomic factors such as mental health, gender, physical ability, caste, sexual orientation, and age. The concept moves beyond notions of material disadvantage or "poverty" to address inequalities in terms of other forms of social power required to live a free and dignified life, such as respect, understanding, citizenship, education, and rights. (Batliwala, 2011b)

Social Justice: The idea of creating an egalitarian society or institution based on principles of equality and solidarity, an understanding and valuing of human rights, and recognition of the dignity of every human being.

Social Privilege: In sociology, **privilege** is a concept used for certain rights or advantages that are available only to a particular person or group of people. The term is commonly used in the context of social inequality, particularly regarding age, disability, ethnic or racial category, gender, gender identity, sexual orientation, religion, and/or social class. Two common examples involve having access to higher education and housing. Under a newer usage of the term, privilege can also be emotional or psychological, regarding comfort and personal self-confidence, or having a sense of belonging or worth in society. It began as an academic concept but has since become popular outside of academia. Researchers have published a substantial body of analysis of privilege and specific social groups, expressing a variety of perspectives. Some commentators have addressed limitations in the term, such as its inability to distinguish between concepts of "spared injustice" and "unjust enrichment", and its tendency to conflate disparate groups.

Social Protection: A group of policy initiatives that ensure the provision of basic needs to vulnerable or precarious sectors usually in the form of social assistance programmes and social safety nets, social insurance and active labour market activities. They protect vulnerable people against livelihood risks and seek to enhance the social status and rights of the marginalised. Transformative social protection does all this and works to ensure that all people realise their rights to the resources needed to maintain and sustain a decent living and security. (IDS 2009)

Social Transformation: Large scale social change as in "cultural reforms" or "transformations"; requires a shift in the collective consciousness of a society - local, state, national or global - so that a new model of existence is envisioned and then fought for through activism.

Socialist Feminism: A current of feminism holding that patriarchy is connected to capitalism and that gender equality should be achieved through ending both the economic and cultural sources of oppression.

Socialisation: Process of social interaction by which people learn their society's way of life and their specific roles in that society.

Socialised: Refers to the "training" process that takes place once birth sex is determined or decided.

Socio-Economic Status: Generally refers to a person's position in society as determined by a combination of factors, such as education and economic means. Socio-economic status is one of the most important sources of disadvantage or privilege but differs from class in that it is assessed with less attention to family lineage and other structural factors that shape economic opportunity and status.

Socio-Economic Violence: Socio-economic violence is both a cause and an effect of dominant gender power relations in societies. Some of the most typical forms of socio-economic violence include taking away the victim's earnings, not allowing her to have a separate income (forced 'housewife' status, working in the family business without a salary), or making her unfit for work through targeted physical abuse. In the public sphere, this can include denial of access to education or (equally) paid work (mainly to women), denial of access to services, exclusion from certain jobs, denial of the enjoyment and exercise of civil, cultural, social, or political rights.

Solidarity Economy: This is an alternative or complement to the market economy consisting of economic enterprises undertaken not for profit but collective benefit. In many instances, women have banded together to produce needed items or coordinate small enterprises such as shops, gardens, neighbourhood kitchens, and childcare or financial cooperatives.

The solidarity economy promotes organisation and a culture of shared decision-making, and can help women access basic economic and social rights such as food, credit, and education. It can also help reduce women's burden of unpaid labour in the care economy.

Son Preference: The practice of preferring male offspring over female offspring, most often in poor communities, that view girl children as liabilities and boy children as assets to the family. This can result in families instilling superiority in male children and inferiority in female children, manifesting in such actions as sending boys to school, especially to higher levels, and not girls or household practices where boys are fed better than girls. The extreme manifestation of son preference is female feticide and sex-selected abortions; in some countries, this has resulted in skewed population sex ratios, with attendant problems such as increased trafficking of females and greater prevalence of sex workers. (See: **Gender-Biased Sex Selection**.).

Special: The term "special", though conforming with human rights discourse, also needs to be carefully explained. Its use sometimes casts women and other groups who are subject to discrimination as weak, vulnerable, and in need of extra or "special" measures to participate or compete in society. However, the real meaning of "special" in the formulation of article 4, paragraph 1 of CEDAW, is that the measures are designed to serve a specific goal.

Stand-alone Gender Programming and Policies: Programming and policies that explicitly address gender inequality to achieve gender equality.

Standpoint Theory: A feminist theoretical perspective that argues that knowledge stems from a social position. The perspective denies that traditional science is objective and suggests that research and theory have ignored and marginalised women and feminist ways of thinking. The theory emerged from the Marxist argument that people from an oppressed class have special access to knowledge that is not available to those from a privileged class. In the 1970s feminist writers inspired by that Marxist insight began to examine how inequalities between men and women influence knowledge production. Their work is related to epistemology, a branch of philosophy that examines the nature and origins of knowledge, and stresses that knowledge is always socially situated. In societies stratified by gender and other categories, such as race and class, one's social positions shape what one can know.

State: Consists of the people, procedures, and institutions of government bound by particular territorial borders. The state's authority and duties and people's access to public decision-making, resources, and opportunities are defined and regulated through laws and policies. Policies and laws are enforced and implemented through government ministries, the police, courts, schools, local government and ministries, and other institutions. Different states exert various levels of control on civil society and the market and regulate relationships in the family through family law. (VeneKlasen and Miller, 2002)

Stereotype: This is an over-generalized belief about a particular category of people. Stereotypes are generalised because one assumes that the stereotype is true for each person in the category. While such generalisations may be useful when making quick decisions, they may be erroneous when applied to particular individuals. Stereotypes encourage prejudice and may arise for several reasons.

Stereotyping: Believing that all people with a particular characteristic are the same.

Straight: A person who is attracted to a gender other than their own. [Commonly thought of as "attraction to the opposite gender," but since there are not only two genders (see **Transgender**), this definition is inaccurate.].

Strategic Gender Interests: Needs and interests identified by women that arise from their subordinate position in society. Strategic interests vary according to context, are related to gendered divisions of labour, power, and control, and may include such issues as legal rights, domestic violence, equal wages, access to contraception, etc. Strategic gender interests question women's socially constructed role, demanding greater equality and a change in existing roles. (See also **Practical Gender Needs**)

Strategic Gender Needs: Requirements of women and men to improve their position or status. Addressing these needs allow people to have control over their lives beyond socially defined restrictive roles. Strategic gender needs for women might include land rights, more decision-making power, equal pay, and greater access to credit.

Strategic Needs: Unlike practical needs, strategic needs arise out of an understanding and analysis of women's subordinate situation in society (conscientisation). Strategic needs are actions and strategies which are required to bring about structural change and empowerment. These may also be variously expressed; a need for political and legislative reform to grant constitutional equality to women; reproductive rights; state accession to CEDAW; a political voice; action on violence against women.

Straw Feminism: Straw feminism is a man argument whereby exaggerated or fabricated elements of feminism are used in an attempt to refute and/or derail feminist arguments. A straw feminist then is a fabricated character used by those arguing against feminism to devalue and derail feminist arguments. Straw feminism often incorporates oversimplifications, misrepresentations, and stereotypes of feminism to easily discredit feminism as a whole.

Straw Feminist: A made-up version of a feminist that doesn't exist, used in straw man arguments against feminist ideas.

Strong Objectivity: This is a term coined by feminist philosopher Sandra Harding, known for her work on feminist standpoint theory. Harding suggests that starting research from the lives of women "actually strengthens standards of objectivity". Strong objectivity can be contrasted with the "weak objectivity" of supposed value-neutral research. Strong objectivity is posited in contrast to scientific objectivity since strong objectivity takes into consideration researcher bias, something that Harding argues can never really be removed; a researcher's life experiences will always be a lens through which they view the world and subsequently their research. From a feminist standpoint, the question of objectivity stems from what kinds of knowledge projects are objective and which aren't, and why; whether or not objectivity is necessary; and how, or if, it is possible to achieve objectivity. These considerations arise at least in part from concerns about sexism and androcentric bias in dominant scientific life and studies. Strong objectivity argues that there is androcentric bias in research because male researchers attempt to be neutral researchers, where Harding argues that is not possible. Harding suggests researcher reflexivity, or consideration of the researcher's positionality, and how that affects their research, as "stronger" objectivity than researchers claiming to be completely neutral. Knowledge and the biases affecting it must be equally judged by the scientific community and located in social history.

Structural Adjustment Programmes (SAPs): Economic policies for developing countries that have been promoted by the World Bank and International Monetary Fund (IMF) and which these countries have to follow to receive loans from these two institutions. SAPs policies reflect the neoliberal ideology that drives globalisation. They aim to achieve long-term or accelerated economic growth in poorer countries through policies that focus on reducing government intervention and pushing export-led growth, privatization, and liberalisation for the efficiency of the free market. The World Bank and IMF pushed SAPs during the eighties and nineties, during which debates emerged about their harmful impact on social sectors. Since then, there has been an acceptance of the problems that SAPs lead to and the importance of balancing economic reform with social priorities and development. The term, which acquired a negative connotation in civil society circles, is not used as often as it has been in the past. But critics of SAPs say that their philosophy and elements continue in the term 'poverty reduction' that financial institutions have used increasingly since the late 1990s. 'Poverty Reduction Strategy Papers, which countries are encouraged to draw up, have taken the place of SAPs. (See also **Feminisation of Poverty**.).

Structural Barriers/Causes: Gender inequalities in social structures, based on institutionalised conceptions of gender differences. Conceptions of masculinity and femininity, expectations of women and men, judgments of women's and men's actions, prescribed rules about behaviour of women and men – all of these, and more, create and maintain gender inequality in social structures. Social and cultural environments, as well as the institutions that structure them and the individuals that operate within and outside these institutions, are engaged in the production and reproduction of gender norms, attitudes, and stereotypes.

Structural Discrimination: A form of discrimination resulting from policies, despite apparently being neutral that have disproportionately negative effects on certain societal groups.

Structural Gender Inequality: Exists where a system of gender discrimination is practiced by public or social institutions. Structural gender inequality is more entrenched if it is maintained by administrative rules and laws, rather than by only custom and traditions.

Structural Racism: The systematic ways through which practices of conferring and withholding benefits based on race are embedded in social institutions.

Subject/Object: A binary combination important to feminist discourse. The subject possesses interiority, is empowered, and in hierarchical societies, dominates others; the object is reduced to the useful tasks they can perform and is marginalised in several ways.

Subjectification: The philosophical concept that refers to the construction of the individual subject attributed to Michel Foucault (1982) has been further elaborated by Gilles Deleuze and Félix Guattari (1987).

Substantive Equality: This focuses on the outcomes and impacts of laws and policies. Substantive equality goes far beyond creating formal legal equality for women (where all are equal under the law) and means that governments are responsible for the impact of laws. This requires governments to tailor legislation to respond to the realities of women's lives. Striving for substantive equality also places a responsibility on governments to implement laws, through gender-responsive governance and functioning justice systems that meet women's needs. Substantive equality is a concept expressed in the Convention on the Elimination of All Forms of Discrimination against Women (CEDAW). It recognises that because of historic discrimination, women do not start on an equal footing to men.

Suffrage: The right to vote in political elections.

Supportive Policies (at the UN): To achieve a balanced representation of women and men, the UN recognises the necessity of having an environment and organisational culture conducive to the balancing of work and life responsibilities. To this end, the UN has some mandatory system-wide entitlements, such as maternity, paternity, sick, and annual leave policies. Promulgation and implementation of other gender-friendly policies are suggested, leaving room for each agency to adopt its variations. A list of these policies can be found on the websites of the Focal Point for Women in the UN system and also of the individual UN entities.

Sustainable Development: There are many definitions of sustainable development, including this landmark one which first appeared in the 1987 United Nations Brundtland Report: "Sustainable development is a development that meets the needs of the present without compromising the ability of future generations to meet their own needs." The United Nations 2005 World Summit Outcome Document refers to the "interdependent and mutually reinforcing pillars" of sustainable development as economic development, social development, and environmental protection.

SWERF: Stands for "sex worker exclusionary radical feminists," referring to feminists who say prostitution oppresses women.

Systems of Oppression: Interlocking societal, economic, moral, and religious values that keep many groups of people down to ensure the power and advantage of a few groups or one group of people. Some systems of oppression in the US and Europe include heterosexism, male supremacy, white supremacy, and the gender binary system.

Temporary Special Measures: This term refers to actions aimed at accelerating de facto equality between women and men that may, in the short term, favor women. Other terms those are often used to refer to such "special measures" in their corrective, compensatory and promotional sense are the terms "affirmative action", "positive action", "positive measures", "reverse discrimination", and "positive discrimination". However, the preferred term within the UN system is temporary special measures.

TERF: The acronym for "trans-exclusionary radical feminists," referring to transphobic feminists.

The CEDAW Convention: (Article 4, paragraph 1) clarifies that "Adoption by States parties of temporary special measures aimed at accelerating de facto equality between men and women shall not be considered discrimination as defined in the present convention, but shall in no way entail as a consequence the maintenance of unequal or separate standards; these measures shall be discontinued when the objectives of equality of opportunity and treatment have been achieved." The concept consists of three parts: Temporary: Such measures should therefore not be deemed necessary forever, even though the meaning of "temporary" may result in the application of such measures for a long period. Temporary special measures must be discontinued when their desired results have been achieved and sustained for a while.

The First Wave of Feminism: Between the late 19th century and the early 20th centuries emerged with the changing scope of global politics and rising urban industrialism. The main goals of this wave were to create more opportunities for women in the public sphere and to gain suffrage.

The Second Wave of Feminism: Took place from the 1960s through the mid-1990s, igniting anti-war movements and the civil rights movements brought on by the growing number of minority groups. The main focus of this movement was to gain just sexuality and reproductive rights, in addition to trying to pass the Equal Rights Amendment to the Constitution, which guarantees social equality regardless of sex.

The Gaze: Asserting dominance by staring at, objectifying, and sexualising those one considers inferior to or merely of use to oneself, transforming them into "other" and objectifying them. In art, the male gaze can be a projection of the artist's fantasy onto a female figure; the white gaze can also be a form of racial intimidation, and the gaze can also be a lesbian or gay projection onto someone so that she/he becomes an object of interest. In the film, the gaze has at least three registers: the eye of the camera registering the POV taken in the film event, the POV of the spectator viewing the film, and that of the characters on the screen gazing at each other.

The Man (or, the boys' club): Vernacular term for male dominance.

The Personal is Political: ***The personal is political***, also termed ***the private is political***, is a political argument used as a rallying slogan of the student movement and second-wave feminism from the late 1960s. It underscored the connections between personal experience and larger social and political structures. In the context of the feminist movement of the 1960s and 1970s, it was a challenge to the nuclear family and family values. The phrase has been repeatedly described as a defining characterisation of second-wave feminism, radical feminism, women's studies, or feminism in general. It differentiated the second-wave feminism of the 1960s and 1970s from the early feminism of the 1920s, which was concerned with achieving the right to vote for white women [*neutrality is disputed*]. The phrase was popularised by the publication of a 1969 essay by feminist Carol Hanisch under the title "The Personal is Political" in 1970, but she disavows authorship of the phrase. According to Kerry Burch, Shulamith Firestone, Robin Morgan, and other feminists who have given credit for originating the phrase have also declined authorship. "Instead," Burch writes, "they cite millions of women in public and private conversations as the phrase's collective authors." Gloria Steinem has likened claiming authorship of the phrase to claiming authorship of "World War II." The phrase figured in women-of-color feminism, such as "A Black Feminist Statement" by the Combahee River Collective, Audre Lorde's essay "The Master's Tools Will Never Dismantle the Master's House", and the anthology *This Bridge Called My Back: Writings by Radical Women of Color*, edited by Gloria E. Anzaldúa and Cherríe Moraga. More broadly, as Kimberlé Williams Crenshaw observes: "This process of recognising as social and systemic what was formerly perceived as isolated and individual has also characterised the identity politics of African Americans, other people of colour, and gays and lesbians, among others."

The Separate Spheres: This is the socially constructed and culturally-perpetuated difference between and man's domain versus a woman's. A man's sphere often consists of going out and getting a job, whereas the woman's sphere is often staying in the house, doing household work, and taking care of the kids. A man's sphere could overlap with a woman's because he had a home life and could still control the woman's sphere. A theory is that the women's sphere of staying in the household came after the Industrial Revolution. In the context of Western feminism, especially US history, 'suffrage' refers to the right to vote and the opportunity to do so with no limitations based on the gender of the individual. With voting rights, also, indirectly comes the capacity to hold public office. In the US, women gained the right to vote, nationally, with the ratification of the 19th amendment in 1920 that prohibited gender-based discrimination in voting practices. However, some states already have laws in practice by then. Notably, women's right to vote was included in international law in 1948 with the Universal Declaration of Human Rights by the U.N.

The Third Wave of Feminism: Focuses on post-modern thinking. Topics like universal womanhood, body image, gender, sexuality, and heteronormativity are applied to the whole of women's roles, not only in today's society but also the historical actions that evolved into women's status today. This status is persistently challenged by this third wave of feminism to help empower women. There are 3 pillars often included in the description of sexual consent, or "the way we let others know what we're up for, be it a good-night kiss or the moments leading up to sex." They are: Knowing exactly what and how much I'm agreeing to, expressing my intent to participate, and deciding freely and voluntarily to participate. To obtain affirmative consent, rather than waiting to say or for a partner to say "no", one gives and seeks an explicit "yes". This can come in the form of a smile, a nod, or a verbal yes, as long as it's unambiguous, enthusiastic, and ongoing. "There's varying language, but the language gets to the core of people having to communicate their affirmation to participate in sexual behaviour," said Denice Labertew of the California Coalition against Sexual Assault." It requires a fundamental shift in how we think about sexual assault. It's requiring us to say women and men should be mutually agreeing and actively participating in sexual behaviour."

Title IX: Protects people from discrimination based on sex in education programmes or activities that receive federal financial assistance.

Tokenism: A policy or practice of attempting to fulfill one's obligations or implement a goal with limited efforts or gestures, especially toward minority groups and women, in ways that give a mere appearance of inclusivity or execution and will not change male-dominated power and/or organisational arrangements. For example, a woman may be given a middle-management position without significant power to make decisions, allowing a company to claim that it does not discriminate against women. (See also **Critical Mass**.).

Tone-Policing: Focusing and critiquing on *how* something is said, ignoring whether or not it's true.

Topfreedom: It is a cultural and political movement seeking changes in laws to allow women to be topless in public places where men are permitted to be barechested, as a form of gender equality. Specifically, the movement seeks the repeal or overturning of laws that restrict a woman's right not to have her chest covered at all times in public. In addition, topfreedom advocates seek to allow nursing mothers to openly breastfeed in public, and women to bathe topless.

Total Fertility Rate (TFR): The average number of children that would be born alive to a woman during her lifetime if the age-specific fertility rates of a given year applied throughout her childbearing years.

Toxic Masculinity: The concept of 'toxic masculinity is used in psychology and gender studies to refer to certain norms of masculine behaviour in North America and Europe that are associated with harm to society and men themselves. Traditional stereotypes of men as socially dominant, along with related traits such as misogyny and homophobia, can be considered "toxic" due to their promotion of violence, including sexual assault and domestic violence. Scholars argue that the socialisation of boys often normalises violence, such as in the saying "boys will be boys" about bullying and aggression. Self-reliance and emotional repression are correlated with increased psychological problems in men such as depression, increased stress, and substance abuse. Toxic masculine traits are characteristic of the unspoken code of behaviour among men in American prisons, where they exist in part as a response to the harsh conditions of prison life. Other traditionally masculine traits such as devotion to work, pride in excelling at sports, and providing for one's family, are not considered to be "toxic". The concept was originally used by authors associated with the mythopoetic men's movement in contrast to a "real" or "deep" masculinity that they say men have lost touch with in modern society.

Traditions: Inherited, established, or customary patterns of thought, action, or behaviour. Some traditions and customs, such as polygamy, are embraced by women and men in one society but might be rejected by them in another. Some traditions and customs accord women status and power, such as healers. But other traditional practices, such as dowry deaths and female genital mutilation, reinforce an unequal and subservient position for women and girls in society and/or violate women's rights. (See also **Dowry**; **Female Genital Mutilation**; **Gender-Based**)

Trafficking in Persons: It was only in November 2000 that an international definition of trafficking was agreed to, under the Protocol to Prevent, Suppress and Punish Trafficking in Persons, Especially Women and Children (Trafficking Protocol), supplementing the United Nations Convention Against Transnational Organised Crime, 2000 (also known as the Palermo Convention): (a) "Trafficking in persons" shall mean the recruitment, transportation, transfer, harbouring or receipt of persons, utilizing the threat or use of force or other forms of coercion, of abduction, of fraud, of deception, of the abuse of power or a position of vulnerability or the giving or receiving of payments or benefits to achieve the consent of a person having control over another person, for exploitation. Exploitation shall include, at the minimum, the exploitation of the prostitution of others or other forms of sexual exploitation, forced labour or services, slavery or practices similar to slavery, servitude, or the removal of organs; (b) The consent of a victim of trafficking in persons to the intended exploitation outlined in subparagraph; (a) of this article shall be irrelevant where any of the means outlined in subparagraph (a) have been used; (c) The recruitment, transportation, transfer, harbouring or receipt of a child for exploitation shall be considered "trafficking in persons" even if this does not involve any of means outlined in subparagraph (a) of this article; (d) "Child" shall mean any person under eighteen years of age. The key features of the United Nations Protocol to Prevent, Suppress and Punish Trafficking in Persons, Especially Women and Children -Defines trafficking as a crime against humanity, marked by the intent to deceive and exploit; -Expands the range of actions considered part of the trafficking process – recruitment, transportation, transfer, harbouring and receipt of persons in end-institutions; -Addresses a wide range of means used, from blatant force to subtle inducements that capitalise on vulnerability, to achieve "consent"; -Makes "consent" to the intended exploitation irrelevant, where any of the means outlined in the definition are used; -Acknowledges men are also trafficked, though it emphasises trafficking in women and children; -Recognises a range of purposes of trafficking, in addition to sexual exploitation; -Contains rights-based and protective social, economic, political and legal measures to prevent trafficking, protect, assist, return and reintegrate trafficked persons, and to penalise trafficking and related conduct; and -Calls for international cooperation to prevent and combat trafficking. (See also **Human Smuggling**.).

Trans Activism: Refers to movements that reject the binary gender norm and demand that nobody should be forced to adjust any aspect of their life to it. Transfeminism originated from and is currently intertwined with, trans activism. Transfeminism is a tradition of ideas that includes trans persons and trans experiences in the analysis and challenges the notions about gender and gender affiliation that are essential to feminism. The participation of trans persons and transfeminism in feminist domains has historically been met with resistance or negligence, something that is still occurring yet to a less extent.

Trans Female/Woman: A male-to-female transition (MTF). [The medical literature tends to use the extremely demeaning term "male transsexual" to mean the same thing. Note that you can tell the preferred form is in use when the gender word comes after the "T" word.].

Trans Feminine: An umbrella term for people who were assigned male at birth, but who identify as Trans and whose gender expression leans towards the feminine.

Trans Inclusivity: The inclusion of transgender women in feminist discussions and safe spaces.

Trans Man/Male: A female-to-male transition (FTM). [The medical literature tends to use the extremely demeaning term "female transsexual" to mean the same thing. Note that you can tell the preferred form is in use when the gender word comes after the "T" word.].

Trans Masculine: An umbrella term for people who were assigned female at birth, but who identify as trans and whose gender expression leans towards the masculine.

Trans Woman: A woman who was assigned male at birth.

Trans/Transgender: An umbrella term for people whose gender identity and/or gender expression differs from the sociocultural expectations of the sex they were assigned at birth. Trans people may or may not choose to alter their bodies hormonally and/or surgically.

Trans-Exclusionary Radical Feminism: Radical feminism excludes transgender women and does not see them as real women. Adherents are referred to as TERFs.

Transfeminism: Defined as "a movement by and for trans women who view their liberation to be intrinsically linked to the liberation of all women and beyond." It's a form of feminism that includes all self-identified women, regardless of assigned sex, and challenges cisgender privilege. A central tenet is that individuals have the right to define who they are.

Transformational Leadership: Transformational leadership enhances the motivation, morale, and performance of followers through a variety of mechanisms. These include connecting the follower's sense of identity and self to the project and the collective identity of the organisation; being a role model for followers that inspires them and makes them interested; challenging followers to take greater ownership for their work, and understanding the strengths and weaknesses of followers, so the leader can align followers with tasks that enhance their performance. Unlike traditional forms of "transactional leadership," transformational leadership is not based on a "give and take" relationship, but on the leader's personality, traits, and ability to make a change through example, articulation of an energising vision, and challenging goals. Transforming leaders are idealised in the sense that they are the amoral exemplar of working towards the benefit of the team, organisation, and/or community.

Transformatory Potential: A gender analysis guided by this approach, applying the analytical framework to development programming, uses the interwoven framework of concepts to assess the transformative potential of a given set of options — which ones are most likely to ensure women get equal access to the resources they need to maximise their productive and reproductive contributions to their households and societies. (See also **Gender Analysis**).

Transgender Person: A person whose self-identification challenges traditional notions of gender and sexuality. Transgender people include transsexuals and others who do not conform to traditional understandings of labels like male and female or heterosexual and homosexual. (Griffin and Harro, 1997)

Transgender: A person whose behaviour, thoughts, or traits differ from society's expectations for his or her sex. Transgenders include cross-dressers, transsexuals (people who physically switch sexes, usually through surgery, and undergo sex reassignment therapy), intersexed individuals, people whose external genitalia or internal reproductive systems fall outside the norms for either male or female bodies, gay men, lesbians, and bisexuals. Terms such as 'gay' and 'homosexual' are often applied to transgenders, but these may not be accurate because more than sexual orientation is involved. Transgenders include men who behave like women, in the clothes they wear and body stores for instance, but who also remain distinct as a 'third sex' category. Transgenders have an entirely distinct lifestyle, neither male nor female, and do not conform to social norms for typical men and women. (See also **Gender Identity; Sexual Identity; Sexual Orientation**.).

Transgenderist: A person who lives either full time or most of the time, in a gender role different than the role associated with their biological or chromosomal sex (a gender nonconformist).

Transition: A complicated, multi-step process that can take years as a transgender person aligns their physical body and/or outward social perception with how they experience their gender identity. This process could include anything from making preferred pronouns known, to hormone replacement therapy, to surgical gender confirmation procedures. Transitioning looks different for every individual; there is no single or correct way to do it. Additionally, the steps one chooses to take or not take do not determine the legitimacy of their gender identity and this process may ultimately include sex reassignment surgery (SRS).

Transmisogyny: A blend of transphobia and misogyny, which manifests as discrimination against "trans women and trans and gender non-conforming people on the feminine end of the gender spectrum."

Transnational Feminism: Examines issues from a global perspective including intersections of oppression across nationalities. Different from Western feminism which emphasizes commonalities and universalism, transnational feminism recognizes inequalities and differences. It's a series of feminisms rather than a uniform movement; see Western privilege.

Transphobia: (1) Discrimination, fear, or hatred of people who blur traditional gender lines that result from the gender/sex binary system. (2) Fear or hatred of transgender people; transphobia can manifest in several ways, including violence, harassment, discrimination, or erasure. Although transphobia is a widely used term to describe the individual or cultural mistreatment of trans and-or gender-nonconforming individuals, it is argued by some to be ableist (marginalising those who experience or are impacted by disability, and expressing the privilege that comes with being able-bodied) because it is using "phobia," a serious and recognised mental health condition, carelessly, incorrectly, and insensitively. People who say and do transphobic things are not doing so out of the presence of a real medical condition, but because they are socialised to hate and fear trans identities.

Transsexual: (outdated) A transgender person who has undergone sexual reassignment surgery and done all the "medical things" (surgery, hormones, etc.), to align their body fully with the gender they identify as. Outdated because it disregards and delegitimizes the identities and experiences of those who choose to identify as transgender and outside the gender binary, and enforces the binary gender options (male and female, man and woman) as the only options.

Transsexual: A term that refers to individuals who may not identify with the sex they were assigned at birth; may identify as genderqueer, transgender, agender, or gender non-conforming.

Transsexuality: May be defined as a variant gender identity in which there is an incongruity between a person's external genitalia and his or her psychological sense of gender. Transsexuals are sometimes defined as individuals who seek to undergo (or have undergone) the transition from their birth sex to that of the opposite sex, usually using gender reassignment therapy or surgery.

Transvestite/Cross Dresser: Individuals who regularly or occasionally wear the clothing socially assigned to a gender not their own, but are usually comfortable with their anatomy and do not wish to change it (i.e. they are not transsexuals). Cross-dresser is the preferred term for men who enjoy or prefer women's clothing and social roles. Contrary to popular belief, the overwhelming majorities of male cross-dressers identifies as straight and often are married. Very few women call themselves cross-dressers. (See also **Sexual Identity; Sexual Orientation**)

Triangle: A symbol of remembrance. Gay men in the Nazi concentration camps were forced to wear the pink triangle as a designation of being homosexual. Women who did not conform to social roles were often believed to be lesbians had to wear the black triangle. The triangles are worn today as symbols of freedom, reminding us to never forget.

Trigger Warnings: A trigger warning does not promise to protect readers from potentially triggering material but provides them with the opportunity to decide whether they need to *protect themselves*. We provide trigger warnings because they give survivors of various stripes the option to assess whether they're in a state of mind to deal with triggering material before they stumble across it.

Trigger: Anything that causes someone to relive a traumatic experience.

Triple Oppression: The early 20th-century theory that three main oppressions faced by black women - racism, sexism, and classism - are connected and must be overcome simultaneously. Also considered as a precursor to intersectionality. Various groups, most notably the feminist movement, have led efforts to change aspects of prevailing gender roles that they believe are oppressive or inaccurate. The term *gender role* was first coined by John Money in 1955, during his study of intersex individuals, to describe the manners in which these individuals expressed their status as a male or female in a situation where no clear biological assignment existed.

Triple Role/ Multiple Burden: These terms refer to the fact that women tend to work longer and more fragmented days than men as they are usually involved in three different gender roles — reproductive, productive, and community work.

Two-Spirit: A holistic term used by some Indigenous communities to encompass sexual, gender, cultural, and/or spiritual identities, including non-heterosexual and non-cisgender identities.

UN System-Wide Action Plan (UN SWAP): The UN-SWAP (UN System-wide Action Plan) is a UN system-wide framework to enhance accountability and measure progress towards the achievement of gender equality and the empowerment of women in the work of the United Nations entities. It is a unified framework that applies equally to all entities, departments, offices and funds, and programmes of the United Nations system. The UN-SWAP includes a set of 15 system-wide performance indicators that establish a common understanding of what it means to achieve gender equality and the empowerment of women and a common method to work towards it. The UN-SWAP also establishes a progressive sliding scale of standards, including the minimum, to which UN system entities are to adhere and aspire to in their work on gender equality and the empowerment of women at the corporate level.

UN Women: In July 2010, the United Nations General Assembly created UN Women, the United Nations Entity for Gender Equality and the Empowerment of Women. In doing so, UN Member States took a historic step in accelerating the Organisation's goals on gender equality and the empowerment of women. The creation of UN Women came about as part of the UN reform agenda, bringing together resources and mandates for greater impact. It merges and builds on the important work of four previously distinct parts of the UN system, which focused exclusively on gender equality and women's empowerment.

Universal Declaration of Human Rights: The Universal Declaration of Human Rights (UDHR) is a milestone document in the history of human rights. Drafted by representatives with different legal and cultural backgrounds from all regions of the world, the Declaration was proclaimed by the United Nations General Assembly in Paris on 10 December 1948 General Assembly resolution 217 A (III) as a common standard of achievements for all peoples and all nations. It sets out, for the first time, fundamental human rights to be universally protected.

Unpaid Care Work: The term unpaid care work encompasses all the daily activities that sustain our lives and health, such as housework (food preparation, cleaning, and laundry) and personal care (especially of children, the elderly, people who are sick or have a disability). These activities are most commonly performed by women in the household for free. According to the United Nations Millennium Campaign to halve world poverty by the

the year 2015, the overwhelming majority of the work that sustains daily life – growing food, cooking, raising children, caring for the elderly, maintaining a house, hauling water – is performed by women, and this work is universally accorded low status and little or no pay. The little social and economic value assigned to this work contrasts sharply with its actual importance to families and society at large. Feminist economists have shown that care is the invisible base of the socio-economic system. However, because care work is considered "women's work" it is mostly unpaid; because it is not assigned a monetary value, it is not measured; because it is not visible, it is not taken into account in policymaking (Orozco, 2010). The Rio+20 Outcome Document recognizes for the first time that unpaid care work contributes substantially to human well-being and sustainable development but poses a disproportionate burden on women and girls (par 153). Unpaid care work supports the market sector by lowering the cost that employers must sustain to maintain employees and their families. It also supports the public sector by offering health services, sanitation, water, and childcare when a public provision of such services is lacking or insufficient.

Unpaid Labor: Refers to time spent on productive activities in which the individual does not receive payment. This category predominantly refers to household maintenance and care work, including care for children, disabled and elderly persons.

Unprotected Sex: Any sexual behaviour that has a degree of risk because partners are not using protection against either pregnancy or STDs. At present, condom use is the only method that can protect these two. (See also **Condom; Safe Sex; Unsafe Sex**.).

Unsafe Abortions: Procedures for terminating a pregnancy performed either by persons lacking the necessary skills or in an environment lacking the basic medical and standard sanitary conditions, or both. A quarter of women worldwide live in countries where there is no access to legal abortion. In countries where abortion is legal, women may not be able to obtain the necessary bureaucratic permission. In these circumstances, women frequently resort to unsafe abortion, which exposes them to an increased risk of mortality or morbidity. (See also **Abortion**.).

Unsafe Sex: Any sexual behaviour that poses risks of transmission of STDs, including HIV and AIDS. There are different levels of risky behaviours, categorised from low to high. Moderate-risk sexual activities include oral-anal contact, oral sex without a condom, sex with multiple partners, and sharing sex toys. High-risk sexual activities include anal and vaginal intercourse without a condom when not in a long-term relationship in which both partners are free from STDs, do not have any other sexual partners, and do not share intravenous drug equipment with others. (See also safe sex.).

Unwanted Sex: Any forced sexual behaviour with an individual without his or her consent. It may also refer to sexual contact in which one of the partners feels obliged to satisfy the other even without overt coercion to do so. (See also **sexual assault**; **sexual violence**) People whose birth sex is female are "socialised" as women although they may or may not.

Verbal Violence: Verbal abuse can include put-downs in private or in front of others, ridiculing, the use of swear words that are especially uncomfortable for the other, threatening with other forms of violence against the victim or somebody or something dear to them. In another sense, verbal abuse is related to the background of the victim, insulting or threatening her based on religion, culture, language, (perceived) sexual orientation, or traditions.

Victim Blaming: 'Victim-blaming' exists to a certain degree with all forms of violence. In order not to question the safety of the world around us when we hear of a violent incident, we may examine the behaviour of the victim and assure ourselves that if we avoid such risks and behaviour (e.g. being out late alone, venturing into certain areas, leaving our door unlocked, dressing in a 'provocative' way) we will avoid violence. This natural act of psychological self-defense, however, focuses our attention on the perceived responsibility of the victim and may neglect to fully question the conduct of the perpetrator. By shifting the blame to the victim in gender-based violence, the focus is on the victim, often a woman, and her behaviour, rather than on the structural causes and inequalities underlying the violence perpetrated against her.

Violence (Domestic): A pattern of abusive and threatening behaviours that may include physical, emotional, economic, and sexual violence as well as intimidation, isolation, and coercion. The purpose of domestic violence is to establish and exert power and control over another; men most often use it against their intimate partners, such as current or former spouses, girlfriends, or dating partners. Forms of domestic violence can include physical violence, sexual violence, economic control, and psychological assault (including threats of violence and physical harm, attacks against property or pets and other acts of intimidation, emotional abuse, isolation, and use of the children as a means of control). Because they occur in intimate relationships, many kinds of abuse are often not recognized as violence. In many places throughout the world, marital rape is still not viewed as sexual assault, because a husband is deemed to have a right to sexual access to his wife. Stalking, as well, has only recently been recognised as a form of violence and a severe threat to the victim.

Violence Against Women (VAW): Article 1 of the UN Declaration on the Elimination of Violence against Women, proclaimed by the UN General Assembly in its resolution 48/104 of 20 December 1993, defines the term "violence against women" as "Any act of gender-based violence that results in, or is likely to result in physical, sexual or psychological harm or suffering to women, including threats of such acts, coercion, or arbitrary deprivation of liberty, whether occurring in public or in private life. Three contexts of violence are differentiated in Article 2: Family, community, and state. The forms shall be understood to encompass, but not be limited to, the following:(a) Physical, sexual and psychological violence occurring in the family: wife-battering, sexual abuse of female children in the household, dowry-related violence, marital rape, and female genital mutilation and other traditional practices harmful to women, non-spousal violence and violence related to exploitation. (b) Physical, sexual, and psychological violence occurring within the general community: rape, sexual abuse, sexual harassment, and intimidation at work and education institutions, trafficking in women, and forced prostitution. (c) Physical, sexual, and psychological violence perpetrated or condoned by the State, wherever it occurs. (See also,

Wage Gap: The difference (disparity) among the amounts of money paid to women and men, often for doing the same work.

Waves of Feminism: Some feminist scholars are moving away from "waves" since it can give the appearance that feminists aren't always actively fighting inequality.

Welfare: This is a term used in a very special way concerning the Women's Equality and Empowerment framework, to refer to the gender gap between women and men in their material well-being. Like the other levels of the Framework, it is an analytic category, so that the "higher" levels of empowerment are by definition excluded. If a project were confined entirely to this welfare level, this would mean that women would be passive recipients of project benefits, since they are not involved in the higher levels of empowerment which denote more active roles in the development process. Although lacking in any degree of empowerment, the welfare level is arguably the most important, since narrowing the gender gap in welfare is the ultimate objective in women's development, to which the process of empowerment must lead.

Wellbeing: The state of being healthy, fulfilled, and thriving. Activism, particularly in risky environments, can put our well-being at risk, and many of us carry out our work at huge personal costs. The personal risks that women face in their homes, communities, and organisations for being empowered and speaking out can be formidable, causing them to withdraw from political roles and involvement so they can avoid stigmatisation and loss of connection to families and other loved ones. Wellbeing becomes an even more critical political issue as economic instability and poverty among women focus their energies on their families' survival. To be sustainable over the long term, feminist organising and social and political change efforts need to acknowledge the importance of the impact of the current moment in which we live on women's bodies and health and incorporate self-care and other opportunities to refresh energies, imagination, and hope. In a broader development context, many feminists and activists argue that the well-being of a population, in terms of access to the various dimensions of quality of life indicators (which includes sustainability), should be the main goal of development rather than economic growth. This perspective serves as one of the bases for calling for an alternative paradigm of development.

Whimpster: Lloyd Dobler in *Say Anything...* A white, wimpy, emo guy who uses his male insecurity to prey on women who want to nurture.

White Feminism: A set of beliefs that allows for the exclusion of issues that specifically affect women of colour; a "one size fits all" feminism, where middle-class white women are the mold that others must fit.

White Privilege: A phrase coined by Peggy McIntosh (1988) to describe "an invisible package of unearned assets" (p.1) advantages that white people possess or are immune to based on skin colour. White privilege reinforces, often unconsciously, hierarchical systems of power and oppression.

Whiteness: Whiteness as a theoretical concept is central within the discipline of critical whiteness studies. It refers for example to whiteness as a norm and ideology with a basis in theories concerning racial affiliation. Thus, the expression 'white' has to do with not only a person's skin colour as it can also be understood as a globally structuring norm that implies that 'being white' brings social, economic, and political benefits. Whiteness or having light-coloured skin becomes a status marker that relates to a normative and hierarchically superior position. This position shows how racialisation processes in societies lead to the development of systems for privileges and superordination. Problematisation of how whiteness is often understood as an 'invisible norm' is central in critical whiteness studies. Similar to other normative positions, whiteness is invisible in particular to those who are positioned within the realms of the norm, i.e. those who are 'white'. Describing whiteness as invisible can be understood as an expression of a whiteness norm in society since this norm is often highly visible to non-whites.

Whitesplaining: The paternalistic lecture given by Whites toward a person of colour defining what should and shouldn't be considered racist, while obliviously exhibiting their racism.

White-Supremacist, Capitalist Patriarchy: Refers to an intersectional matrix of domination that oppresses people based on race, class, and gender.

WID (Women in Development): It is an approach developed in the early 1970s as a reaction to women having been left out of the development process. WID evolved from a (primarily) North American liberal feminist framework and was also heavily influenced by the work of women researching development, such as Esther Boserup (Women's Role in Economic Development, 1970). WID gave primacy to women's productive roles and stressed the integration of women into the market economy, as it was based on the premise that women's subordination was directly linked to their exclusion from the formal marketplace. Early WID approaches focused on "women in isolation" and took on mostly women-based projects and research, for example, regarding women's economic contribution and women's contribution to agricultural productivity. The most common incarnations of WID policy were the anti-poverty and the efficiency approaches, which viewed women's participation in development as necessary only insofar as their participation in the market was required for the rapid economic growth sought by development agencies and international monetary institutions.

Wiki gender: A global online collaborative platform linking policymakers and experts from both developed and developing countries to find solutions to advance gender equality. It provides a centralised space for knowledge exchange on key emerging issues, with a strong focus on the Sustainable Development Goals (SDGs), and in particular on SDG 5 (Achieving gender equality and empowering all women and girls). Both English and French speakers worldwide can discuss current issues, relevant research, and emerging trends on gender equality.

Wittigian: Relating to French feminist author Monique Wittig (1935-2003).

Woke Misogynist: Nona Willis Aronowitz paints an all-too-familiar picture of the guy who acts like he's all about gender equality, but then turns around and demeans, degrades, and harasses women. His misogyny may not always be overt, but it's there. He's a feminist poser.

Woke: Educated and aware of social justice issues.

Wollstonecraftian: Relating to English protofeminist author Mary Wollstonecraft (1759-1797).

Woman: A woman is a female human being. The word 'woman' is usually reserved for an adult, with a girl being the usual term for a female child or adolescent. The plural women are also sometimes used for female humans, regardless of age, as in phrases such as "women's rights". Women with typical genetic development are usually capable of giving birth from puberty until menopause. There are also Trans women (those who have a male sex assignment that does not align with their gender identity), and intersex women (those born with sexual characteristics that do not fit typical notions of male or female).

Womanism: A social and ecological change perspective that emerged out of Africana women's culture and women of colour around the world.

Women of Colour Feminism: A form of feminism that seeks to clarify and combat the unique struggle women of colour face. It's a feminism that struggles against intersecting forms of oppression.

Women of Colour: A political term to unite women from marginalised communities of colour who have experienced oppression. It could include women of African, Asian, Latin, or Native American descent.

Women's Economic Empowerment: Gender equality in the economy refers to the full and equal enjoyment by women and men of their economic rights and entitlements facilitated by enabling policy and institutional environments and economic empowerment. Economic empowerment is a cornerstone of gender equality that refers both to the ability to succeed and advance economically and to the power to make and act on economic decisions. Empowering women economically is a right that is essential for both realising gender equality and achieving broader development goals such as economic growth, poverty reduction, and improvements in health, education, and social well-being.

Women's Human Rights: The Universal Declaration of Human Rights adopted by the United Nations General Assembly in 1948 outlines what is considered in this century to be the fundamental consensus on the human rights of all people to matters such as security of person, slavery, torture, protection of the law, freedom of movement and speech, religion, and assembly, and rights to social security, work, health, education, culture, and citizenship. The human rights delineated by the Universal Declaration are to be understood as applying to women. However, tradition, prejudice, social, economic, and political interests have combined to exclude women from prevailing definitions of "general" human rights in practice and to relegate women to secondary and/or "special interest" status within human rights considerations. During the United Nations Decade for Women (1976-1985), women from many geographical, racial, religious, cultural, and class backgrounds took up organising to improve the status of women. The United Nations-sponsored women's conferences, which took place in Mexico City in 1975, Copenhagen in 1980, and Nairobi in 1985, convened and took up the first steps to evaluate the status of women and to formulate strategies for women's advancement. In 1979, the UN General Assembly adopted the Convention on the Elimination of All Forms of Discrimination Against Women (CEDAW), which is often described as an international bill of rights for women. Consisting of a preamble and 30 articles, it defines what constitutes discrimination against women and sets up an agenda for national action to end such discrimination. Following this historic breakthrough, women in many diverse countries worked to get CEDAW ratified by their countries and began developing analytic, political, and legal tools for enforcement. The Vienna Conference on Human Rights in 1993 finally recognised women's rights as integral and indivisible from all human rights and launched a process for developing legal alternatives for enforcement, including the Optional Protocol for the CEDAW, which enables women to take their country to court for failure to enforce CEDAW. Today, women's movements continue to use the human rights system and frameworks to push their governments to recognise and enforce their basic rights.

Women's Political Participation: Women's political participation refers to women's ability to participate equally with men, at all levels, and in all aspects of political life and decision-making. Women's participation and access to formal political power structures vary across countries. There is a steady upward trend in women's political participation and representation in developed countries, particularly in Nordic countries. Out of twelve countries where women's representation in parliament is more than 33%, nine of them are ranked in the high human development category.

However, the improvements in medium and low human development countries are not significant. The structural and functional constraints faced by women are shaped by social and political relations in a society. The common pattern of women's political exclusion stems from (a) social and political discourses, (b) political structures and institutions, and (c) the socio-cultural and functional constraints that put limits on women's individual and collective agency.

Women's Studies: "Women's Studies are not simply the study of women," the Hunter College Women's Studies Collective explained, "It is the study of women which places women's own experiences in the center of the process. It examines the world and the human beings who inhabit it with questions, analyses, and theories built directly on women's experiences." As an academic field, women's studies developed alongside not only the women's liberation movement but the civil rights, antiwar, and student movements of the late 1960s. The emerging interdisciplinary field, therefore, gathered young faculty and graduate students who viewed scholarly work as incontestably political and anti-establishment. Although the field soon widened to encompass many perspectives, its pioneering scholars represented the radical sector of the academy. By 1970 women's studies courses, mainly in the liberal arts, were taught on college campuses, and within a few years, the numbers grew at such a rate that the first undergraduate majors were established. By the decade's end, programs in women's studies totaled approximately 350. Specialised journals appeared, such as Feminist Studies, Women's Studies, Signs, Frontiers, and the Women's Studies Newsletter. The National Women's Studies Association was formed in 1977, and by the early 1980s, its annual meetings drew between 1,000 and 2,000 participants. The major professional organisations, such as the American Psychological Association, Modern Languages Association, and American Historical Association, housed feminist or women's caucuses by the mid-1980s. Although feminist scholars began in the late 1960s by criticising the male bias of contemporary disciplinary literature, a sizable sector turned to study the origins and nature of women's oppression and asked questions concerning women's historical agency. Drawing on older works, such as Simone de Beauvoir's *The Second Sex* (1949), Mary Ritter Beard's *Woman as Force in History* (1946), or Friedrich Engels's *The Origin of the Family, Private Property, and the State* (1884), they came upon an earlier scholarly tradition influenced by historical materialism. Feminist anthropologists, sociologists, and historians, in particular, centered their initial analyses on the sexual division of labour in its specific cultural and historic forms as a guide to understanding the status of women and the relations between the sexes. A groundbreaking contribution was Margaret Benston's essay "The Political Economy of Women's Liberation," which appeared in Monthly Review in 1969. Employing Marxist terminology, Benston analyzed women's oppression as a function of their particular place in capitalist production, namely their assignment to the production of use-value in the home. Because the value of domestic work remains unrecognised in a capitalist economy, she argued, women carry the stigma of their distance from commodity production. Although Benston's specific analysis suffered a series of criticisms, her demonstration of the connections between women, the family, and the larger society inspired other scholars to make the study of political economy an important facet of their work. This framework stood out in the early scholarship in the field of anthropology and especially so in the work of Michelle Rosaldo. Although Rosaldo discarded Engels's dictum that women's subordination occurred only with the institution of private property in favor of a theory of universal female subordination, she nevertheless took a materialist approach. Rosaldo studied social and cultural organisation as a function of the sexual division of labour and reasoned that women's reproductive function and responsibility led to a "differentiation of domestic and public spheres of activity." Women's oppression and agency depended, in Rosaldo's analysis, on the degree of "sexual asymmetry." The concept of distinct "spheres," structural divisions by private and public, showed itself prominently in early feminist scholarship in the field of history. In the influential essay "The Social Relations of the Sexes: Methodological Implications of Women's History," published in 1976, Joan Kelly (1928-82) speculated that when the differentiation between family and society was minimal, women's status more nearly approximated that of men; when there was a sharp break between the private and public spheres, sexual inequality increased. The historical scholarship of the early 1970s incorporated this line of argument, which generated, in turn, a major subfield, women's labour history. Shop-floor studies in trades with high rates of female participation, analyses of women's role in specific strikes and unions, and a new perspective on the significance of women's domestic labour, all highlighted a challenge made by women scholars to traditional as well as Left labour historiography. Feminist scholars, Rosaldo and Kelly among the most articulate, did not, however, simply transpose the materially determinist frameworks of earlier generations onto their work. They insisted that sex, class, and race were co-equally integral and interactive concepts. Outside the social sciences, the influence of the Left has been more circuitous. Feminist literary criticism began in the late 1960s by criticising the canon for its virtual exclusion of women writers and exposing the misogynist handling of female characters by male authors. Scholars proceeded to uncover a lost tradition of women writers, the Feminist Press under Florence Howe's leadership in the 1970s playing the leading role in reprinting primary sources. By the mid-1980s an entirely different approach had taken over the field. In a loose combination of Marxism, psychoanalysis, and deconstruction, many scholars proposed new lines of interpretation. The historical materialist approach yielded to theories of representation that highlighted the ambiguity of the text in light of the triumph and subsequent fragmentation of Western thought.

Women-Only Space: A **women-only space** is an area where only women are allowed, thus providing a place where they do not have to interact with men. Historically and globally, many cultures had, and many still have, some form of female seclusion.

Women's Suffrage: The right of women to vote in elections.

Womon; Womyn: An alternative spelling of woman/women, coined to exclude the word "man". Frequently used by TERFs as a euphemism for their views.

Womyn: The word ***womyn*** is one of several alternative spellings of the English word *women* used by some feminists. There are other spellings, including ***womban*** or ***womon*** (singular), and ***wimmin*** (plural). Some writers who use such alternative spellings, avoiding the suffix"-man" or "-men", see them as an expression of female independence and a repudiation of traditions that define women by reference to a male norm. Historically, "womyn" and other spelling variants were associated with regional dialects.

Womyn-Born Womyn (WBW): This is a term developed during second-wave feminism to designate women who were identified as female at birth, were raised as girls, and identify as women (or womyn, a deliberately alternative spelling that challenges the centering of male as a norm). Events and organisations that have womyn-born-womyn-only policies bar access to anyone who was assigned male at birth: male children of attendees, Trans women, gay men, and heterosexual men. These women-only spaces have raised a several concerns from transgender groups.

Womyn's Land: Womyn's land (also called **lesbian land**, **wimmin's land**, **landdyke communities**, or **women's land**) is a term that refers to intentional communities organised by women to empower women. These communities mainly exist in rural areas where land is utilised to establish counter-cultural, women-centered space, often without the presence of males. The first known women's land community in the US was the Sanctificationists, later known as the Woman's Commonwealth, which was established in Texas in the late 1870s to 1880s. In the 1970s, women's land-based communities that explicitly welcomed lesbians were established in the US, Australia, New Zealand, and Western Europe. Many still exist today. Womyn's land-based communities and residents are loosely networked through social media; print publications such as newsletters; Maize: A Lesbian Country Magazine; Lesbian Natural Resources, a not-for-profit organisation that offers grants and resources; and regional and local gatherings to form a social movement variously called the lesbian land movement, womyn's land movement, and/or landdyke movement. Some womyn's lands practice lesbian separatism, an idea that emerged as a result of the Radical Feminist movement in the late 1960s. Lesbian separatism is based on the idea that women must exist separately from men, socially and politically, to achieve a true feminist or lesbian utopia. The radical feminist group Cell 16 is often credited for establishing the base of ideas that define lesbian separatism. These separatist communities exist as a way for women to achieve female liberation by separating themselves from a mainstream patriarchal society. Men are not allowed to live in or enter these communities. Some communities ban male infants and/or male relatives. Womyn's lands, as well as lesbian separatism, have generated a wide range of criticisms. These criticism center around, but are not limited to, the lack of acceptance by many residents of bisexual and heterosexual women; the exclusion of transgender and transsexual women for not being biological females; ideological conflicts with local communities that include violence and threats of violence targeting residents of womyn's land; and local community concerns about social change, e.g. rising divorce rates and expanded lesbian visibility. Examples of present-day womyn's lands include Hawk Hill Community Land Trust, HOWL, Susan B. Anthony Memorial Unrest Home (SUBAMUH) and Sugar Loaf Women's Village. Today, these communities are facing decline as the founders' age, as well as the struggle to connect with younger generations of women.

World Economic Forum's (WEF): India slipped 21 places on the World Economic Forum's (WEF) Global Gender Gap index to 108, behind neighbours China and Bangladesh, primarily due to less participation of women in the economy and low wages. Moreover, India's latest ranking is 10 notches lower than its reading in 2006 when the WEF started measuring the gender gap. According to the WEF Global Gender Gap Report 2017, India has closed 67% of its gender gap, less than many of its international peers, and some of its neighbours like Bangladesh ranked 47th while China was placed at 100th. Globally also, this year's story is a bleak one. For the first time, since the WEF began measuring the gap across four pillars — health, education, the workplace, and political representation — the global gap has widened. "A decade of slow but steady progress on improving parity between the sexes came to a halt in 2017, with the global gender gap widening for the first time since the WEF's Global Gender Gap Report was first published in 2006," it said. The findings in this year's report, published today, showed that an overall 68% of the global gender gap has been closed. This is a slight deterioration from 2016 when the gap closed was 68.3%. At the current rate of progress, the global gender gap will take 100 years to bridge, compared to 83 last year. The case is worse in terms of a workplace gender divide, which the report estimates will take 217 years to close. On a positive note, however, some countries are bucking the dismal global trend as over one-half of all 144 countries measured this year have seen their score improve in the past 12 months, the report noted.

Yes Means Yes: A paradigm shift in the way we look at rape, moving beyond "no means no" toward the contradictory idea that consent must be open.

References

Agarwal, B. (1994), 'Gender and Command over Property: A Critical Gap in Economic Analyses and Policy in South Asia' World Development 22(10): 1455-1478.

Agarwal, B. (1997), 'Bargaining and Gender Relations: Within and Beyond the Household', Feminist Economics 3(1): 1-51

Agarwal, B. (1998), 'A Field of One's Own-Gender and Land Rights in South Asia', UK, New Delhi: Cambridge University Press and Foundation Books.

Alam, M.S. (2011), 'Unequal They Stand: Decision-Making and Gendered Spaces within Family' in S.Raju and K.Lahiri-Dutt (eds), Doing Gender, Doing Geography. New Delhi and Abingdon: Routledge, pp229-247.

Alcoff, Linda. 1989. 'Cultural Feminism versus Post-Structuralism: The Identity Crisis in Feminist Theory.' Pp. 295–325 in Feminist Theory in Practice and Process, ed. Micheline Malson, et al. Chicago, Illinois: University of Chicago Press.

Alesina, P. Giuliano and N. Nunn (2013), 'On the origins of Gender Roles: Women and the Plough'

Amin, H (2010), 'Analysis of Gender Roles in Home Management and Agricultural Development: A Case Study of Faisalabad Tehsil'. Unpublished Thesis, Department of Agricultural Extension University of Agriculture, Faisalabad. Pakistan.

Angela Harris (1990), Race and Essentialism in Feminist Legal Theory, 42 Stan. L. Rev. 581.

Anne Bottomley (1987), Susie Gibson and Belind Meteyard, 'Dwrokin; which Dworkin? Taking Feminism Seriously' 14 Journal of Law and Society 47 .

Bacharch, P and Baratz, M.S. (1970), 'Power and Poverty: Theory and Practice New York': Oxford University Press

Baden, S. and Goetz, A. 'Who needs (sex) when you can have (gender) 2 In: Feminist Review', Vol 56,(Summer), pp 3-25. Routledge, 1997.

Badran, Margot (1996), Feminists, Islam, and nation: gender and the making of modern Egypt, Princeton University Press

Bagchi, D. (1993), 'The Household and Extra-household Work of Rural Women in a Changing Resource Environment in Madhya Pradesh, India,' in S.Raju and D. Bagchi (Eds.) Women and Work in South Asia: Regional Patterns and Perspectives, London, Routledge.

Banerjee, N (1999) 'Can Markets Alter Gender Relations,' Gender, Technology and Development Vol 3 no1,103-122

Barbau., R. (2007) 'Doing Focus Groups', London, Thousand Oaks, New Delhi, Singapore: Sage Publications.

Basu, P. (2006), 'The Gender of Successful Development, ' The International Journal of The Interdisciplinary Social Sciences 1(1): 61-68.

Behura, D. D, Nayak and D, Jena. (1999), 'An Economic Assessment of Role of Women in Traditional Farming Society in Orissa: A Case Study', Indian Journal of Agricultural Economics 54(3): 306.

Benjamin J. (1998). 'The Bonds of Love : Psychoanalysis, Feminism, and the Problem of Domination', 304 pp New York Pantheon Books

Bhuvaneswari and K. Kannan (1999), 'Women in Agriculture and Rural Development', Indian Journal of Agricultural Economics 54(3): 324.

Boochever, A (2011), 'The Influence of Family Structure on Women's Role in Agriculture in Two distinct Societies of South West China.' Independent Study Project (http: //digitalcollections.sit.edu/isp-collection) (ISP) Collection. Paper 1126

Bose M.L, A. Ahmed, M. Hossain (2009), 'The Role of Gender in Economic Activities with Special Reference to women's participation and Empowerment in Rural Bangladesh', Gender, Technology and Development 13(1): 69-102.

Bose M.L, Ahmad, A, Hossain,M (2009), 'Feed the Future: Women's Empowerment in Agriculture Index', Ophi: USAID, International Food Policy Research Institute.

Bose, M.L., Alia Ahmad and Mahabub Hossain, (2009), 'The Role of Gender in Economic Activities with Special Reference to Women's Participation and Empowerment in Rural Bangladesh,' Gender, Technology and Development 13(1): 69-102.

Boserup (2007), 'Woman's Role in Economic Development with New Introduction' by N. Kanji, Su Fei Tan, Camilla Toulmin, London: Earth scan.

Bossen, L (2002), 'Chinese Women and Rural Development: Sixty Years of Change in Lu Village,' Yunnan, Lanham MD: Rowman & Littlefield.

Braidotti, R., E. Charkiewicz., S. Häusler., S. Wieringa. (2004), 'Women, the Environment and Sustainable Development', Towards a Theoretical Synthesis, London, New Jersey: Zed Books in association with Instraw.

Bulter J.(1990). 'Gender Trouble: Feminism and the Subversion of Identity'. 172 pp. New York : Routlege, Chapman and Hall.

Burton, M. and K. Reitz (1981), 'The Plow, Female Contribution to Agricultural Subsistence and Polygyny: A Log-Linear Analysis' Behaviour Science Research 16 (4): 272-305.

C.O.N. Moser (1993), 'Gender Planning and Development', Theory, Practice and Training, London and New York: Routledge.

Carranza, E. (2012), 'Soil Endowments, Production Technologies and Missing Women in India' Policy research Working Paper, The World Bank South Asia Region Human Development Unit.

Carrie Menkel-Meadow (1997), 'Portia in a Different Voice: Speculations on Women's Lawyering Process, in: Hilaire Barnett (ed.,) On Feminist Jurisprudence, London: Cavendish Publishing Limited (1997), pp. 194-196.

Castree, N. (2001), 'Socializing Nature: Theory, Practice and Politics,' in Social Nature: Theory, Practice and Politics. UK: Blackwell Publishers Co.

Catherine A. MacKinnon, 'Difference and Dominance: On Sex discrimination' in: Feminism Unmodified: Discourse on Life and Law, Cambridge: Harvard University Press, pp. 32-36, at 45.

Chakravarti, U. (2009), 'Gendering Caste: Through a Feminist Lens.' Calcutta: Stree.

Chatterjee, B. and Ghosh, D.K. (2003), 'Towards a District Development Report for West Bengal,' Kolkata: Centre for Rural Research.

Chodorow N.J.(1989). 'Feminism and Psychoanalytic Theory'. 286 pp. New Haven: Yale University Press.

Chowdhry, P. (2012), 'High Participation, Low Evaluation: Women and Work in Rural Haryana', in P. Swaminathan (ed) Women and Work New Delhi, Orient Blackswan Private Limited and Economis and Political Weekly, pp. 89-118.

Cornwall, A. E. Harrison and A. Whiteheads (2007), (Eds.) 'Feminisms in Development, Context and Challenges', London, Zed Books.

Cropanzano, R and M. S. Mitchell (2005), 'Social Exchange Theory: An Interdisciplinary Review', Journal of Management 31(December), pp. 874-900.

Currie, D. Hand Vernooy, R. (2010), 'Social and Gender Analysis in Development Practice: Lessons from the Field' Gender Technology and Development Vol 14(1): 1-23.

Datar, C (2011). 'Eco feminism Revisited Introduction to the Discourse.' Rawat Publications Jaipur.

De Beauvoir S.(1974). 'The Second Sex'. 814 pp. Trans. & ed. H.M. Parshley. New York: Vintage Books.

Deere, C.D (2005), 'The Feminization of Agriculture? Economic Restructuring in Rural Latin America' (Occassional Paper 1) Geneva: United Nations Research Institute for Social Development.

Del Casino, Jr, V.J (2009), 'Social Geography: A Critical Introduction Malden,' Oxford, Victoria:Wiley Blackwell.

Desai, N. (1996), 'Women's Employment and their Familial Role in India' in Social Structure and Change, Volume 2: Women in Indian Society, New Delhi: Sage Publications, pp. 98-112.

Deshmikh-Ranadive, J. (2002), 'Spaces for Power: Women's Work and Family strategies in South and South-EastAsia' Noida, Delhi, Ahmedabad: Rainbow Publishers in collaboration with Centre for Women's Development Studies.

Deskmukh-Ranadive, J. (2002), 'Space for Power Women's Work and Family Strategies in South and South-East Asia,' New Delhi: Rainbow Publishers in collaboration with Centre for Women's Development Studies.

Dinnerstein D. (1976). 'The Mermaid and the Minotaur: Sexual Arrangements and Human' Malise. 288 pp. New York: Harper and Row.

Dolan, C. and Sorby, K. (2003), 'Gender and Employment in High Value Agriculture industries'. (Agriculture and Rural Development Working Paper 7) Washington DC, World Bank.

Domosh, M. and J. Seager. (2007), 'Women at Work' in, The Introductory Reader in Human Geography: Contemporary Debates and Classic Writings. Malden, Oxford, Victoria: Blackwell Publishing Ltd.

Dyck, I. (2011), 'Embodied Life' in A Comparison to Social Geography. Oxford, West Sussex, Malden, Wiley Blackwell. pp. 346-361.

El-Bushra, J (2000), 'Rethinking gender and development practice for the twenty first century'. Gender and Development, 8(1), 55-62.

Elliot, J.A. (2013), 'An Introduction to Sustainable Development,' London and New York: Routledge.

Elsh J.B. (1981), 'Public Man , Private Womam: Women in Social and Political Thought'. 378 pp Princeton University Press.

Engels F.(1972). 'The Origin of the Family, Private Property and the State'. 191 pp. New York Pathfinder Press.

Fabiyi, EF. B.B Dauladi, K E Akande and Y Mahmood(2007). 'Role of Women in Agricultural Development and their constraints:' A Case Study of Biliri Local Government Area, Gaube State.

FAO (2004), 'Rural Households and resources: A guide for extension workers' SEAGA Socio Economic and Gender Analysis Programme Rome: FAO.

FAO. (2013), 'Understanding and Integrating Gender Issues into Livestock Projects and Programmes: A Checklist for Practitioners'. Rome: FAO.

Felny, S. (1993), 'Division of Labour and Women's Work in a Mountain Society: Hunja Valley in Pakistan', in S.Raju and D. Bagchi (Eds.) Women and Work in South Asia: Regional Patterns and Perspectives, London, Routledge.

Foord, J and N. Gregson (1986), 'Patriarchy: Towards a Reconceptualisation,' Antipode 18 (2): 186-211Gender and Equity Strategy: Background proposals for the CGIAR Research Progress on Livestock and Fish.

Friedan, Betty (1963). 'The Feminine Mystique'. New York: Norton.

Geeta, V. (2009), 'Patriarchy', Calcutta, Stree Publishers.

Gibson-Graham J.K (2008), 'Diverse Economies: Performative practices for other worlds', Progress in Human Geography 32 (5): 613-632.

Gilligan, Carol (1982), In a Different Voice: Psychological Theory and Women's Development'. Cambridge, Mass.: Harvard University Press, 1982;

Goodman, Robin Truth (2010). Feminist Theory in Pursuit of the Public: Women and the "Re-Privatization" of Labor. New York: Palgrave Macmillan, 2010.

Grace, J. (2004), 'Gender Roles in Agriculture: Case studies of five villages in northern Afganisthan, Afganisthan Research and Evaluation Unit Case studies series.

Groenhout, Ruth E.(2002), 'Essentialist Challenges to Liberal Feminism.' Social Theory and Practice 28:1 , 51-75;

Hanoi (2004), 'Gender mainstreaming guidelines in national policy formulation and implementation towards gender equality in Vietnam through gender responsive national policy and planning' vie 01-015-01 Project 'Gender in Public Policy' National Committee for the Advancement of Women in Vietnam.

Haslanger, Sally (2002), 'On Being Objective and Being Objectified.' In Louise Antony and Charlotte Witt, eds., A Mind of One's Own: Feminist Essays on Reason and Objectivity. Boulder, Colo.: Westview, 2002, 209-53;

Held, Virginia. 'The Obligations of Mothers and Fathers.' In Mary Vetterling- Braggin, ed., "Femininity," i'Masculinity," and "Androgyny": A Modern Philosophical Discussion.

Hirway, I. (2000), 'Tabulation and Analysis of the Indian Time use Survey Data for improving measurement of pain and Unpaid Work', United Nations Secretariat, Statistics Division, Gender Issues in the Measurement of Paid and Unpaid Work: Expert Group Meeting on Methods for Conducting Time Use Survey.

Huang, Y. (2012), 'From the feminization of agriculture' to the ageing of farming populations': Demographic transition and farming in a central Chinese village', Local Economy 27(1): 19-32.

J Acharya (2003): 'Gendered Spaces: Craftswomen's Stories of Self-Employment in Orissa, India' Dr. Polit Thesis 2003, Department of Geography, Faculty of Social Sciences and Technology Management, Norwegian University of Science and Technology, NTNU Trondheim.

Jackson, S (1998), 'Feminist Social Theory', in S. Jackson and J. Jones, (eds) Contemporary Feminist Theories, New York: New York University Press, pp. 12-33.

Jeckoniah, J.N. Mdoe, C. Nombo (2013), 'Mapping of Gender Roles and Relations along Onion Value Chain in Northern Tanzania', International Journal of Asian Social Science 3(2): 523-541.

Joan Williams (1997), 'Deconstructing Gender, in: Hilaire Barnett (ed) Sourcebook on Feminist Jurisprudence, London: Cavendish Publishing Limited, pp. 268-275.

Joshi, C.K and M.R.Alshi (1985), 'Impact of High Yielding Varieties of Employment Potential of Female Labour. A study in Akola District (Maharashtra)', Indian Journal of Agricultural Economics 40 (3): 230-234.

Kabeer, N. (1994), 'Reversed Realities: Gender Hierarchies in Development Thought.' London: Verso Publications.

Kabeer, N. (1999), 'Resources, Agency Achievements: Reflections on the Measurement of Women's Empowerment', Development and Change 30: 435-464.

Kandiyoti, D. (1988), 'Bargaining with Patriarchy', Gender & Society 2 (3): 274-290.

Kapadia, K. (1995), 'Gender, Caste and Class in Rural South India.' Boulder, Colorado: West view Press.

Katherine A. MacKinnon (1989), 'Consciousness Raising,' in: Toward a Feminist Theory of the State, Cambridge: Harvard University Press , pp. 83-106.

Kimberle Crenshaw (1992), 'Race, Gender and Sexual Harassment,' 65 Cal. L. Rev. 1467. Her critique had practical implications for US antidiscrimination law.

Kimberle Crenshaw, 'Demarginalizing the Intersection of Race and Sex: A Black Feminist Critique of Antidiscrimination Doctrine, Feminist Theory and Antiracist Politics,' 1989 U. of Chi. Legal Forum 139.

Kit Kniports (1991), 'Evidence Engendered,' 1991 U. of Ill. L Rev. 413.

Krolokke, Charlotte; Anne Scott Sorensen (2005). "Three Waves of Feminism: From Suffragettes to Grrls". Gender Communication Theories and Analyses: From Silence to Performance.

Kumwar, D.S (1999), 'Women's Access to and Management of Natural Resources: A Case Study for Kenya', Indian Journal of Agricultural Economics 54(3): 312.

L Bondi, J Davidson. (2007), 'Situating Gender' in L Nelson and J Seager (eds) A Companion to Feminist Geography pp. 15-31.

Lahiri-Dutt, K. (2011), 'Doing Gender' in Geography: Exploring Contemporary Feminist Methodologies in S. Raju and K. Lahiri-Dutt (eds), Doing Gender, Doing Geography: Emerging Research in India. New Delhi, Abingdon:Routledge, pp. 45-83.

Lahiri-Dutt, K. (2012), 'Large dams and changes in an agrarian society: Gendering the impacts of Damodar Valley Corporation in Eastern India', Water Alternatives 5(2): 529-542.

Lastarria-Corntriel, S. (2006), 'Feminization of Agriculture: Trends and Driving Forces', Background Paper for the World Development Report 2008.

Leidner, R. (2006), 'Identity and Work', in M. Korczynski, R. Hodson and P. Edwards (eds), Social Theory at Work, Oxford: Oxford University Press, pp. 424-63.

Leslie Bender (1998), 'A Lawyer's Primer on Feminist Theory and Tort, 38 J. Legal Educ. 3.

Little, J. (2002), 'Gender and Rural Geography: Identity, Sexuality and Power in the Countryside', Essex, Pearson Education Ltd.

Longwe, S.H. (1991), 'Gender Awareness: The Missing Element in the Third World Development Project', in T.Wallace with C. March (eds), Changing Perceptions: Writings on Gender and Development, Oxford: Oxfam.

Marothia, D.K and S.K Sharma (1985), 'Female Labour Participation in Rice Farming System of Chattisgarh Region', Indian Journal of Agricultural Economics 40 (3): 235-237.

Martha Minow (1990), Making all the Difference: Inclusion, Exclusion and American Law. She has argued that differences should be seen relational rather than intrinsic, and that instead of objectivity we should look at different perspectives, especially at perspectives of those mostly affected.

Mazumdar, V. (1978), 'Roles of Rural Women in Development', Report of Seminar held at.

McLafferty S.L. (1995), 'Counting for Women', The Professional Geographer, 47(4): 436-442.

Mead, M. (1949), 'Male and Female: A Study of the sexes in a changing world'. Oxford: William Morrow.

Mehta, M. (1996), 'Our Lives are no different from that of our buffaloes' 'Agricultural change and gendered spaces in a central Himalayan valley' in D. Rocheleau, B. Thomas-Slayter, and E.

Ministry of Women and Child Development National Mission for Empowerment of Women, Available atnmew.gov.in

Momsen, J. (2010), 'Gender and Development'. London and New York: Routledge.

Momsen, J.H. (1999), 'Women and Development in the Third World'. London and New York: Routledge.

Mosedale, S. (2003), 'Towards a framework for assessing empowerment', Paper prepared for the international conference, New Directions in Impact Assessment for Development: Methods and Practice Manchester UK 24 and 25 November 2003.

Moser, C.O.N. (1993), 'Gender Planning and Development: Theory, Practice and Training'. London, New York: Routledge.

Moss, P. and P.J. Moss (2002), 'Feminist Geography in Practice: Research and Methods' OECD Publishing.

NABARD Consultancy Services Pvt Ltd (2012), 'State Agriculture Plan for West Bengal'.

Nayak, D.K and A.Ahmad. (1984), 'Female Participation in Economic Activity: A Geographical Perspective with Special Reference to Rural Areas in India', The Indian Geographical Journal 59(2): 262-267. New Delhi, California, London, Singapore: Sage Publications, pp. 15-31.

Oakley, A. (1972), 'Sex, Gender and Society' London: Mawrice Temple Smith Ltd.

Okali, C. (2012), 'Gender Analysis: Engaging with Rural Development and Agricultural Policy Processes' Working Paper 026, Future Agricultures.

Oorthuizen, J. (2003), 'Water, Works and Wages: The everyday politics of irrigation management reform in the Phillippines'. Wageningen University Water Resources Series. New Delhi, India: Orient Longman.

Ortner, S.B. (1978), 'The Virgin and the State Feminist Studies'. 4(3): 19-35.

Paris, T.R (1998), 'Technology and Policy Needs of Poor Women in Asian Rice Farming', Gender Technology and Development 2(2):187-218.

Patricia A. Cain, 'Feminist Jurisprudence: Grounding the Theories,' 4 Berkley Women's L.J. 191 (1989-90).

Peterman, A., J.Behrmen, A Quisumbing, A. (2010), 'A Review of Empirical Evidence on Gender Differences in Non Land Agricultural Inputs. Technology and Services in Developing Countries', IFPRI Discussion Paper 00975.

Pica-Ciamarra, U. and M.Dhawan. (2009), 'A Rapid Rural Appraisal of the Family based Poultry Distribution Scheme of West Bengal', South Asia Pro Poor Livestock Policy Programme, Document 023.

Sylvia A. Law (1988), 'Homosexuality and the Social Meaning of Gender', Wis. L. Rev 187 at 195.

Taylor, Verta; Rupp, Leila J. (Autumn 1993). "Women's Culture and Lesbian Feminist Activism: A Reconsideration of Cultural Feminism". Signs (The University of Chicago Press)

Totowa, N.J.: Rowman and Littlefield, 1982, 242-58; Illinois Coalition against Sexual Assault. University of Sussex. Bombay: Allied.

Wangari (eds), 'Feminist Political Ecology: Global Issues and Local Experiences'. London and New York: Routledge.

Websites

http://arabstates.undp.org/contents/file/GenderMainstreamingTraining.pdf)

http://depts.drew.edu/wmst/CoreCourses/WMST112/WMST112_Glossary.htm

http://en.wikipedia.org/wiki/Difference_feminism

http://ezinearticles.com/?Definition-of-Feminism&id=1697184

http://feminism.eserver.org/about/overview.html

http://global.finland.fi/julkaisut/taustat/nav_gender/glossary.htm

http://obgyn.ucla.edu/menopause

http://uninstraw.org

http://uninstraw.org

http://www.amnestyusa.org/humanrights/page.do?id=1031002

http://www.awid.org/ywl/glossary/index.php?term=Gender%2FSex%20disaggregated %20data

http://www.chicanas.com/defs.html

http://www.coe.int/t/dghl/monitoring/trafficking/Docs/Convntn/CETS197_en.asp# P99_4163

http://www.cwgl.rutgers.edu/globalcenter/policy/csw01/csw01priority.html

http://www.cwluherstory.com/CWLUArchive/crcwlu.html

http://www.dur.ac.uk/postgraduate.english/ElizabethWrightArticleIssue14.htm

http://www.generoyambiente.org/ES/publicaciones_uicn/equidadi/Mod9i/mod9i.htm

http://www.grcc.edu/womensstudies

http://www.hc-sc.gc.ca/english/women/exploringconcepts.htm

http://www.idrc.ca:8080/biodiversity/tools/gender1_e.cfm ILO

http://www.ifad.org/gender/glossary.htm

http://www.ilo.org/public/libdoc/ILO-Thesaurus/

http://www.ilo.org/public/libdoc/ILOThesaurus/english/tr2698.htm)

http://www.internationaldisabilityalliance.org/CRPD.

http://www.iom.int/jahia/jsp/index.jsp

http://www.ohchr.org/EN/UDHR/Pages/introduction.aspx

http://www.oxfordbibliographies.com/view/document/obo-9780199756384/obo-9780199756384-0138.xml

http://www.peacewomen.org/assets/file/AdvocacyEducationTools/genderglossary_migs_aug2005.pdf

http://www.peacewomen.org/assets/file/AdvocacyEducationTools/genderglossary_migs_aug2005.pdf

http://www.peacewomen.org/assets/file/AdvocacyEducationTools/genderglossary_migs_aug2005.pdf

http://www.siyanda.org/static/bridge_conceptsdefinitions.htm

http://www.siyanda.org/static/bridge_conceptsdefinitions.htm

http://www.siyanda.org/static/bridge_conceptsdefinitions.htm

http://www.un.org/disabilities/documents/convention/convoptprot-e.pdf.

http://www.un.org/documents/ecosoc/docs/1997/e1997-66.htm

http://www.un.org/documents/ga/res/48/a48r104.htm

http://www.uncjin.org/Documents/Conventions/dcatoc/final_documents_2/convention_%20traff_eng.pdf,

http://www.undp.org/gender/docs/GenderAnalysisTrainModule.pdf

http://*www.unfpa.org/icpd/icpd_poa.htm#ch7*

http://www.ungei.org/resources/files/Glossary_of_Gender_Terms_and_Concepts.pdf.

http://www.unwomen.org/en/news/in-focus/csw59/feature-stories.

http://www.who.int/mediacentre/factsheets/fs241/en/

http://*www.who.int/reproductive-health/gender/glossary.html*

http://www.who.int/reproductive-health/gender/glossary.html)

http://www.womenlobby.org/SiteResources/data/MediaArchive/position%20papers/Sexual%20Rights%20position%20paper_EN.pdf

https://data.oecd.org/emp/labour-force.htm

https://en.wikipedia.org/wiki/Boy

https://en.wikipedia.org/wiki/Dowry

https://en.wikipedia.org/wiki/Dowry_death

https://en.wikipedia.org/wiki/Gender_budgeting

https://en.wikipedia.org/wiki/Malnutrition

https://en.wikipedia.org/wiki/Man

https://en.wikipedia.org/wiki/Monogamy

https://en.wikipedia.org/wiki/Old_age

https://en.wikipedia.org/wiki/Polyandry

https://en.wikipedia.org/wiki/Role_conflict

https://en.wikipedia.org/wiki/Sati_(practice)

https://en.wikipedia.org/wiki/Sexism

https://en.wikipedia.org/wiki/Single_person

https://en.wikipedia.org/wiki/Woman

https://grccwomenstudies.files.wordpress.com/2010/09/a-glossary-of-womens-studies-terms.pdf

https://grccwomenstudies.files.wordpress.com/2010/09/a-glossary-of-womens-studies-terms.pdf

https://medlineplus.gov/menstruation.html

https://nashvillefeministcollective.com/resources/glossary-of-feminist-terms/

https://nashvillefeministcollective.com/resources/glossary-of-feminist-terms/

https://pdf.usaid.gov/pdf_docs/Pnadl089.pdf

https://rationalwiki.org/wiki/Feminist_glossary

https://rationalwiki.org/wiki/Feminist_glossary

https://smartsexresource.com/topics/gender-glossary

https://sustainabledevelopment.un.org/topics/genderequalityandwomensempowerment.

https://trainingcentre.unwomen.org/mod/glossary/view.php?id=36

https://trainingcentre.unwomen.org/mod/glossary/view.php?id=36&mode=letter&hook=G&sortkey=&sortorder=&fullsearch=0&page=1

https://trainingcentre.unwomen.org/mod/glossary/view.php?id=36&mode=letter&hook=G&sortkey=&sortorder=&fullsearch=0&page=1

https://trainingcentre.unwomen.org/mod/glossary/view.php?id=36&mode=&hook=ALL&sortkey=&sortorder=&fullsearch=0&page=-1

https://www.britannica.com/topic/standpoint-theory

https://www.cbd.int/gender/decisions/terminology.shtml

https://www.genus.se/en/wordpost/functionality-functional-variation-and-ableism/

https://www.genus.se/en/wordpost/gender/

https://grccwomenstudies.files.wordpress.com/2010/09/a-glossary-of-womens-studies-terms.pdf

https://www.genus.se/en/wordpost/functionality-functional-variation-and-ableism/

https://www.genus.se/en/wordpost/gender/

https://www.marxists.org/glossary/terms/w/o.htm

https://www.google.com/search?ei=uI2cXITsC7Hfz7sP74uE8Ao&q=dowry+&oq=dowry+&gs_l=psy-ab.3..0i67j0l4j0i67j0l4.2033.2033..3464...0.0..0.122.122.0j1......0....1..gws-wiz.......0i71.Ko1AAcN4f7Y

https://www.google.com/search?hl=en-IN&authuser=0&ei=W5-lXMToFYzor-QGHgKjIBg&q=male+domination+definition&oq=male+domination+definition&gs_l=psy-ab.3...3911.20703..21475...0.0..0.1114.12894.0j12j1j2j0j6j6j1....2..0....1..gws-wiz.......0i67j0i131j0i131i67j0j0i70i249j0i10.peVUXhC7lME

https://www.marxists.org/glossary/terms/w/o.htm

https://www.marxists.org/glossary/terms/w/o.htm

https://www.thoughtco.com/matriarchy-3026402

https://www.unicef.org/gender/training/content/resources/Glossary.pdf.

https://www.uvm.edu/wid/writingcenter/tutortips/GSWSPage.pdf

https://www.uvm.edu/wid/writingcenter/tutortips/GSWSPage.pdf

www. ngo.fawco.org

www.glbtq.com

www.ltcconline.net/lukas/gender/pages/exoticsgen.htm

www.nic.in/empwomen.htm.

www.thecommonwealth.org/shared_asp_files/uploadedfiles/{EEEA4F53-90DF-4498-9C58-73F273F1E5EE}_PovertyEradication.pdf)

www.un.org/womenwatch/daw/cedaw

www.wildforhumanrights.org

Index

A

Ableist Language, 17
Abstinence, 17
Academic world, 137
Access, 18
Access and Control Over Resources, 17
Accession, 18
Accountable systems, 47
Activist (for justice), 18
Adolescence, 18
Adolescent Health in All Policies, 18
Adolf Loos, 61
Adoption, 18
Advancement of Women, 44
Advocacy, 18
Affirmative action, 19
Affirmative Consent, 19
African Americans, 164
Ageism, 19
Agency, 19
Agender, 20
AIDS, 20
Alaska, 51
All Forms of Discrimination Against Women, 73
American feminist, 65, 153
American Historical Association, 180
American Psychological Association, 180
Anarcha-Feminism, 20
Androcentric, 20
Androcentrism, 21
Androcracy, 21
Androgen production, 112
Androgynous Mind, 21
Androgyny, 21
Anti-war movements, 163
Antifeminism, 21
Antioppression, 22
Antonio Gramsci, 95
Aromantic, 22
Asex, 22
Asexual, 22
Asexuality, 22
Asian Americans, 92
Assigned Female, 22
Assigned Male, 22
Association of Women's Rights in Development, 59
Atheism Plus, 22
Australia, 183
Australia and Canada, 108
Autonomy, 22
Autonomy in Decision-making, 22

B

Bamboo Ceiling, 22, 92
Bangladesh, 47, 183
Bechdel Test, 22, 110
Beijing, 73
Beijing Conference, 23
Beijing Declaration and Platform for Action, 23
Beijing Platform, 104

Beijing Platform for Action, 38
Benevolent Sexism, 23
Bernie Sanders, 113
Biantagonism, 23
Big capitalists, 119
Binary, 23
Binary assumptions, 39
Binary Thinking, 23
Biological appearance., 155
Biological characteristics, 146
Biological Determinism, 24
Biological Sex, 24, 151
Biphobia, 24
Birth control, 24
Bisexual, 24, 65
Bisexuality, 24
Black Feminism, 24
Black Feminist Statement, 50, 164
Bloomerism, 24
Bodily Autonomy, 24
Body Positivity, 25
Brass Ceiling, 25
Bride burning, 47
British and American, 145
Broflake, 25
Bropriation, 25
Bropropriating, 25
Business ownership, 147
Butlerian, 25

C

Cairo Conference, 105
California, 51
Canada, 112
Capabilities Approach, 25
Capitalism, 26
Capitalist Patriarchy, 177
Carceral Feminism, 26
Care (Informal), 26
Care Economy, 26
Care Work, 27
Career Woman, 27
Carol Gilligan, 84
Caroline Moser, 131
Casual sex, 27
Catholicism, 65
Celibacy, 28
Characteristics, 151
Chemical agent, 34
Chicana Feminism, 28
Chief Executives Board, 104
China, 183
Christian Egalitarianism, 28
Christian feminism, 28
Christian feminists, 29
Christianity, 65
Chromosomes, 151
Cinderella Complex, 29
Circular and Linear Thinking, 29
Circular Thinking, 29
Cisgender, 29
Cissexism, 29
Citizen and Citizenship, 29
Civil society, 30
Civil society actors, 47
Cold War, 100
Colonial ideology, 129
Colorado, 51
Commission on the Status of Women, 31
Commodity Feminism, 31
Common analysis, 118
Common sense, 95
Common vision and agenda, 118
Community Managing Role, 31
Community Organising, 32
Community Politics Role, 32
Community-supported policies, 141
Complementarianism, 32
Complementary research, 154
Compulsory Heterosexuality, 32

Concept and international consecration, 143
Condition and Position, 76
Conflict theories, 33
Congenital condition, 102
Connecticut, 51
Conscientisation, 33
Consciousness Raising, 34
Conservative Feminism, 54
Constituency Building, 34
Consumerism, 34
Contraceptive, 33, 34
Copenhagen, 72, 179
Coretta Scott, 113
Counter narratives, 35
Crimes of Honour, 35
Critical Consciousness, 35
Critical cooperation, 118
Critical mass, 36
Cross Dresser, 171
Cross-dressing, 36
Cult of True Womanhood, 36
Cultural Appropriation, 36
Cultural Capital, 36
Cultural Critic, 36
Cultural feminism, 37
Cultural Hegemony, 37
Cultural prejudice, 119
Culture, 37
Customary Law, 37

D

Dalit movement, 101
Date rape, 37
Dating partners, 174
De Facto Discrimination, 38
De Jure Discrimination, 38
Decent Work, 38
Decision-Making and Participation, 38
Deconstruction, 39
Democracy, 39
Democratic regimes, 60
Derailing, 39
Development agencies, 177
Development Data Base, 86
Development Framework, 117
Development Index, 77
Development Objective, 72
Development process, 97
Development Studies, 146
Dichotomy, 40
Difference Feminism, 40
Differences in legal status, 41
Direct and Indirect, 42
Disability, 41
Disabled, 41
Disadvantaged groups, 41
Disaggregated Data (Sex), 41
Discrimination (Systemic), 43
Discrimination against Girls and Women, 43
Discrimination Against Women, 42, 52, 148, 179
Displaced Women, 43
Division for the Advancement of Women, 44
Domestic responsibilities, 44
Domestic violence, 44, 45, 174
Domestic Work, 45
Domestic Worker, 45
Dominant group, 122
Donald Trump, 113
Dorothy Pitman Hughes, 145
Double Burden, 46
Double Consciousness, 46
Double Day, 46
Double Standard, 46
Dowry deaths, 46
Dowry-related violence, 86
Dworkinian, 47

E

Ecofeminism, 47
Economic activities, 65
Economic Autonomy, 47
Economic control, 174
Economic Democracy, 47
Economic Development, 177
Education and health, 48
Education Fund, 108
Education levels, 147
Educational attainment, 48
Electro-shock, 91
Electronics, 47
Elimination of Violence, 175
Elisabeth Schüssler Fiorenza, 107
Emergency contraception, 48
Emergency contraception pill, 48
Emosogynist, 48
Employing Marxist terminology, 181
Empowerment, 77
Empowerment Feminism, 48
Empowerment of Women, 49, 172
Empowerment of Women and Girls, 48
Engendered Citizenship, 49
English and French speakers, 177
Epistemic Advantage, 49
Epistemology, 50
Equal Opportunities, 53
Equal Pay, 51
Equal relationships, 137
Equal Rights Amendment, 51, 163
Equality, 53
Equality between women and men, 72
Equality of Opportunity, 52
Equality of Outcome, 52
Equity Feminism, 54
Escalating levels, 60
Essentialism, 55
Ethnic and sectarian violence, 100
Eve teasing, 55
Executive Chairman, 94
Exorbitant energy costs, 59
Extractive Industries, 55

F

Family planning, 55
Family planning programmes, 55
Family planning services, 55
Fat feminism, 56
Fat-shaming, 56
Fatphobia, 56
Félix Guattari, 161
Female children, 158
Female dowry deaths, 47
Female feticide, 158
Female Gaze, 56
Female Genital Mutilation, 56, 175
Female genital organs, 57
Female Infanticide, 57
Female political leadership, 93
Female-headed household, 57
Female-to-Male, 65
Female-to-male transition, 168
Feminine Labour, 58
Feminine Mystique, 58
Femininity, 58
Feminisation, 63
Feminisation of Migration, 58, 63
Feminisation of Poverty, 58
Feminism and modern architecture, 61
Feminism movement, 51
Feminist Advocacy, 61
Feminist domains, 167
Feminist Epistemology, 50, 61
Feminist ethical principles, 120
Feminist Leadership, 61
Feminist Movement-Building, 62
Feminist Movements, 62
Feminist Popular Education, 62
Feminist scholarship, 62

Feminist Studies, 180
Feminist Theory, 63
Feminist Transgression, 63
Fertilisation, 48
Financial cooperatives, 157
Financial power and control, 88
Finland, 93
First Wave Feminism, 63
First Wave of Feminism, 163
Focal Point, 162
Food and healthcare, 100
Fourth World Conference on Women, 104
Fourth-Wave Feminism, 64
Free Trade, 64
Free-Market, 64
Free-market principles, 64
French feminist, 178
Friedanian, 65
Friedrich Engels, 113
Full-time employment, 80
Fundamentalist discourses, 65
Funeral custom, 144

G

Gas Lighting, 66
Gay Activist Alliance, 108
Gay men, 182
Gender (or Sexual) Division of Labor, 66
Gender - Nonconformity, 66
Gender Accommodating, 67
Gender Action Plan, 67
Gender Analysis, 68
Gender Analytical Information, 68
Gender and Development, 68, 76
Gender Apartheid, 68
Gender as Cultural Construction, 68
Gender Audit, 69
Gender Aware-Policies, 69
Gender Awareness, 69, 82
Gender Balance, 69
Gender Bias, 70
Gender Binary, 70
Gender blind, 79
Gender Blindness, 70
Gender budgeting, 70
Gender Characteristics, 70
Gender Confirmation Surgery, 151
Gender Conformity, 71
Gender Discrimination, 42, 71, 148
Gender Disparities, 71
Gender Division of Labour, 71
Gender Effect, 71
Gender Empowerment Measure (GEM), 72, 77
Gender Equality, 72, 73, 77, 104, 172
Gender Equity, 73
Gender Essentialism, 74
Gender Expression, 74
Gender Fluid, 75
Gender Fluidity, 75
Gender Focal Point, 75, 104
Gender Gap, 75
Gender Gap Index, 93
Gender Gap Report, 183
Gender Harassment, 150
Gender Identity, 75, 96
Gender Identity (Changes), 81
Gender Image, 74
Gender in Development, 76
Gender inequality, 110
Gender Issues, 44, 77
Gender Lens, 77
Gender Mainstreaming, 77
Gender Needs, 78
Gender Neutrality, 79
Gender Non-binary, 80
Gender Non-conforming, 80
Gender Norms, 79
Gender Parity, 79

Gender Parity Index, 79
Gender Pay Gap, 79
Gender Performativity, 80
Gender perspective, 80
Gender Planning, 78, 80
Gender Policies, 80
Gender Presentation, 80
Gender Programming and Policies, 158
Gender Queer, 80, 81
Gender related Development Index, 72
Gender Relations, 81
Gender Role, 82
Gender Role Stereotyping, 82
Gender roles, 84
Gender Roles and Responsibilities, 82
Gender Sensitisation, 83
Gender Sensitivity, 82, 83
Gender Socialisation, 83
Gender Stereotypes, 84
Gender stratification, 85
Gender Studies, 85
Gender Training, 85
Gender Transformative, 89
Gender Violence, 86
Gender- Critical, 71
Gender- Neutral Language, 78
Gender-Based Constraints, 87
Gender-Based Violence, 39, 87
Gender-Based Violence in Emergencies, 88
Gender-Biased Sex Selection, 88
Gender-Blind, 88
Gender-Blind Policies, 88
Gender-Blindness, 88
Gender-differentiated impact, 88
Gender-disaggregated data, 89
Gender-dominated occupations, 89
Gender-Neutral, 89
Gender-Neutral Programming and Policies, 89
Gender-neutral Pronouns, 89
Gender-Nonconformity, 89
Gender-Redistributive Policies, 90
Gender-Related Development Index, 40
Gender-related Development Index, 90
Gender-Responsive Budgeting, 90
Gender-Responsive Programming and Policies, 89
Gender-Sensitive, 89
Gender-Sensitive Budgets, 90
Gender-Sensitive Programming and Policies, 91
Gender-Sensitivity, 91
Gender-Socialisation, 91
Gender-Specific Torture and Ill Treatment, 91
Gender-Transformative Programming and Policies, 91
Genderfuck, 89
Genderqueer, 89
Generation process, 154
Geographic Location, 91
Gilles Deleuze, 161
Gilmanian, 92
Glass Ceiling, 92
Glass Escalator, 92
Global Care Chains, 93
Global Gender Gap Index, 93, 183
Global Gender Gap Report, 183
Global women's movement, 52
Grand Rapids Community College, 49, 95
Greta Gaard, 139
Guerrilla Girls, 95
Gynocriticism, 95

H

Hawk Hill Community, 183
Health experts, 48
Hegemonic Masculinity, 95
Hegemony, 95

Heteronormative, 95
Heteronormativity, 96
Heteropatriarchy, 96
Heterosexism, 96
Heterosexual, 96
Heterosexual men, 182
Heterosexual norms, 97
Heterosexual Privilege, 96
Heterosexuality (Compulsory), 96
Hidden Hetero gender Curriculum, 96
Hidden Sexuality Curriculum, 96
Hierarchical, 97
High Level Committee, 104
High Level Panel, 129
High-risk sexual activities, 173
Hillary Clinton, 113
Hinduism, 65
Homonormativity, 97
Homophobia, 97
Homosexual, 97
Homosexual females, 109
Homosexuality, 97
Honour Killing, 35, 98
Hooksian, 98
Hostile Sexism, 98
Household maintenance, 98
Housewife, 98
Human development index, 40
Human Development Report, 72, 77
Human Immunodeficiency Virus, 97
Human Papillomavirus, 99
Human Rights, 57, 99, 179
Human rights Vienna, 72
Human Rights with a Gender Perspective, 99
Human Rights-Based Approach, 100
Human Security, 100
Human sexuality, 152
Human smuggling, 100
Hypermasculinity, 101

I

Identity Politics, 101
Illinois, 51
Impairment, 102
Implantation, 48
Incest, 102
Index ranges, 77
Indigenous communities, 172
Indigenous Feminism, 102
Individualist Feminism, 102
Indonesia, 145
Inequalities in economic participation, 102
Inequalities in political power, 102
Informal Economy, 102
Informal Labour, 103
Informal sector, 103
Inheritance, 103
Institutional Power, 103
Institutional Racism, 103
Institutionalised Oppression, 103
Institutionalised Sexism, 104
Institutions and Development Data Base, 86
Inter-Agency Network, 104
Intermediate barriers, 104
Internal governance, 118
Internalised Oppression, 105
Internalised Racism, 105
Internalised Sexism, 105
International agreement, 35
International Conference, 105
International consultants, 75
International Day of the Girl Child, 106
International Domestic Workers Network, 45
International Financial Institutions, 106
International Labour Organisation, 38
International Monetary Fund, 128, 160
International Training Centre, 69

Internet communications technologies, 94
Interpersonal Racism, 106
Intersectional Analysis, 106
Intersectional Feminism, 106
Invisibility of Feminine Labour, 107
Invisible minority, 107
Iowa, 51
Ireland, 93
Islam, 65

J

Joint actions, 118
Judaism, 65
Judith Butler, 125

K

Kanye West, 113
Karl Marx, 113
Kellyanne Conway, 54
Knowledge creation, 39
Knowledge production, 129

L

Labour and services, 142
Labour force, 107
Lactivism, 108
Lambda Legal Defence, 108
Land and employment, 48
Lateral Violence, 108
Latin America, 108
Laura Mulvey, 111
Le Corbusier, 61
Lesbian Country Magazine, 183
Lesbian Feminism, 109
Lesbian Natural Resources, 183
Liberal Feminism, 109
Liberal feminist, 109
Lipstick Feminism, 109
Literacy rate, 147
Livelihood, 109
Logocentrism, 109
London, 78
Low-income countries, 106

M

Mainstream Feminism, 109
Mako Mori Test, 110
Male as Norm, 110
Male Chauvinism, 111
Male Gaze, 111
Male guards, 91
Male Privilege, 111
Male supremacy, 111
Male-dominated power, 165
Male-Dominated Society, 111
Male-to-Female, 118
Male-to-female transition, 168
Malestream, 111
Malnutrition, 111
Mansplain, 112
Mansplaining, 112
Mansplainy, 112
Marginalisation, 113
Marginalised Group, 113
Maria Suarez, 104
Marital rape, 175
Marital relations, 96
Market Economies, 64
Market-oriented processes, 119
Marxist feminism, 113
Maryland, 51
Masculinity, 113
Mass media, 84
Master Narrative, 35, 116
Material benefits, 40
Maternity leave, 79
Matriarchy, 114
Matrilineal, 114
Matrilocal, 114
Matrix of Domination, 114

Maxine Molyneux, 131
Medical conditions, 107
Medical students, 148
Men's Rights Activists, 115
Men's Rights Movement, 116
Menstrual blood, 116
Menstrual Hygiene Management, 116
Michelle Rosaldo, 181
Micro-aggression, 116
Millennium Development Goals, 116
Minority women, 92
Misogynic attitudes, 105
Misogyny, 117
Missing women, 117
Mitch McConnell, 113
Modern Languages Association, 180
Money or goods, 47
Monique Wittig, 178
Monogamy, 118
Monosexism, 118
Montana, 51
Movement, 118
Movement-Building, 118
Multiple Burden, 171
Multiple Discrimination, 119

N

Nairobi, 179
National assemblies, 128
National Women's Studies Association, 180
Naturalisation process, 119
Nepali shamanism, 65
Neurodiversity, 120
New Zealand, 93, 183
Nicaragua, 93
Nice Guy, 121
Nike Foundation, 71
Nineteenth Amendment, 121
Non-Binary, 121
Non-cisgender identities, 172
Non-Productive Activities, 121
Nona Willis Aronowitz, 178
Nonspousal violence, 86
Normal vaginal bleeding, 116
North America, 166

O

Objectification, 121
Occupational Segregation, 121
Old French, 56
Oppression, 122
Optional Protocol, 28, 179
Oregon, 51
Out of the closet, 122
Outreach (for organising), 122
Ovulation, 48

P

Pacific Islander, 55
Paglian, 122
Pakistan, 47
Pansexual, 122
Paradigm, 123
Parity in Education, 123
Participant Observer, 123
Participation, 123
Participation of women, 58
Participatory Action Research, 123
Participatory Development, 123
Participatory Poverty Assessments, 124
Participatory Rural Appraisal, 124
Patriarchal Resistance, 124
Patriarchy/Patriarchal, 124
Patricia Hill Collins, 114
Pay equity, 125
Penis Envy, 125
Performative, 125
Performativity, 125

Personal factors, 61
Petro-sexual politics, 126
Phallocentric, 126
Phallocentrism, 126
Phallogocentrism, 126
Philippines, 93
Phyllis Chesler, 68
Physical anatomy, 126, 130
Physical characteristics, 55, 136
Physical device, 34
Physical violence, 126
Pink-collar worker, 127
Planned parenthood, 127
Policy claims, 34
Political activists, 117
Political Economy of Women's Liberation, 181
Political equality, 51
Political institutions, 119
Political leadership, 124
Political movement, 165
Political participation, 72
Political representation, 184
Political struggle, 118
Politics of Location, 127
Polyamory, 128
Polyandry, 128
Polygamy, 128
Polyurethane, 33
Positive parenting, 128
Post feminism, 128
Post–modernism, 130
Post-2015 Development Agenda, 128
Post-Op, 130
Post-colonialism, 129
Postmodern feminism, 130
Potential financial donors, 104
Power within, 131
Practical and Strategic, 78
Practical Gender Needs, 131
Practical Needs, 131
Pre-natal sex selection, 132
Pre-Op, 132
Preferential treatment, 115
Prejudice, 132
Present, 132
Prevention of fertility, 34
Primary healthcare, 141
Private and public spheres, 132
Privatisation, 132
Privatisation and liberalisation, 160
Privilege, 132
Pro-choice, 133
Problematise, 133
Production, 133
Productive Roles, 133
Productive Work, 133
Profeminism, 134
Programme, 134
Project purpose, 134
Prostitute, 134
Prostitution, 134
Protofeminism, 134
Proxy wars, 100
Psychoanalysis, 135
Psychological assault, 174
Psychological challenge, 46
Psychological harm, 39
Psychological manifestation, 117
Psychological violence, 135
Public/Private Spheres, 135
Purity Culture, 135
Purple Washing, 135

Q

Qualitative Methods, 135
Quantitative Methods, 135
Queer, 136
Queer and intersex, 65
Quotas, 136

R

Racial intimidation, 163
Racialisation, 137
Radical Feminism, 137
Radical feminist group, 183
Radical Feminist movement, 183
Rainbow Flag, 138
Rape (Date), 138
Rape (Marital), 138
Rape Culture, 138
Rape schedule, 138
Refrigerator, 47
Religious consideration, 39
Repression, 139
Reproductive age, 139
Reproductive health, 77, 139
Reproductive health rights, 35
Reproductive Justice, 139
Reproductive Rights, 140, 141
Reproductive Roles, 141
Reproductive Tax, 141
Reproductive Work, 141
Research and Training Institute, 44
Resistance, 142
Resonance, 142
Resources, 142
Respectability Politician, 142
Respectability Politics, 143
Richian, 143
Rights, 143
Rights (Sexual), 143
Role conflict, 143
Rosaldo and Kelly, 181
Rosie the Riveter, 144
Rwanda, 93

S

Safe motherhood, 144
Safe sex, 144
Safe Space, 144
Sati or suttee, 144
Second Shift, 145
Second Wave Feminism, 145
Second Wave of Feminism, 163
Secondary sex, 151
Self-Identify, 145
Self-identify as women, 145
Self-Reliance, 145
Senate majority leader, 113
Separate Spheres, 164
Separatist Feminism, 146
Sex and Gender, 146
Sex apartheid, 68
Sex discrimination, 117
Sex Identity, 102, 147
Sex plus disability discrimination, 119
Sex Positive, 147
Sex Role Stereotype, 147
Sex Roles, 147
Sex Strike, 147
Sex Typing, 147
Sex worker, 134
Sex Worker-Exclusionary Radical Feminism, 147
Sex-Disaggregated Data, 147
Sex-Positivity, 148
Sex-Reassignment Surgery, 148
Sex-Shaming, 148
Sexism against women, 104
Sexism in Medicine, 148
Sexual abuse of girls, 86
Sexual and domestic violence, 148
Sexual and Reproductive Health, 140
Sexual and Reproductive Health and Rights, 149
Sexual apartheid, 68
Sexual Assault, 149
Sexual attraction, 153
Sexual behaviour, 152, 174
Sexual Consent, 149

Sexual contact, 37, 152, 174
Sexual Division of Labour, 149
Sexual Exploitation, 150
Sexual Harassment, 86, 150
Sexual Health, 150
Sexual identities and consent, 148
Sexual Identity, 150
Sexual inequality, 181
Sexual intercourse, 33
Sexual minority, 151
Sexual Objectification, 151
Sexual organ, 138
Sexual Orientation, 59, 109, 151
Sexual penetration, 138
Sexual Reassignment Surgery, 151
Sexual Rights, 151
Sexual Violence, 152, 174
Sexuality, 152
Sexually active people, 99
Sexually transmitted diseases, 144
Sexually transmitted infection, 33, 99, 152
Shakespeare's Sister, 152
Showalterian, 153
Sick family members, 46
Single men, 153
Single parent, 153
Single person, 153
Sisterhood, 153
Situated knowledge, 154
Slovenia, 93
Slut-Shaming, 155
Social and Cultural Rights, 38
Social Capital, 155
Social Construction, 155
Social Constructionism, 156
Social exclusion, 156
Social gender, 151
Social Justice, 156
Social protection, 156
Social Transformation, 157
Socialisation, 157
Socialised, 157
Socialist Feminism, 157
Socio-Economic Status, 157
Socio-Economic Violence, 157
Solidarity Economy, 157
Son Preference, 158
South Africa, 136
South Asia, 101
Spanish colonizers, 108
Specific ideology, 65
Spiritual identities, 172
Standpoint theory, 158
Status of women, 179
Stereotype, 159
Stereotyping, 159
Strange person, 35
Strategic Gender Interests, 131, 159
Strategic Gender Needs, 159
Strategic Needs, 159
Straw Feminism, 160
Straw Feminist, 160
Strip searching of women, 91
Strong Objectivity, 160
Structural adjustment programmes, 160
Structural Barriers, 161
Structural Discrimination, 161
Structural Gender Inequality, 161
Structural Racism, 161
Suarez and Miller, 142
Subjectification, 161
Substantive Equality, 161
Supportive Policies, 162
Suppress and Punish Trafficking in Persons, 167
Sustainable Development, 54, 162
Sustainable Development Goals, 67, 177
Sweden, 93
System of decision making, 39

T

Targeted recruitment, 115
Taylor Swift, 113
Teasing the girls, 55
Technical workers, 93
Technocratic institutions, 120
Temporary Special Measures, 162, 163
The History of Sexuality, 152
Third Wave of Feminism, 165
Tone-Policing, 165
Top freedom, 165
Total fertility rate, 166
Toxic Masculinity, 166
Trade barriers, 94
Traditional circumcisers, 57
Traditional epistemologies, 50
Traditional practices, 166
Traditional understanding, 145
Trafficking in Persons, 166
Trans Activism, 167
Trans Female, 168
Trans Feminine, 168
Trans Inclusivity, 168
Trans Masculine, 168
Trans Woman, 168, 182
Trans-Exclusionary Radical Feminism, 168
Transfeminism, 167, 168
Transformational Leadership, 168
Transformatory Potential, 169
Transgender, 65, 66, 151, 159, 168, 169
Transgender people, 151
Transgender Person, 169
Transgender rights, 101
Transgenderist, 169
Transition, 169
Transmisogyny, 170
Transnational Feminism, 170
Transphobia, 170
Transportation, 167
Transsexual, 32, 170
Transsexuality, 170
Transvestite, 171
Triangle, 171
Trigger, 171
Trigger Warnings, 171
Triple Role, 171
Turkey, 112

U

U.S. Centers for Disease Control, 99
Uma Narayan, 49
Umbrella term, 109
UN Development Agenda, 128
UN entities, 162
UN General Assembly, 104, 179
UN System Task Team, 128
UN System-wide Action Plan, 172
UN Women, 44, 104, 172
Uniform groups, 137
United Kingdom, 108
United Nations, 43, 51, 67, 73, 77, 92, 166, 172
United Nations Brundtland Report, 162
United Nations Decade for Women, 179
United Nations Development Fund, 44
United Nations Development Programme, 40
United Nations Economic and Social Council, 38
United Nations General Assembly, 104, 172, 179
United Nations offices, 104
United Nations Protocol, 167
United Nations system, 51
United States, 80, 103, 136, 139, 153
Universal Declaration of Human Rights, 51, 73, 172, 179
University of Brighton, 146
Unpaid Care Work, 172
Unpaid Labor, 173

Unprotected intercourse, 48
Unprotected sex, 173
Unprotected sexual contact, 97
Unsafe abortions, 173
Unsafe sex, 173
Unwanted sex, 174

V

Value judgment, 40
Verbal abuse, 174
Verbal Violence, 174
Vibrant social movements, 101
Victim Blaming, 174
Video Music, 113
Vienna Conference, 179
Vietnam, 145
Violence (Domestic), 174
Violence Against Women, 39, 175
Violent civil and political conflicts, 100

W

Wage Gap, 175
West distinction, 129
Western civilisation, 74
Western philosophers, 117
Whimpster, 176
White Feminism, 176
White Privilege, 176
Whiteness, 176
Whitesplaining, 177
WID approach, 76
Wife-battering, 86
Wittigian, 178
Woke Misogynist, 178
Wollstonecraftian, 178
Woman, 178
Womanism, 178
Women and feminism, 115
Women in Development, 76, 177
Women in isolation, 177
Women of Colour, 178
Women of Colour Feminism, 178
Women-In-Development, 115
Women-Only Space, 182
Women's Economic Empowerment, 178
Women's Equality & Empowerment, 35
Women's Equality & Empowerment Framework, 54
Women's Human Rights, 179
Women's Political Participation, 179
Women's Studies, 180
Women's Suffrage, 182
Womyn-born womyn, 182
World Bank, 94, 160
World Economic Forum, 75, 94, 183
World Trade Organisation, 94
Wyoming, 51

Z

Zach Braff, 48
Zero-sum game, 49